INDIA IN THE 21ST CENTURY

WHAT EVERYONE NEEDS TO KNOW®

INDIA IN THE 21ST CENTURY

WHAT EVERYONE NEEDS TO KNOW®

MIRA KAMDAR

OXFORD
UNIVERSITY PRESS

OXFORD
UNIVERSITY PRESS

Oxford University Press is a department of the University of Oxford. It furthers the University's objective of excellence in research, scholarship, and education by publishing worldwide. Oxford is a registered trade mark of Oxford University Press in the UK and certain other countries.

"What Everyone Needs to Know" is a registered trademark of Oxford University Press.

Published in the United States of America by Oxford University Press 198 Madison Avenue, New York, NY 10016, United States of America.

Library of Congress Cataloging-in-Publication Data
Name: Kamdar, Mira, author.
Title: India in the 21st century / Mira Kamdar.
Description: Oxford ; New York : Oxford University Press, 2018. |
Series: What everyone needs to know
Identifiers: LCCN 2017046723 | ISBN 9780199973590 (pbk. : alk. paper) |
ISBN 9780199973606 (hardback : alk. paper)
Subjects: LCSH: India—History—21st century.
Classification: LCC DS480.853 .K3635 2018 | DDC 954.05/3—dc23
LC record available at https://lccn.loc.gov/2017046723

1 3 5 7 9 8 6 4 2

Paperback printed by LSC Communications, United States of America
Hardback printed by Bridgeport National Bindery, Inc., United States of America

CONTENTS

Part I
How India Got to the Twenty-First Century

Part II
Will the Twenty-First Century Be India's Century?

4 Society   107

5 Economy 142

6 Politics 166

7 Geopolitics   196

AUTHOR'S NOTE

I first traveled to India from America in 1960 on the *Jalagopal*, a cargo ship owned by the Scindia Steamship and Navigation Company. Founded in 1919, Scindia was the first Indian-owned and -operated large-scale shipping company, and bore the name of the proud clan that led the Maratha Confederacy, which fought the British in a series of wars beginning in 1775.

I was three years old when we set out from Seattle to Bombay. Of all we experienced on that journey, what I remember most distinctly is the wooden lip that kept the china from skittering off the edge of the dining table as a storm-tossed Pacific Ocean rolled the great freighter from side to side, and the kindness of the crew, who doted on me and my sister. My Danish-American mother had married an engineering student from India, and we were off on a great journey from the West Coast of the United States to visit my father's family. Passage in the very comfortable officers' quarters on a freighter was cheaper than flying—a luxury my parents could not then afford. In those days, my parents communicated with my father's family by letter or telegram. The rare phone calls went through international operators, who announced: "Hello, India. This is the United States calling."

Over the years, I have lived off and on in India. I continue to visit the country frequently, tied by family and friendship and an enduring fascination with one of the most confounding and diverse countries in the world. I speak, read, and write (slowly) Hindi, and I understand a little Gujarati, one of India's regional languages. I have published books on India, and I have written articles on India for major publications in India, in Europe, and in the United States. As an Overseas Citizen of India, I may soon be able to vote in India's elections.

Still, distilling India as it moves into this uncertain twenty-first century into one compact book is no easy task. This brief book can only scratch the surface of one of the most ancient cultures and complex countries in the world. Even so, it seeks to give the reader a better understanding of how India got to where it is today, and of how it may evolve going forward. Structured as a series of questions about what I feel are the most essential things to know about India, this book offers what I can best describe as freeze-frame images of a country traveling at multiple speeds on multiple tracks, hurtling forward but sometimes also simultaneously backward, sideways, or cyclically. A tale that originated in ancient India may help explain how I hope this book will work. Versions of the tale are retold in various religious traditions important in India, including Hinduism, Jainism, Sufism, and Buddhism. The tale entered the Western canon in the form of a poem by the nineteenth-century American poet John Godfrey Saxe called "The Blind Men and the Elephant." In Saxe's poem, as in the traditional tale, several blind men touch a different part of an elephant, and each comes to a different conclusion about what the beast is. The man who touches the tail believes the elephant is a rope. The man who touches an ear concludes the elephant is a fan. The man who touches a leg is sure the elephant is a pillar, and so on. None of them can see the elephant in its totality, and therefore none of them is able to perceive what the elephant really is. This book offers glimpses into India's past, its present, and where it may be headed in the future. I hope that, taken together, these glimpses will give the reader a good sense of how India arrived at where it is today and what its future may hold.

ACKNOWLEDGMENTS

I am enormously grateful to my editor at Oxford University Press (OUP) in New York, Timothy Bent, for his patience during the long period this book was put on hold. As it turned out, had the book been published on schedule before the election of Narendra Modi in 2014, it would have been almost instantly obsolete. Sincere thanks as well to Rajesh Kathamuthu at Newgen and Mariah White at OUP for their help in transforming my manuscript into a finished book.

I also wish to thank Brendan Mark Foo for his assistance with initial research for the book while an intern at the World Policy Institute in New York, as well as former Institute colleagues Michele Wucker, Belinda Cooper, Claudia Dreifus, and Kate Maloff for their early support. Thanks also to Ajith Francis, who fact-checked the draft manuscript for me in Paris.

I sincerely thank eminent India scholars Christophe Jaffrelot, Sumit Ganguly, Ananya Vajpeyi, and Ines Zupanov for their generous friendship and support throughout and for taking time from busy schedules—as also did Catherine Servan-Schreiber—to read or have read anonymously, on a quick deadline, sections of the book for accuracy. I take responsibility for any errors that remain.

In addition to these scholars, this book benefited from my exchanges with my network of scholars, journalists, authors, artists, and activists with deep connections to India, many of whom I am honored to call my friends. Too numerous to cite here, I thank specially, in no particular order, Mallika Sarabhai, Basharat Peer, Ganeve Rajkotia, Neeta Gupta, Ingrid Therwath, Aliette Armel, Noopur Tiwari, Ramachandra Guha, Pratap Bhanu Mehta, Rajiv Desai, Stanley Wolpert, Narendra Pachkedhe, Tridip Suhrud, Manu Bhagavan, Meena Alexander, David Lelyveld, Marina Budhos, Zette Emmons, Siddharth Dube, Ishaan Tharoor, Kanishk Tharoor, Dina Siddiqi, David Ludden, Radhika Balakrishnan, Mallika Dutt, Zeyba Rahman, Judi Kilachand, Devinder Sharma, Bénédicte Manier, Sujata Parekh, Atul Kumar, Vinod Jose, Dilip d'Souza, Vibha Kamat, Naresh Fernandes, Salil Tripathi, Leela Jacinto, Kavita Nandini Ramdas, Sheela Bhatt, Samir Saran, Malvika, Tejbir Singh, Mukul Kesavan, Salman Rushdie, Barkha Dutt, Amitav Ghosh, Shashi Tharoor, Sooni Taraporewala, and Thrity Umrigar..

My Indian family, both in India and in the diaspora, also helped me keep my finger on the pulse of the country these past few years, as well as providing me with warm welcome and sustenance during my travels. I must also express deep gratitude to my parents, Prabhakar Kamdar and Lois Eagleton, for giving me a lifelong connection to India. Finally, I thank my children, Alexander and Anjali Claes, and my husband, Philippe Fabbri, for being in my life. You are what matters most.

INDIA IN THE 21ST CENTURY

WHAT EVERYONE NEEDS TO KNOW®

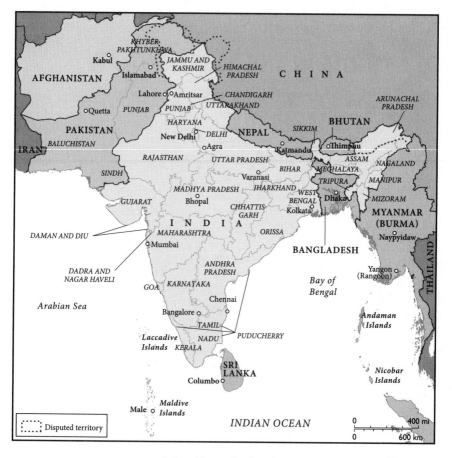

India and Surrounding Countries

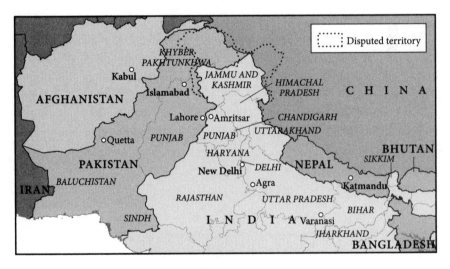

Northern India

INTRODUCTION

India enchants the world with its culture, excites with its potential, and intrigues with its traditions. It perplexes with its complexity, and it shocks with its violence, poverty, and corruption, yet it comforts much of the world—Western democracies in particular—with its large English-speaking population and its democratic institutions. While it is impossible to write a book detailing everything there is to know about a country as ancient and complex as India, it is essential for everyone to know some basic things about it, given that India is bound to shape our twenty-first-century world.

By the middle of this century, India will be the most populous country on earth and the world's second-largest economy. Its 1.7 billion people will consume resources and produce goods and services on a scale that will dwarf all but that of China. The impact of India on the twenty-first century cannot be underestimated. India's prime minister, Narendra Modi, whose Bharatiya Janata Party swept to power in May 2014, firmly believes that "the twenty-first century is India's century." Many, and not just Indians, agree with him.

Like all centuries, the twenty-first will be defined as much by humanity's failures as by its achievements. In no area will this be more true than in how the world deals with the effects of climate change. Every country on earth will be forced to grapple with the effects of global warming. India will be on the front lines, both in terms of the severity of what climate change is predicted to inflict and in terms of finding solutions to avert the worst scenarios—even as it tries to develop and industrialize its economy. India's leadership in developing renewable energy sources, such as wind and solar, will be key to its future and may help bring the cost of these technologies down for the entire world.

As India's population grows over the coming decades, so will the world's. The latest projections see global population continuing to increase through the end of the twenty-first century. If those projections hold, there will be 11 billion people on earth by 2100. The combination of ever-larger numbers of people, the havoc wreaked by climate change, and dwindling global resources will test humanity as never before. India will struggle to create jobs, provide housing, feed, educate, and care for the health of its own burgeoning population in a world where competition for resources will be fierce. In tackling these problems, India has the potential to discover innovative solutions applicable to other developing countries, and that may help developed countries make do with fewer resources in a crowded world.

India is also poised to play a key role in information and communication technologies. With the majority of its massive population still not connected to the Internet—and with China's strict control of Internet access effectively cutting that country's market off to U.S. giants such as Google, Facebook, and Twitter—India is the largest potential market for these technologies. It also has the potential to be a leader in creating new information and communication technologies, especially ones that are adapted to meeting the needs of the global poor and the world's emerging middle classes—for example, helping more people get an education and access healthcare.

India faces the twenty-first century as a fractious, diverse democracy. The Republic of India is a federation of twenty-nine states, many created along linguistic lines in a country that counts twenty-two official languages. Many of these states have their own literatures and movie industries, television, radio, and news media in their different languages. While about 80 percent of Indians are Hindus, India is also home—as of the 2011 census—to some 172 million Muslims, 28 million Christians, 21 million Sikhs, 8 million Buddhists, and 4.5 million Jains.

It bears remembering that India is a young republic, independent only since 1947. Skeptics then predicted that democracy could never work in a country with so many poor and illiterate people. Yet India's democracy has flourished. There were no fewer than 1,866 officially registered political parties in India in 2015. The 2014 general elections saw a record-setting 540 million Indians cast their vote.

Still, India's democracy is a rough-and-tumble affair. More than a third of the members of India's parliament elected in 2014 were at the time charged with crimes, including assault, kidnapping, and even murder. A series of spectacular corruption scandals touching the highest reaches of India's government contributed to the defeat of India's National Congress Party in 2014 by the Bharatiya Janata Party. Founded in 1885, the Congress Party was the midwife to India's independence in 1947 and governed the country for most of the following years. Its future is now uncertain. At the same time, a host of regional and caste-based parties wield real political clout.

India's prime minister, Narendra Modi, campaigned for the winning Bharatiya Janata Party in 2014 on a promise of economic liberalization and good governance that resonated with much of India's electorate, eager for a government that could give concrete shape to the aspirations of a nation whose full potential has remained stubbornly frustrated. That promise helped Modi's party win a decisive victory, taking the helm of a government that had not been in the hands of a single party for thirty years.

Yet it will not be easy for the prime minister to fulfill his campaign promises. Since Modi's election in 2014, India's growth has declined from over 7 percent to under 6 percent.

While this is still a very high rate of growth compared to developed countries, it is not nearly enough to lift millions of Indians out of poverty, especially since that growth has not narrowed inequalities. Moreover, the global economic outlook is uncertain, and China's growth has also stalled. Though Modi's government has moved aggressively to reform India's tax regime and facilitate foreign investment, it has not been able to create enough new jobs, a critical task in a country where in 2015 nearly 50 percent of the population was under the age of twenty-five (compared to 30 percent in China).

What the Bharatiya Janata Party and allied Hindu nationalist groups have been able to accomplish since Modi was elected in 2014 is advance their cultural agenda. They have moved swiftly to reform India's school and university curricula, change the staffing and orientation of India's cultural institutions, and try to regulate cultural practices, such as couples holding hands in public or the consumption of beef. Ministers in Modi's cabinet have vowed to "cleanse" India of Western and other non-Hindu "pollution," and to rewrite the country's textbooks, accepted history, and even internationally accepted scientific theories to reflect their view that India's ancient Hindu epics, the Ramayana and the Mahabharata, are documents of historical fact. Their goal is nothing less than to restore India to the imagined glory of its ancient past, without which, they believe, India cannot achieve its rightful place in the world. This is not the modernizing, globalizing India most Westerners imagine.

As India struggles to reconcile modernity with traditional cultural norms, its women are among the main beneficiaries—and the main victims—of wrenching social change. India's growing economy and urbanization have brought young women onto university campuses and into the workforce in record numbers. But the easy mixing of young men and women outside the home alarms conservative Indians, who have reacted by trying to impose restrictions on women's freedom to wear what they want, see whom they want, go out when they want, and—the ultimate taboo for many Indian parents—marry whom they want. Village councils have even banned young women from using cell phones—in the country with the fastest-growing cellular phone market in the world.

A brutal gang rape resulting in the death of a twenty-three-year-old college student on her way home with a male friend from watching a movie in New Delhi in 2012 brought thousands of Indian citizens into the streets. The event made international headlines. Too many of India's women and girls experience lifelong discrimination. The traditional joint-family system, by which sons stay in the family home and support aging parents while daughters are married off, often with onerous dowries, has led to women being perceived as financial liabilities and resulted in girls receiving less education and, in poorer communities, less food and medical care. As a consumer-based society took hold in India at the end of the twentieth century and families put even more value on discretionary income, a new trend of discrimination against women began to emerge: sex-selective abortion. The result is a growing number of "missing girls": India's 2011 census indicated only 877 girls for every 1,000 boys in the state of Haryana, for example. Sexual violence and gender discrimination will be major issues for India in the twenty-first century.

India is slowly transforming itself from a largely agrarian country into a nation of megacities. It is estimated that more than 800 million Indians will live in cities by 2050. Choked roads, polluted air, chronic water shortages, electricity blackouts and brownouts, little planning for public goods such as parks, sidewalks, post offices, fire stations, schools, or hospitals—the current state of India's already burgeoning cities does not bode well for the quality of life of urban Indians as the century progresses. The trend for those who can afford it is to opt out, living in private, gated, self-sufficient communities where everything they need is at their doorstep and they never need to leave their comfortable cocoon to face the poverty and chaos outside. Joining a global trend, Prime Minister Modi has promised technology-enhanced "smart cities" as a solution to India's urban crisis. This is an ambitious project, but whether as a result all Indians will have equitable access to efficient, clean cities remains to be seen.

Economically, and in terms of life opportunities as basic as education, healthcare, and decent housing, India is divided by stark inequalities. The World Bank's 2015 report on economic inequality in South Asia pointed to an exceptional concentration of wealth in India, where a handful of billionaires account for 12 percent of gross domestic product. Meanwhile, more than 450 million Indians live on less than $1.25 per day, and India has one of the highest rates of child malnutrition in the world, higher than in sub-Saharan Africa.

Feeding its growing population will be one of India's biggest challenges in the century ahead. India is one of the most productive agricultural areas in the world. It is the largest producer of milk and an important exporter of meat, cotton, rice, pepper, and sugar. But India must import a portion of its food, and Indian agriculture faces tough times ahead as global warming causes monsoon rains to become less predictable, increases the severity of both droughts and floods, and threatens yields of wheat and rice. An alarming number of India's farmers resort to suicide when their crops fail: 11,458 of them committed suicide in 2016, according to India's government. India's water crisis doesn't help: underground aquifers are being pumped dry, and farmers must share groundwater with the growing demands of India's cities. More than half of India's people still make a living from agriculture, yet it contributes less than 15 percent of India's gross domestic product. With few employment alternatives aside from casual labor, India's farmers are facing a grim future unless steps are taken to boost their incomes.

Determined to assume a role on the world stage commensurate with its population and the size of its economy, India also has to contend with what one former minister of external affairs called its "dangerous neighborhood." India has fought wars with both Pakistan and China, and has border disputes with both. All three are nuclear powers. India's military spending is dwarfed by China's, but it is one of the world's largest arms purchasers, aggressively seeking to modernize and expand its military capabilities.

As the twenty-first century unfolds, India will use its growing military clout to project its power across South Asia, and perhaps beyond. It is joining other emerging countries to press for a world order tailored to the needs and interests of countries too long denied a role in the institutions of global governance set up in the mid-twentieth century. As part of that effort, India is seeking a permanent seat on an expanded United Nations Security Council.

India will continue to benefit from a global diaspora that numbers more than 30 million people. Diaspora Indians play a significant role in shaping policies toward India in the countries where they reside, in making Indian culture familiar to non-Indians, and in investing their skills and their wealth in India. In no country is this more true than in the United States, where the number of Americans of Indian origin has now reached nearly 3 million. The population of Indian Americans is expected to double every decade if U.S. immigration policies before the election of President Donald Trump in 2016 remain in place. Indian Americans are the most highly educated and have the highest household incomes of any immigrant group in the United States—and they are increasingly visible in the media and active in politics, with five winning election to Congress and the Senate in 2016. Former South Carolina governor Nikki Haley, appointed U.S. ambassador to the United Nations in 2017, is the daughter of Indian immigrants to the United States.

The multiple changes India is undergoing and the speed with which these are occurring are mind-boggling. There is terrific promise in this moment as India seeks to invent itself anew, lift millions out of poverty, and assert itself on the global stage. Yet the environmental and economic challenges

India faces will not be easy to overcome. Meanwhile, a battle is raging in India over what kind of nation it should seek to be, with Hindu nationalists empowered as never before to shape India to their vision. How India manages the aspirations of its diverse people and the many challenges it faces in the twenty-first century matters deeply, not only to India but also to the peace, prosperity, freedom, and perhaps even survival of our world.

Part I

HOW INDIA GOT TO THE TWENTY-FIRST CENTURY

1

INDIA'S CIVILIZATIONAL LEGACY

How has India's geography shaped its history?

The Indian subcontinent is a distinct geographic area, connected to yet largely separate from the vast continent of Eurasia. At once accessible and protected, the subcontinent's geography and topography allowed a unique and multifaceted civilization to develop over thousands of years. The Himalayas, the world's highest mountains, bestride its northern boundary, their mighty peaks a bulwark against cold sweeping down from the Arctic and all but the most determined people. To the west, what was once known as the Great Indian Desert cuts a sere swath between mountain and sea. Still further west, snow-capped mountains rise again in what is now Afghanistan and western Pakistan. The Indian subcontinent extends south some 2,000 miles from the Himalayas into the Indian Ocean, ending in a triangular point at 8°4' north of the equator.

India takes its name from the Indus River. The name Indus comes from the Sanskrit word *sindhu*, "river" or "waterway." The Persians pronounced this "hindu." The Indus, which courses through Pakistan today, starts its 3,000-mile course to the Arabian Sea high in the Himalayas. Other great rivers—the Ganges, the Brahmaputra, and the Yamuna—flow down from these mountains to water the plains below. Farther south, across the great Deccan Plateau that takes up most of the center of the Indian subcontinent, the Narmada, Betwa, Cauveri, Godavari, and Krishna Rivers wind through valleys and forests before emptying into the Arabian Sea to the west, or the Bay of Bengal to the east.

Monsoon rains sweep up from the Indian Ocean, moving northward in a great annual procession, bringing life-giving water to a land parched by summer's searing heat, turning barren riverbeds into rushing torrents, filling lakes and ponds. India's agriculture developed to the seasonal cadence of the monsoon. The arrival of the eagerly awaited annual rains and the cyclical rhythms of planting and harvest have been celebrated in India's rites, festivals, songs, and literature from time immemorial.

India is gifted with rich biodiversity. Temperatures, soils, and precipitation change dramatically down the slopes of the Himalayas and onto the vast plains, across the massive central plateau, and along the long coastlines. Ecological islands thrive in river deltas, protected valleys, on windswept mountain slopes. An impressive variety of plants and animals flourishes in India's diverse environments. Some can scarcely be imagined separately from India: the Bengal tiger, the Indian elephant, the Brahma bull, the king cobra, not to mention the banyan tree and the Alphonso mango. India's civilizational roots plunge deeply into a fertile and ecologically varied land.

Since the dawn of India's history, those roots were fed by contact with the world beyond the subcontinent. For more than 5,000 years, the subcontinent's long coastlines and natural ports have facilitated seafaring trade with Southeast Asia to the east, and with Africa, Persia, the Gulf of Arabia, and the Mediterranean to the west. Traders traveled overland across the mountains and the great deserts, connecting India with China, Southeast Asia, Central Asia, and the Levant. Ancient India's considerable riches attracted a series of invaders and settlers. By the time Alexander the Great marched his armies into India in 326 BCE, India had a long history of interaction with the rest of the ancient world.

What was the Indus Valley civilization?

Between 2300 and 1700 BCE, a sophisticated, urban civilization emerged in the Indus River Valley, spreading into the present-day Indian states of Rajasthan and Gujarat. Traces of this civilization can be found in the archaeological ruins of the cities of Mohenjo-daro and Harappa, now located in Pakistan. These cities supported populations of about 40,000 people each. The Harappans lived in houses of fired bricks, some two stories tall, with bathrooms that had running water. The buildings were laid out in neat grids along streets. The water and sewage systems in these cities, built four millennia ago, were superior to what Indian cities offer many of their residents today.

Northwestern India and Pakistan's climate was much wetter 4,000 years ago than it is now. The river valleys were fertile, and agriculture was advanced enough to support urban populations. Farmers delivered barley, millet, rice, and wheat to city granaries. They brought fresh melons, pomegranates, and peas to city markets. They also grew cotton. Cotton was first domesticated and cultivated in the Indus Valley 7,000 years ago. Cotton fabric produced in India was traded throughout the ancient world, and the history of cotton and the history of India have been intimately bound together ever since.

The people who lived in the Indus Valley enjoyed many of the attributes of civilized life we associate with modernity: municipal planning and administration, precise systems of weights and measures, civil engineering, and long-distance commerce. The Indus River was a vital artery for trade. Boats transported cargo up and down the river, between the cities and the sea, and beyond. Archaeological evidence that the people of the Indus Valley civilization gave special importance to the cow—held sacred to Hindus—to ritual bathing, and to fertility goddesses tantalizingly hints at the ancient roots of Hinduism. Due to a shift in monsoon rains that led to a 200-year-long drought, the Indus River Valley civilization had largely collapsed by 1500 BCE, when the Aryans arrived on the Indian subcontinent.

Who were the Aryans?

The *Rig Veda* is a collection of 1,028 hymns composed between 1700 and 1100 BCE. It was transmitted orally for centuries before being written down in Sanskrit around 300 BCE. Hindus recite the hymns of the *Rig Veda* to this day. *Rig Veda* means "verse of knowledge." It sheds an intriguing light on the origins of India's ancient civilization. The word *arya* appears thirty-six times in the *Rig Veda*. This Sanskrit word means "noble." An Aryan is a person of nobility. The ancient culture evoked in the *Rig Veda* is referred to as Vedic culture. Philology and comparative linguistics connect the *Rig Veda* with the arrival in the Indus Valley of a group of nomadic tribes called Aryans, after references to *arya* in the ancient hymns. It is believed that these tribes, who spoke a proto-Indo-European language that in India would become Sanskrit, dispersed from Central Russia into South Asia and across Central Asia and Persia into Europe around 2000 BCE. Traveling with their herds of cattle, the Aryans arrived on the Indian subcontinent around 1500 BCE.

It was nineteenth-century European Indologists, through their study and translation of the *Rig Veda*, who formulated the theory that the Aryans were a race of lighter-skinned, nomadic people who invaded and conquered weaker, darker, sedentary indigenous peoples, finding clues in the *Rig Veda* that the indigenous peoples of India were assimilated to an existing Aryan social hierarchy. This hierarchy was organized according to descending classes of people according to their *varna*, a word that means "color" in Sanskrit. It is believed that India's caste system emerged over many centuries out of the layered assimilation of different peoples to the Aryan hierarchy of *varnas*. In Vedic culture, Brahmins occupied the pinnacle of the Aryan social hierarchy, where they composed, transmitted, interpreted, and enforced the sacred texts that laid out the social rules and structures to which every member of society was bound.

The theory of the Aryans as a conquering Indo-European race has been used to explain all kinds of ideologies of racial and cultural superiority, from the natural superiority of Brahmins in India to the racial theories of the Nazis. This theory is highly contested by some Hindus who date the origins of their faith on the Indian subcontinent to the dawn of time, if not the beginning of the cosmos, instead of to the arrival of cattle-herding nomadic tribes. There are also those who believe that Vedic culture developed in the Indus Valley from a syncretism of Aryan culture and vestiges of the older Harappan civilization. In any case, without some knowledge of the controversies surrounding the Aryan invasion of India, it is impossible to understand some of the bitterest contemporary political and social conflicts—between North and South India, between rural and urban India, about caste, or concerning India's Adivasi tribes, believed to be the original inhabitants of India.

The *Rig Veda* is the founding narrative of Indian Hindu civilization. It provides ancient evidence of some of the key notional concepts and ritual practices of Hinduism, a religious faith that is inseparable from prescriptions for individual moral conduct and the right structure of society. The *Rig Veda* recounts the creation of Being out of Chaos, breathed into life, it tells us, as thought kindles desire. Indra is the hero of the Vedic gods. He is the lord of war, of rains, and of tempests. He is the slayer of Vritra, who had blocked the rivers and brought drought upon the world. Aditi is the great mother goddess, the mother of all the gods. Her name means "unbound." She is what gives divine form to cosmic energy. Agni, the god of fire, is at the center of Vedic religious rituals. Hindus still worship these and many other gods and goddesses who appear in the *Rig Veda* and in other Hindu literature.

What is Hinduism?

The vast majority of Indians, 80 percent, are Hindus. Hinduism is a polytheistic religion. The main divine trilogy consists of Brahma, the creator; Vishnu, the preserver; and Shiva, the destroyer. Other major gods include Krishna, Ganesh, and Ram, while Saraswati, Lakshmi, and Kali are important goddesses. The number of Hindu gods is popularly said to be 330 million, but this is more to drive home the point that the divine spirit has infinite manifestations than it is meant to be an actual number. Hinduism consists as much in its rituals and in its prescriptions for the organization of human society and how individuals should conduct their lives as it does in its explanations of existence and the cosmos in its many sacred texts. In addition to the *Rig Veda* and other Vedas from roughly the same ancient period, the major sacred texts of Hinduism are the *Puranas*, the *Baghavad Gita*, the *Mahabharata*, the *Ramayana*, and the *Upanishads*. These texts began as orally transmitted hymns, poetic cycles, and epics. They were written down at different times by different authors and have been translated into all of India's regional languages, of which there are twenty-two recognized by India's constitution.

The *Mahabharata* and the *Ramayana* are epic tales, with divine heroes and heroines who wrestle with the ethical demands of kingship, war, married life, parenting, and kinship. These epics tackle the question of how to live an ethical life in accordance with the divine structure of the cosmos, a concept known to Hindus as *dharma*. Tales from these epics are recounted, performed, and celebrated across India, and every Hindu knows the major storylines. Many Hindus, male and female, are named after the gods and goddesses, kings and queens, and princes and princesses in these well-known stories.

Hinduism is profoundly grounded in the geographic space and the topography of India. The exploits recounted in the *Mahabharata* and the *Ramayana* are set on the Indian

subcontinent. Hindus living in India inhabit the same physical world as the one in which the action of their most sacred
epics takes place. Locations mentioned in these epics abound,
and many of the holiest are marked with temples, shrines,
and pilgrimage sites. Trees—especially the pipal tree, as it
was under the shade of one of these that the Buddha is said
to have achieved enlightenment—rivers, and certain animals,
including the cow, the rat, the elephant, and the cobra, are
imbued with sacred significance. The holiest river in India is
the Ganges. The river itself is a goddess, the goddess Ganga,
and every drop of its water is considered sacred to Hindus.
The birth of the goddess Ganga is recounted in one of the
Puranas. Sprung from Vishnu's foot and passing through the
abode of Brahma, the Ganges falls from heaven onto the god
Shiva's long hair, from where it is channeled to its bed. The
purifying properties of Ganges water are believed to remove
all sin. Devout Hindus bathe in the Ganges and immerse the
ashes of their dead into the sacred river, notably in the city of
Varanasi.

The physical world of the Hindu is alive with sacred energy,
and even the most mundane tasks are connected to the cosmos.
In rituals performed daily, at specific times of year, with phases
of the moon, or on the occasions of birth, marriage, and death,
Hindus connect their individual lives with a universe pulsing
with divine energy.

The divine trilogy of Brahma, the creator; Vishnu, the preserver; and Shiva, the destroyer represents cosmic creation, existence, and annihilation, an ongoing, infinite process. Each of
these gods has a distinct personality and appears in different
manifestations or avatars. Hinduism's epics and hymns tell an
extraordinarily rich and complicated collection of tales about
the exploits of these gods in their different guises.

The major Hindu goddesses are consorts of the gods. Hindu
gods are commonly represented in ancient temple sculptures,
as well as in contemporary images, as divine couples. The

simplest depiction of the cosmic union of male and female divine energies is in the *yoni-lingam* sculptures found in temples and shrines dedicated to the god Shiva, which depict the union of male and female sex organs. Shiva, the destroyer, is a virile god. The animal he is associated with, his "vehicle," is Nandi, a Brahma bull. His divine power is represented as a phallus (*lingam*), its mighty power anchored in an abstract circular form representing a woman's sex organs (*yoni*).

Female cosmic energy, called *shakti*, is an important aspect of Hindu cosmology, and goddesses, called *devis*, play an important role. There is Devi, the great mother goddess, as well as many other devis. Lakshmi, the goddess of wealth, is displayed in every Hindu-owned business in India so she can bless the enterprise with good profits. Saraswati is the goddess of learning and music. The goddess Kali, closely associated with Shiva, appears in ancient Hindu texts on the battlefield as protagonists prepare to wage their divine battles; her name means "black," and she is commonly depicted with black skin.

The most famous divine couples in Hinduism are Shiva and Parvati, Krishna and Radha, and Rama and Sita. Krishna is a beloved, mischievous, life-loving avatar of the god Vishnu. He is portrayed with blue skin. The music of Krishna's divine flute is as irresistible to the lovesick milkmaids of Hindu sacred legend as his divine message is to his disciples. The state of ecstatic worship that Krishna inspires is called *bhakti*. Krishna is closely associated with cows, an animal whose sacred status dates back to Vedic times. As a baby, he delighted in stealing ghee, or clarified butter, from his mother's kitchen, and images of plump baby Krishna laughingly eating butter are a common sight in India. Ganesh, the elephant-headed god, who is the son of Shiva and his goddess consort Parvati, is worshipped as a god of filial piety, success, and new beginnings.

The *Ramayana* is the epic tale of the trials of Rama and his wife, Sita. Rama is an avatar of the god Vishnu and the king of Ayodhya. His wife, Sita, is an avatar of the goddess Lakshmi. Sita is kidnapped by the demon Ravana, who carries her off to his kingdom in Lanka, where she spurns his advances. The faithful monkey god Hanuman flies across the sea to Lanka, rescues the queen, and brings her back, only to have Rama doubt her virtue after her sojourn with Ravana. To prove her purity, Sita undergoes a trial by fire, which she passes, and the couple takes their rightful place as king and queen of Ayodhya. After the birth of their twin sons, Rama once again questions Sita's fidelity. She asks Mother Earth to swallow her up.

Sita is considered to be a model of Hindu womanhood: a virtuous wife devoted to her husband. While Hindus worship powerful female goddesses, and women, especially mothers, can wield real power within—and increasingly outside—the home, Hindu orthodoxy, like that of many other religions, maintains women in roles that perpetuate patriarchal privileges.

While early Hinduism in the Vedic and Puranic phases spoke of women on the battlefield or of Brahmin women wearing the sacred thread and reciting prayers, Hindu women's lives and conduct were severely restricted by the time the *Laws of Manu* was written down. A Hindu treatise on the rules of right conduct (*dharma*) compiled between 400 and 200 BCE, the *Laws of Manu* defined women first and foremost as wives subservient to husbands they should treat as their god. According to Manu's laws, the only purpose of a woman's life is her husband. A woman should never be independent. She must be subservient to her father, then to her husband, and, if her husband dies before she does, to her sons. Manu's laws go into detail of how a Hindu woman should lead her day-to-day life: she should get up before everyone else, prepare food for her family and take care of all their needs, and eat only after everyone else has finished. She should follow her husband like a shadow and obey him like a slave.

In orthodox Hinduism, Brahmin widows are not allowed to remarry and child marriages, illegal but still practiced by members of some communities in India, mean some women become widows as young girls. A husband's death can easily be considered the fault of his wife: she might have committed some sin, if not in this life, then in a previous life, that brought bad luck. The practice of *sati*, widow burning, was widespread, though not frequent, in northern India well into the nineteenth century, and there have been isolated incidences since. In *sati*, the widow, still very much alive, threw herself onto her dead husband's funeral pyre and burned with him so that her soul might follow his. The practice was outlawed by the British and remains illegal.

The key concept in Hinduism is *dharma*. *Dharma* defines the duties and privileges of every human that allow him or her to act in accordance with the divine principles of the universe, a harmony that is reflected in good social order. Those duties and privileges are both eternal and situational. They differ according to gender, caste, and stage of life. There are four basic stages of life that define how upper-caste Hindus should live: *brahmacharya*, a premarital (celibate) stage dedicated to study (traditionally of the Vedas); *grihastha*, the stage of married life, running a home, raising children, and making money; *vanaprastha*, a stage of religious observance and withdrawal from active life; and *samnyasa*, a stage of renunciation of this world.

The challenge of *dharma*, right conduct, is the primary theme of the *Bhagavad Gita*. In the *Bhagavad Gita*, set before the epic battle of the *Mahabharata*, the god Krishna illustrates the situational aspect of *dharma* as he explains to Arjuna how killing someone, even a family member or a teacher, may be permissible in the context of a just war. *Dharma* is connected with the forces governing reincarnation, or the transmigration of souls. Hindus believe that the soul, *atman*, is reborn into a new body after death. Reincarnation, the ceaseless birth and rebirth of the soul, is called *samsara*. *Karma*, whose Sanskrit root means "action," is the notion that human beings can choose to perform good actions, those that are in harmony with *dharma*, or bad actions, those that are against *dharma*, and that the balance sheet of these good and bad actions determines the form and status of the soul's next rebirth.

What is the caste system?

As we have seen, the notion of caste, a system of social stratification, has its origins in India's ancient Vedic culture. The Vedas set forth a social hierarchy divided into four major categories or *varnas*. In descending order, these are Brahmins (priests), Kshatriyas (warriors), Vaishyas (merchants and landowners), and Shudras (artisans and laborers). Brahmins, the perpetuators of religious knowledge and ritual and the composers and keepers of Hinduism's sacred texts, occupy the highest place in this social hierarchy. Next come Kshatriyas, the defenders of the social order, and then Vaishyas, the creators of material wealth and well-being. These three *varnas* are said to be "twice born," referring to rituals they are allowed to perform that initiate them formally into the *varna* into which they were born. Vedic texts are very clear that only the twice-born are allowed to recite or hear recited the sacred texts of the Vedas.

Last in the hierarchy of *varnas* are the Sudras: craftsmen and menials whose labor serves the upper three layers of society. In addition to the four *varnas*, there are outcasts, referred to in the past as "untouchables" because the work they were condemned to perform, such as handling dead animals and cleaning drains, was considered unclean according to Hindu notions of purity and pollution. The term "untouchables" is no longer used today. It has been replaced by the name Dalits, which means "oppressed."

The hierarchy of the *varnas* is a descending ladder from the purest, the Brahmins, to the least pure, the Dalits. Orthodox upper-caste Hindus believed that direct contact with Dalits, with something they had touched, with food they prepared, or even with their shadow put them at risk of losing their *varna*. Only elaborate rituals, performed or prescribed by Brahmins, could purge the contaminated individual of the "pollution" contracted from contact with a Dalit. Dalits who so contaminated an upper-caste Hindu, even accidentally, faced severe punishment, including death. Article 19 of India's constitution outlawed untouchability in 1950. Yet Dalits, who make up over 24 percent of India's population, continue to suffer terrible discrimination. Their struggle for dignity and equality is far from over.

The four *varnas*, or broad caste categories, include some 4,000 specific *jatis*, or specific castes recognized by the Indian government. *Jati* simply means "birth" in Sanskrit. Caste is transmitted from parents to their children. One does not choose one's caste; one is born into it. Traditionally hereditary vocations—from the priesthood to commerce, from barbering to leatherworking—have their own castes, and they may be divided into even more specific subcategories. Indians belong to the caste of their birth, even if they never exercise the hereditary vocation associated with that caste.

What is Jainism?

Jainism is a very ancient religion in India, perhaps having its origins in a religious culture parallel to Vedic culture. The name Jain derives from the Sanskrit word *jina*, meaning "victor," and refers to an individual who has vanquished the endless cycle of reincarnation with all its suffering on earth. Though there is no proof of any connection, there are statuettes dating back to the Indus Valley civilization of naked standing male figures and of seated figures in a yogic position that uncannily resemble later depictions of Jain *tirthankars*, or "realized souls." Born as human beings, *tirthankars* achieved, through meditation and fasting, the liberation (*moksha*) of their souls (*atman*) from the endless cycle of reincarnation (*samsara*).

There are twenty-four *tirthankars*. The last one to achieve this state of liberation was Mahavir. Born Prince Vardhamana into a Kshatriya family in 599 CE (some scholars say fifty or so years later), Mahavir left home at the age of thirty to lead the life of an ascetic. After twelve and a half years of fasting and meditation, his soul achieved *moksha*, or liberation from his body and from rebirth. His name means "great hero." Mahavir's legacy included communities of monks and nuns who built temples across India. Another *tirthankar* is Bahubali, the legendary son of the *tirthankar* Rishabha. In 981 CE, a fifty-seven-foot-tall monumental statue of Bahubali, carved from a single block of granite, was erected at Shravanabelagola, a town in the Indian state of Karnataka. Every twelve years, a major ceremony is held during which the statue is anointed with milk, saffron paste, and sugarcane juice and showered with flowers. There are also important Jain temple complexes in Palitana, in the state of Gujarat, and on Mount Abu, in Rajasthan.

Jainism is divided into two main sects, Digambars and Swetambars. The differences between the two revolve around disagreements over Mahavir's genealogy and the biographical details of his life. To show their utter indifference to the material world and to the body, Digambar monks do not wear clothes. Digambar nuns and Swetambar monks and nuns wear white cotton clothing. Swetambars hold that women can become realized souls, and that Mallinath, one of the twenty-four *tirthankars*, was a woman.

Though they venerate the *tirthankars*, Jains do not worship any god, gods, or goddesses. Each Jain is responsible for the progression of his or her own soul toward *moksha*. The Jains have extensive and ancient libraries, and reading and studying the texts of Jain doctrine and the teachings of the *tirthankars* and later sages is essential to Jain religious practice.

Jains believe in the sanctity of all life, *jiva*, and in the principle of *ahimsa*, nonviolence. Like Hindus, Jains believe in karma, and that acts of *himsa*, violence, produce bad karma. In order not to harm living beings, practicing Jains are lacto-vegetarians, and many in the West are vegans. For Jains, the act of eating implies doing violence—if only plucking leaves or seeds from a plant—to something that is alive. For Jains, fasting is an important way to cease the violence of eating, and fasting to death is an admired way of leaving the current body. Some orthodox Jains do not eat after sunset, when it is believed that more microorganisms are out and about. They avoid all root vegetables because harvesting these involves killing the plant by pulling it up by the root as well as disturbing microorganisms in the soil. Garlic and onions are considered to give "heat" to passions, a major source of actions that promote bad karma. Restaurants in India frequently offer "Jain" dishes on their menus that do not contain onions, garlic, or root vegetables. Mahatma Gandhi, who made *ahimsa* a core part of his philosophy, was born in Gujarat, where Jainism is prevalent. Gandhi corresponded with the Jain sage Srimad Rajchandra on philosophical and religious topics, and considered him one of his teachers.

Another key notion in Jainism is *anekantavada*, non-absolutism or the principles of relativism and pluralism. The parable of the blind men and the elephant in the introduction to this book illustrates the Jain notion of *anekantavada*: humans attempting to understand the meaning of life or the nature of the soul or of the cosmos are like blind men able to perceive, in a sense-limited way, only a small part of the whole. Discussions of questions such as "What is the meaning of life?" or "What is the nature of the soul?" can only ever yield partial, imperfect answers because humans cannot be omniscient.

The emperor Chandragupta Maurya (340–248 BCE), after conquering and unifying a good part of what is now north-western India, Pakistan, and Afghanistan to create the first major Indian empire, converted to Jainism and fasted to death. Between the eighth and eleventh centuries, Jainism came under pressure from Hinduism, and many Jains converted. Muslim invasions of India in the eleventh and twelfth centuries constrained Jainism further, as Muslim raiders destroyed or damaged Jain temples, burned Jain manuscripts, and forced conversions, as they did with Hindus and Buddhists.

According to the 2011 census of India, there are 4.8 million Jains in India today, which is a tiny percentage of India's population. However, the same census showed Jains have the highest literacy rate—at 94.1 percent—of any of India's religious groups. Almost no one escapes caste in India, and Jains are assimilated into the Hindu caste hierarchy. Most Jains in

Gujarat and north India are Vaishyas, members of the merchant caste. Jains have traditionally worked in trading, banking, and other businesses, such as diamond dealing. Jains control a third of the rough diamond trade in Antwerp, Belgium, where they have built the largest Jain temple outside India.

Who was the Buddha?

India is also the home of Buddhism. Siddhartha Gautama was born a Hindu into a wealthy Kshatriya family in southern Nepal in circa 560 BCE (though some scholars date his birth to as late as 400 BCE). He is reputed to have been an uncommonly handsome man. Legend has it that at the age of thirty, having spent his life in coddled luxury, he saw four things that caused him to realize that all human life is *dukkha*, "suffering": a sick man, an old man, a corpse, and a religious ascetic.

Siddhartha Gautama believed in several of the core precepts of Hinduism: *samsara*, or endless birth and rebirth of the soul into physical bodies, and the operation of *dharma*, which, as we've seen, is the harmony of personal action with the divine order of the cosmos. However, whereas in Hinduism living in accordance with one's *dharma* means respecting the duties and privileges of the *varna* into which one is born, the Buddha believed that every human being could free himself from the suffering of endless birth and death, of *samsara*, and therefore from *dukkha*, suffering, no matter his caste. This view brought the prince Gautama into direct conflict with Hindu orthodoxy.

After a dispute with a Brahmin over the connection between *varna* and *dharma*, Siddhartha Gautama embarked on a quest for meaning that took him to the Ganges Valley in India. At the age of thirty-five, he attained *nirvana*, enlightenment, after meditating under a pipal tree in Bodh Gaya for forty-nine days. The tree is known as the Bodhi tree. When Siddhartha Gautama attained enlightenment, he became the Buddha, the enlightened one. What the Buddha grasped on his path to nirvana forms the core canon of Buddhism. They are known as the Four Noble Truths: (1) life is suffering, (2) suffering is caused by desire, (3) desire can be vanquished, and (4) the way to vanquish desire is not self-mortification or ascetic sacrifice. The Buddha realized this fourth truth after failing to attain nirvana by extreme deprivation. Legend has it he broke his fast by accepting a meal a young woman presented to him in a golden bowl. Buddhism's so-called middle way, or moderate path to enlightenment, was born.

Gautama Buddha spent the rest of his life preaching what he had learned. Core to the teachings of Buddhism are eight precepts known as the Eightfold Path, all of them dealing with notions of "rightness" or "balance." The Eightfold Path consists of (1) right understanding, (2) right thought, (3) right speech, (4) right action or behavior, (5) right livelihood, (6) right effort, (7) right mindfulness, and (8) right concentration or absorption.

Chandragupta Maurya's grandson the emperor Ashoka Maurya (304–232 BCE) played an important role in encouraging the spread of Buddhism in India. Our knowledge of Ashoka comes from Buddhist texts, including the *Ashokavadana* or "Story of Ashoka," written in Sanskrit in the second century, as well as from a number of edicts Ashoka had carved on stone boulders and pillars. Ashoka is said to have converted to Buddhism after being appalled by the massacre of thousands during the war between the Maurya Empire and the kingdom of Kalinga in 262–261 BCE. By that time, Buddhism was already an important religious and social movement in northern India. Ashoka's edicts proclaimed the Buddhist notion of *dhamma*, or *dharma*, as the responsibility of human beings for each other. *Dhamma*, as expounded in Ashoka's edicts, did not exclude any religious path or sect. Ashoka put tolerance of differences between peoples and between different religious beliefs at the core of *dhamma*. He also described the responsibilities and actions of a ruler who cared about the welfare of his people. With Ashoka's death in 232 BCE, the Mauryan Empire went into decline, but Buddhism continued to flourish, spreading throughout Asia.

In the sixth century, a Buddhist king in Sumatra endowed a monastery at Nalanda, located near the city of Patna in what is now the Indian state of Bihar. Nalanda's complex of brick buildings, including dormitories, classrooms, and a library, has been excavated. The largest center of Buddhist learning in India, Nalanda hosted some 10,000 students in its heyday, attracting students from China and Southeast Asia. Its vast library held collections of Buddhist manuscripts but also treatises on astronomy, mathematics, grammar, and medicine. Revenue collected from the monastery's estates and neighboring villages supported the monastery, and students were provided with free room, board, and education.

Nalanda flourished from the sixth through the ninth centuries. At the end of the twelfth century, the complex was sacked by the Turk Bakhtiyar Khilji. A contemporary Arabic account reports that thousands of students were burned alive or beheaded and that the library burned for days. The destruction of Nalanda dealt a major blow to Buddhism in India, which was already declining, with Hindu gods regaining popularity in areas where Buddhism had spread.

Though Buddhism remained strong elsewhere in Asia, it all but disappeared from India after the thirteenth century. It was revived by the scholar and Dalit leader B. R. Ambedkar in the twentieth century. Seeking a way out of Hinduism's caste system and its civilizational oppression of Dalits, Ambedkar converted to Buddhism, along with some 400,000 Dalits gathered for the occasion, in Nagpur, India, on October 14, 1956. Today 8 million Indians consider themselves Buddhists, most following the precepts laid out by Ambedkar in his book *The Buddha and His Dhamma*.

Did Indians invent the concept of zero?

The oldest writing on mathematics in India is found in the *Sulab Sutras*, first written in 800 BCE. The authors of the *Sulab Sutras* stress that they were merely committing to writing knowledge that had existed for a very long time. Vedic culture required the construction of elaborate temples for fire worship and developed advanced geometry, trigonometry, and algebra that served the architectural requirements of these temples. Vedic Indians were adept at using fractions and used advanced accounting, including calculating profit and loss.

By far the most important mathematical invention attributed to ancient Indians is the concept of the number zero. The first written evidence of this dates to between 200 and 400 CE, but the concept was certainly in use well before. Ancient Arabs, who traded with India and who were also gifted mathematicians, transmitted these concepts to Europeans. The word *algebra* comes from the Arabic *al-gibr*. As for the word *zero*, the Arabs translated the Sanskrit word *sunya* as *cifr*, from which we have the word *cipher* but also, via the Latin word *zephirum*, the word *zero*.

Mathematics continued to develop separately in India for centuries after the Vedic age, and Indian mathematicians invented an original system of symbols and words for mathematical concepts, including addition, subtraction, multiplication, division, and mathematical roots. India is still known as a country with a pronounced bent toward mathematics, producing a remarkable number of gifted mathematicians and engineers. One of India's most famous mathematical geniuses was Srinivas Ramanujan (1887–1920), who, without any formal training, rediscovered a number of known theorems and solved new ones.

What about the history of South India?

While Buddhism and Nalanda flourished in northern India, South India also has its own rich and diverse history. Ashoka's edicts reference some of the kingdoms of South India. Ancient South Indian dynasties included the Pandyas, the Cholas, and the Cheras. These dynasties reigned from 300 BCE to between the ninth and thirteenth centuries. South India, with its long coastlines and road connections to the kingdoms in the north, was a center for trade. Roman and Arab ships docked at South Indian ports, while Indian ships sailed to Southeast Asia in search of spices. As trade grew, so did the merchant class and the cities. Vedic culture influenced local elites, who built elaborate stone and rock-cut Hindu temples. The Tamils worshipped the Hindu god Murugan, also known as Subramanya and Kartikeya in neighboring regions of the South. Murugan is a perennially handsome god of war associated with snakes and peacocks. Other popular gods included many in the Vedic Hindu pantheon: Indra, Surya (the god of the sun), Lakshmi, Shiva and his consort Parvati, Hanuman, and Vishnu. Jainism and Buddhism, popular with the merchant class, also flourished in southern India.

Some 80 million people, mainly in South India, speak Tamil. The earliest Tamil writing is found in inscriptions dating from the third century BCE. Tamil belongs to the Dravidian group of languages. Over the centuries, many Sanskrit words were adopted into Tamil and many Tamil words found their way into Sanskrit—and even, intriguingly, into Hebrew. Tamil was first written down in the Prakrit, Brahmi, and Sanskrit scripts. Ancient Tamil epics include *Cilappatikaram* and *Manimekalai*.

The Sangam Age refers to a period between 300 BCE and the fourth century CE, when Tamil culture flourished in South India. The Pandyas, a major dynasty, encouraged academies in the city of Madurai, where poets gathered to compose and recite their poetry. The poetry is divided into two main genres: *akam*, "interior," and *puram*, "exterior." The *akam* poems speak of love in all its forms, its transports, its complications, and its disappointments. The *puram* poems deal with war, the deeds of kings, and the wisdom of the bards.

A *bhakti* cult of ecstatic worship focused on the Hindu gods Vishnu and Shiva arose between 500 and 900 CE, sparking a literary boom as *bhakti* saints traveled all over South India singing devotional poems set to music. Tamil began to be written in its own script at this time. Temples, sponsored by the dynastic kings, became the major centers of religious activity, with

Shaivism, or the worship of Shiva, predominating, though Vishnu was also popular, as was Murugan. The caste system rooted in Vedic culture became firmly entrenched. Trade guilds spanning the Indian subcontinent and extending to Sri Lanka and into Southeast Asia were established. The ancient Chola kingdom entered a phase of glory when King Aditya defeated the Pandyas in 885, making the Chola Empire the largest in the South. Carnatic music, mostly vocal and originating with the hymns of the *Rig Veda* as set to musical notation in the *Sama Veda*, became a distinctive musical tradition of South India. In Karnataka, another great dynasty, the Chalukyas, came to power in the sixth century, and with them the Kanada language took on new importance. The Cholas and the Chalukyas dominated the political scene of South India until the advent of the Vijayanagara state in 1336 on the Deccan Plateau.

Who were the Rajputs?

Meanwhile, far from the Deccan Plateau, in northwestern India, the Rajputs were expanding their power. The Rajputs emerge onto the scene of Indian history in the ninth century. Four Rajput clans claim to have descended from a mythical progenitor who rose out of a sacrificial fire on Rajasthan's sacred Mount Abu. The Agnivanshi, or fire clan, includes the Pariharas, the Chauhans, the Solankis, and the Pawars. There are also Rajput clans that claim to descend from the sun, the Suryavanshis, and from the moon, the Chandravanshis. Each clan or *kul* has a clan goddess or *kul devi*. The Rajputs may have descended from the Huns, equestrian nomads who had conquered Afghanistan, or from tribes who entered India with the Huns in the fifth century. Warriors, the Rajputs were assimilated into the Kshatriya caste.

The name Rajput comes from *raja*, "king," and *putra*, "son," presumably a nod to primogeniture, with kingship passing to the eldest son. The Rajputs clans warred among themselves. After the establishment of the Delhi Sultanate and Mughal rule in northern India, many of the Rajputs became vassals to the sultanate. The Rajputs of Mewar and Marwar—the more recent rulers of Udaipur and Jodhpur in Rajasthan—remained defiant. The princely states of what the British called Rajputana, which included Rajasthan and the Saurashtra region of the state of Gujarat today, came under the British Raj (*raj* means "rule") only in 1818. The Rajputs were allowed to continue to administer their princely holdings and to keep a good part of their revenues on the condition they pass along a portion of these to the British. The fabulous wealth, fairy-tale palaces, polo teams, and incredible jewels of Rajput rajas and maharajas (kings and great kings), not to mention the ranis and maharanis (queens and great queens), made the Rajputs enduring images of Indian royal exoticism. Deprived of their privy purses and feudal privileges in 1971—a year we will read more about later—many former Rajput kings and queens have converted their palaces into luxury hotels. Some have successfully run for elected office in the areas they once ruled. The Rajputs cling to their heritage and clan lineages with fierce pride.

When did Christianity come to India?

Legend has it—and some faithful believe—that Christianity arrived in India when Saint Thomas landed on the Malabar Coast of southwestern India in 52 CE. Villages across Kerala have their own local Saint Thomas traditions still today. In any case, sea trade between India and the Mediterranean via the Persian Gulf beginning around that time would have brought Indians into contact with the early Christian world. The Syrian Christians of Kerala trace their history back to 345 CE when Thomas of Kana, a rich Syrian Christian merchant, arrived with seventy families at Cranganore. There are some 7 million Syrian Christians in India today.

Christianity in India got another big boost after the Portuguese explorer Vasco da Gama put down anchor at

the port of Calicut in 1498, opening a direct sea route between Europe and the riches of India. For pious Portuguese,
commerce and conversion to Christianity went hand in hand.
Following close on the heels of the Portuguese came the
Jesuits. Saint Francis Xavier, one of the founders of the Society
of Jesus, arrived in Goa in 1542 and traveled throughout Asia,
spreading the word of the Christian gospel until his death in
1552. Other Jesuits followed in Saint Xavier's footsteps. They
were the first Western scholars of India, learning Indian languages, translating Indian sacred texts, and documenting
their observations of Indian political, social, and cultural life
in detailed reports. They opened colleges and seminaries for
training Indian converts to be priests.

The British brought the Anglican Church to India in the
early seventeenth century. Other Protestant faiths followed
British colonial expansion. American Protestant evangelicals
arrived in India in the nineteenth century. There is a strong
tradition in India of fine Catholic-run educational institutions
that have educated generations of Indian Hindus. The 2011
census of India counted 28 million Christians, or 2.3 percent of
India's total population.

What about Jews in India?

The history of the Jews in India is ancient and distinct: Jews
were never persecuted in India for their religion. There were
three different Jewish communities in India. The Cochinim,
Jews settled in Cochin, Kerala, traced their roots to merchants
who came to India during the time of King Solomon in search
of spices, peacocks, and other exotic commodities. A pair of
engraved copper plates given by the Kerala king Varman
conferred specific rights to Jews settled in Kerala in 1000 CE.
By the seventeenth century, there were eleven congregations
of Cochin Jews with their own synagogues.

A second group, the Bene Israel, believes their ancestors
were one of the ten biblical lost tribes of Israel whose flight

from persecution brought them to India's shores when their ship was wrecked off the coast of Kerala in 175 BCE. Though the Bene Israel conserved elements of Judaism through long centuries of estrangement from other Jews, their Jewishness was debated until 1964, when Israel officially recognized them as Jews.

Another group of Jews arrived in India much later, in the eighteenth century, by which time European expansion in India was in full swing. These so-called Baghdadi Jews hailed from Baghdad but also from Basra, Aleppo, and other points throughout Persia and the Middle East. Jewish traders established a synagogue in the port city of Surat, a major hub for European trade with India, on the coast of modern-day Gujarat in 1730, and Jewish communities flourished from the end of the eighteenth century in Kolkata and Mumbai. The community counted five synagogues in Calcutta. In Bombay, the Jewish merchant and philanthropist Jacob Sassoon financed the construction of the Keneseth Eliyahoo synagogue. Mumbai's Sassoon Docks bear his name.

By the late 1940s, there were an estimated 30,000 Jews living in India. After the creation of the state of Israel in 1948, the vast majority of India's Jews emigrated. Today, the once thriving Jewish communities in Cochin, Calcutta, and Mumbai are reduced to tiny remnants, and India's total Jewish population stands at less than 5,500 individuals.

When did Muslims arrive in India?

Arabic traders frequented India well before the birth of the Prophet Muhammad and the advent of Islam. Converts to Islam among these traders began arriving in India between the seventh and the eighth centuries, mainly on the Malabar Coast. Some settled in port cities. In the early eleventh century, lured by tales of India's incredible wealth and fired by anti-idolatrous zeal, Mahmud of Ghazni made a series of raids into the Indian subcontinent. A Turkoman sultan, Mahmud founded an empire that covered Afghanistan, Pakistan, parts of northwestern India, and western Iran. Mahmud's mercenary cavalry was highly mobile and effective but also expensive, and Mahmud held out the prospect of loot to inspire his fighting force. He also had ambitions for Ghazni, which he sought to transform from a dusty trading town into an imperial capital.

Hindu temples in northwestern India were well-known repositories of treasure, filled with gold and jewels deposited by pious and prosperous merchants. In 1026, Mahmud's raiders swept across Punjab, Sind, and Gujarat to raid the Shiva temple at Somnath on the coast of Gujarat. While they were there, they broke part of the roof, causing the central idol that hovered mysteriously in midair between the ceiling and the floor (perhaps held by delicately balanced opposing magnets) to fall to the ground. They also killed a great many people, captured prisoners to be sold as slaves, and carried off an enormous amount of loot. Mahmud of Ghazni and other Muslim raiders of this period defaced Hindu, Jain, and Buddhist temple sculptures, which they viewed as idolatrous.

The history of Mahmud of Ghazni's raids into India, the resistance of Rajput clans, and Mahmud's destruction and defacement of Hindu temples—especially the temple at Somnath—has become part of a highly politicized narrative in India around the claims and goals of Hindutva ("Hinduness" or "the way of life of the Indian people") and Hindu nationalism. One of Hindutva's goals is to restore the stature of India's Hindus from the damage done by Muslims, beginning with the sack of the temple at Somnath.

Despite the brutality of Mahmud's raids, Muslim traders, including Bohras, Ismailis, and Kohjas, lived peacefully among Jain and Hindu traders in Somnath and other coastal areas of Gujarat. Hindus also fought as part of Mahmud's mercenary army, living in Ghazni in their own neighborhood, and Hindu and Jain merchants participated in trading networks across the Muslim world.

Following Mahmud of Ghazni, other invaders from Central Asia, Iran, and Afghanistan came to India, conquered territory, and stayed. The Delhi Sultanate brought a series of successive Muslim dynasties to Delhi between 1206 and 1526: the Mamluks, the Khiljis, the Tughlaqs, the Sayyids, and the Afghan Lodis. The tombs of the Lodi kings can be seen today in New Delhi's beautiful Lodi Gardens. The Delhi Sultanate ended with the defeat of the last Lodi king at Palipat by Babur, the first of the Mughals to rule, in 1526.

Who were the Mughals?

The Mughals were highly Persianized Turkic Mongols who brought the Persian language and Persian aesthetic sensibilities to India. The golden age of the Mughals in India during the sixteenth and seventeenth centuries left a lasting legacy, including some of India's most renowned architectural monuments, poetry, and painting. The Mughals were as transformed by India as India was by their rule, producing a new, distinctly Indian culture of exquisite artistic achievement to which Indian Hindus, Jains, and Zoroastrians made major contributions. The Mughals married Hindu Indian princesses, brought Indians of different faiths into their courts, and forged administrative relationships and alliances with Hindu rulers. The impact of the Mughals on the language, food, dress, manners, administration, and political map of India was transformative. It is impossible to imagine India as we know it today without the legacy of the Mughals.

The Mughals got off to a rocky start. Babur lasted only four years in India before being succeeded by his son Humayun. Humayun's reign was checkered as well. Succeeding his father in 1530, he fled into exile to Sind in 1540. His son Akbar, born in 1542, ascended to the throne in 1556 at the tender age of fourteen after his father died, having just retaken Delhi from the Hindu king Vikramaditya. Humayun's tomb is one of the architectural splendors of Delhi.

What is sometimes called the High Mughal era began with Akbar, who ruled for fifty years, until 1605. He transformed a fragile collection of fiefdoms into an empire that sprawled from Afghanistan in the west to Bengal in the east, and south to the Godavari River on the Deccan Plateau. Akbar held his realm together by a well-oiled military machine and a canny administration, but he also treated his subjects with a degree of fairness and respect. He was a curious man, interested in different faiths, who sponsored open debates between Hindu, Jain, Zoroastrian, and Christian priests and scholars, as well as with leaders of different Muslim sects. He abolished a humiliating tax on non-Muslims and married several Rajput princesses, giving members of their families high positions in his court.

Akbar was interested in architecture and had a royal city constructed at Fatehpur Sikri, located near Agra. Built from delicately carved and shaped red sandstone, Fatehpur Sikri incorporated Persian and Indian architectural elements into an enchanting series of courtyards and airy pavilions, with areas for music and dance performances, a giant outdoor chessboard, and water channeled to fill pools and feed fountains.

Akbar was also keenly interested in trade, including trade with Europe. He was aware of the growing Portuguese settlements in Goa, where the Portuguese defeated the local sultan in 1510, and of the interest of other European powers in trade with India. Akbar invited a community of Armenians to settle in Agra, where they were allowed to keep their Christian faith. The Armenians served as middlemen in the textile trade between India and the Levant, and Akbar wanted to expand exports of Agra's famous printed cotton textiles. He married an Armenian woman, Mariam, whose sister was the physician to the women in his harem. He also allowed the Jesuits to set up a college in Agra, and he gave them regular gifts of money to support their projects. The Christian cemetery in Agra, located on part of an estate given by Akbar to the Jesuit mission, still exists. Many of the Armenians Akbar invited to

Agra are buried there, as are a number of French, British, and other Europeans who made Agra their home over the centuries.

Akbar's son Jahangir succeeded to the throne after his father's death. He maintained his father's traditions of courtly life. An alcoholic addicted to opium, he gradually ceded much of his rule to his wife, Nur Jehan. Nur Jehan was, by all accounts, a remarkable woman. Beautiful, well educated, artistically inclined, and politically ruthless, Nur Jehan could hunt and ride a war elephant with the best of the Mughal men. The Mughals did not practice primogeniture; male rulers had many wives and concubines, and many sons who vied for a throne they could obtain only by eliminating their siblings and other family rivals. Shah Jehan ascended to the throne in 1628 after vanquishing his half-brother Shariyar (Nur Jehan's son-in-law and Jahangir's son) in a pitched battle. He secured his rule by executing Shariyar and locking up his stepmother.

Shah Jehan is best remembered as the man who commissioned the building of the Taj Mahal on the banks of the Yamuna River in Agra. A tomb for his beloved wife Mumtaz, who died giving birth to their fourteenth child, the Taj Mahal and its surrounding mosques and gardens took thirty years to complete. Built of white marble, with delicately carved floral panels and inlays of semiprecious stones, the Taj Mahal is considered to be one of the world's most exquisite architectural monuments. Passages from the Koran are inlaid on the monument's exterior and within the interior of the tomb in Persian script rendered in black marble and jasper. In order to preserve the monument's appearance of perfect symmetry, the size of the calligraphy as well as the pitch of the delicate minarets at the four corners of the tomb are calibrated so that they appear equal and straight to the viewer at ground level, though in fact they are not. A team of architects oversaw the Taj Mahal's construction. Master craftsmen and exquisite materials were brought to Agra from across India, Afghanistan, Persia, and Nepal. The Taj Mahal is the most visited tourist destination in India, a symbol of undying love to this day.

Shah Jehan's reign crowned the golden age of Mughal rule in India, begun by his grandfather Akbar. In addition to collectors of land revenues and taxes, the Mughals were avid traders, maintaining fleets of ships that sailed from port cities in Gujarat and Bengal, both of which Akbar conquered during his reign. The Mughal period corresponded with the arrival of Europeans and their trading companies in India. It was Jahangir who granted permission to the British East India Company in 1615 to set up a trading center in Surat, Gujarat, giving the British their first foothold in India. Competition for the India trade was cutthroat, not only between rival European powers but also between Europeans and the Mughals. Still, the Mughals amassed wealth beyond any ever before seen on the Indian subcontinent, spending it on administering, defending, and expanding their empire as well as on a courtly life of incredible luxury and refinement.

In addition to building the Taj Mahal, Shah Jehan expanded the fort in Agra, and built a similarly massive fort of red sandstone in Delhi, called the Lal Qila, or Red Fort, and, opposite the fort, the Jama Masjid, Delhi's most famous mosque. Under his reign, Delhi became a great imperial city. Shah Jahan also inherited his great-grandfather Babur's love of pleasure gardens and built the exquisite Shalimar Gardens in Lahore, now located in Pakistan.

Akbar established an atelier of court calligraphers, painters, and bookbinders called the *kitab khana*, literally "book house." His son and grandson continued this courtly tradition. Painters sponsored by these three generations of Mughal rulers left a legacy of exquisite miniature paintings depicting scenes of courtly life as well as scenes from literary works. Poetry and literature flourished under the Mughals. Jahangir was particularly fond of history, and several important histories were written during his reign. Persian was the court language and the language of Mughal administration as well as the privileged language of courtly poetry, whose legacy includes the great tradition of Urdu poetry. Urdu, written with Persian

Nasta'liq script, evolved under Turkic and Mughal rule on the Indian subcontinent. These rulers wrote the local Hindustani language in Nasta'liq script, and over time that language absorbed many Persian and Arabic words and expressions. Urdu is the national language of Pakistan and one of the official languages of India.

The Mughal courts were centers of pan-Indian and international culture. Literature in Sanskrit and other Indian languages was translated into Persian. Europeans visiting the Mughal courts were consulted by the Mughal rulers and their courtiers, and wrote about what they saw there. One of the most famous European accounts of the court of Shah Jehan was penned by the French Protestant diamond dealer Jean-Baptiste Tavernier, who brought a fabulous 112.75-carat violet Indian diamond, later known as the Hope Diamond, back to France, where he sold it, along with other precious Indian jewels, to Louis XIV. Tavernier described in his memoirs the stunning Peacock Throne. Built to Shah Jehan's specifications, the gold throne, encrusted with jewels and pearls, featured two peacocks whose tails shimmered with precious stones. It was carried off as booty by Nadir Shah when he raided the Mughal Empire in 1738, and it disappeared after his death, its stones and gold surely scattered to many a fortune-seeker's content.

There was constant cross-fertilization and exchange between the Mughal court and the courts of Rajput and other Hindu rulers. Literature in India's regional languages, including Hindi, Bengali, and Brajbhasha (the last of these the language of the Bundela kings at Orchha), underwent a renaissance during this period, as did miniature painting of Hindu themes, many taken from the great epics the *Ramayana* and the *Mahabharata*. Hindu kings constructed their palaces and forts with a hybrid architecture, incorporating Hindu and Mughal-Persian elements. There were also important advances in mathematics and astronomy during the Mughal period. The Rajput king of Jaipur, Jaisingh II, who cannily kept his kingdom intact in close proximity to the Mughals, constructed astronomical observatories that tracked the movements of the stars and the planets with astonishing accuracy. The largest of these observatories is in Jaipur. Another is in Delhi.

Shah Jehan fell ill in 1658. With his illness, Mughal India took a turn from which it never recovered. Shah Jehan's son Dara Shikoh assumed the throne as his chosen regent. Dara Shikoh's brothers Aurangzeb, Shuja, and Murad, perhaps believing their father was dead already, swooped upon Agra with their armies to dislodge the favored brother. Aurangzeb assembled the larger army and defeated all his brothers. He had Murad executed. Shuja was also killed. Dara came in for special treatment.

Dara Shikoh was, by all accounts, rather the opposite of his brother Aurangzeb. He was cultured and open-minded. His religious beliefs tilted toward the mystical attractions of Sufism. He befriended the leading Sikh guru of his day and personally translated verses of the Hindu *Upanishads* into Persian so that Muslim clerics and scholars could read them for themselves. He sponsored miniature painters and calligraphers, and collected an important album of the best of their work, some of which survives. He built a library in Delhi that still exists. He was fond of the performing arts, sponsoring corps of musicians and dancers.

None of this sat well with Aurangzeb. Well versed in Persian and Arabic, Aurangzeb was a pious but intolerant man. He resented his father's favoritism of Dara Shikoh. When his sister Jahanara accidentally burned herself, Shah Jehan, keeping vigil at her bedside, summoned Aurangzeb to court. Enraged when Aurangzeb appeared in his battle gear, Shah Jehan stripped his son of his title and gave the privilege he had enjoyed of using red tents to Dara Shikoh. Every military campaign Aurangzeb undertook under his father's orders ended in defeat or humiliating compromise. At every turn it seemed his brother Dara Shikoh got the better deal. When he finally outmaneuvered him, Aurangzeb brought Dara Shikoh in chains to Delhi, where he had him executed.

As for Shah Jehan, he partially recovered from his illness but never regained his kingship. He was surely in shock from the murder of his three sons, including his favorite and the one he had chosen to rule. Aurangzeb did not kill his father, as he well might have done. Instead, he locked him up in Agra Fort in a sumptuous apartment from which Shah Jehan could see the Taj Mahal, the tomb of his beloved wife.

Aurangzeb snuffed out the Mughal courtly pleasures enjoyed by his forefathers, banning the drinking of alcohol, dancing, gambling, and music. In contrast with his ancestors, he waged a kind of holy war against every religion in India that was not Islam. Aurangzeb reinstated the hated tax on non-Muslims. He ordered the destruction of scores of Hindu temples, stopped the support of the Christian mission in Agra, destroyed Christian settlements near the new European trading posts (called factories), and enslaved Christian converts. Meanwhile, he went on a campaign of imperial expansion, conquering former allied kingdoms now in revolt and pushing the limits of the Mughal Empire ever farther into the Deccan. With the successful siege of Golconda and the possession of its diamond mines, Aurangzeb became perhaps the richest man in the world.

Though he spent far less than his ancestors on expensive courtly luxuries, Aurangzeb's constant military campaigning and the revolt it provoked on every flank of the empire took a heavy toll, plunging the Mughal treasury into penury. Everywhere Aurangzeb turned, he faced hostile neighbors seething with resentment. He incurred the wrath of the Sikhs by executing Tegh Bahadur, the ninth Sikh Guru, in 1675. British pirates attacked and looted some of his ships returning from Mecca. Jats rose up in revolt in Bharatpur. The armies Aurangzeb marshaled against Shivaji on the Deccan Plateau were like traveling cities, his soldiers accompanied by cooks, cobblers, smiths, entertainers, and as many as 50,000 camels and 30,000 elephants, all of which, along with the horses, had to be fed and the men paid their salaries. Military expeditions on this extravagant scale bled dry the treasury of what had been one of the richest empires ever seen. Wobbling within the loosening bonds of its overextended territory, and reeling from rebellions on every front, the Mughal Empire met its match in the Marathas and their leader, Shivaji Bonsle.

By the time he died at the age of eighty-eight in 1707, Aurangzeb had outlived the rivals of his younger days. But the empire he had coveted so much that he had been willing to kill his brothers and imprison his father to rule it had reached a tipping point from which it would never recover. Though it would limp along until the mid-nineteenth century, the Mughal empire in India was effectively over.

Who were the Marathas?

The Marathas are one of the major peoples of India, whose historic homeland is roughly centered in what is now the Indian state of Maharashtra. The most famous Maratha was the afore-mentioned Shivaji Bonsle, who believed from an early age that he was destined to wrest Hindu India from regions controlled by the Mughals. Aurangzeb temporarily quelled Shivaji's ambitions and took him and his son prisoner at his court in Agra. But after a cunning escape in 1666, in which the two hid in baskets of sweets being carried out of court for the poor, Shivaji redoubled his efforts to take territory from the Mughals. In 1674 he had himself made emperor, or *chhatrapati*, of a Maratha kingdom, over which he reigned until 1680. After Shivaji's death in 1707, an alliance of Maratha kings, known as the Maratha Confederacy, revived Maratha power and sustained it until the early nineteenth century, when the British destroyed it. Still, from the later part of the seventeenth century through the early nineteenth century, the Marathas were a major political force in India.

Shivaji is considered a hero by Maharashtrians. His statue is ubiquitous in Maharashtra's capital, Mumbai, where the main railway station, formerly called Victoria Terminus, is now called Chhatrapati Shivaji Terminus.

What is Sikhism?

Sikhism is a religion born in Punjab from the fifteenth-century cauldron of simmering dissent between Islam and Hinduism. Rejecting each religion but embracing elements of both, Guru Nanak (1459–1539) preached that God is one and eternal, and that the faithful have a duty to social welfare. Nine gurus followed in Guru Nanak's footsteps. Guru Ram Das founded the sacred city of Amritsar, which means "Nectar of Immortality," and oversaw the construction of a water tank and a temple at Amritsar. Covered in gold leaf, the Golden Temple is Sikhism's holiest site. The last guru, Guru Gobind Singh, composed the *Guru Granth Sahib*, a collection of hymns that is the culmination of the teachings of Sikhism's ten Gurus. This sacred book was written down in a unique cursive script called Gurmukhi in 1678. Since God is without form, Sikhs do not worship any divine images. They gather in temples and meeting halls called *gurudwaras* to pray and sing verses from the *Guru Granth Sahib*. Sikh *gurudwaras* are famous for their *langar*, communal meals open to anyone.

Guru Nanak traveled widely and peaceably throughout India, preaching his message of life in truth. But these peaceful beginnings were not to last. The growing popularity of Sikhism in the Punjab was viewed by the Mughals as a threat to Islam and to their rule. Jahangir ordered the execution of Guru Arjan in 1606, and his grandson Aurangzeb had the ninth Sikh guru, Guru Tegh Bahadur, executed in 1675. Chafing under Mughal rule and determined to defend his faith, Guru Gobind Singh, the tenth and last Sikh guru, created the "army of the faithful" or Khalsa in 1699. The Sikhs, whose reputation as unbending adherents to their faith was already secure, became a people of martial renown. Initiation into the

Khalsa involves the adoption of five outwardly signs: (1) *kesh*, not cutting one's hair; (2) *kanga*, a wooden comb; (3) *kara*, an iron bracelet; (4) *kachera*, cotton briefs; and (5) *kirpan*, a small dagger. Orthodox Sikh men are recognizable by their flowing beards and often brightly colored turbans that conceal their long hair.

By the end of the eighteenth century, Sikh militarism had evolved into a full-fledged empire, stretching over what is now Afghanistan, Pakistan, and northwest India under the rule of the Sikh king Ranjit Singh. The territory covered by the Sikh Empire at its height gradually came under British control in the first part of the nineteenth century.

Who are the Parsis?

There is a beautiful legend about the arrival of the Parsis in India. Zoroastrians fleeing Muslim conversion in Persia, the Parsis navigated their way to the shores of Gujarat on the Arabian Sea. The precise date of their arrival is debated. It could have been as early as 716 BCE or as late as 936 BCE. As legend has it, the Parsis sent a request to the local Hindu king, asking for refuge. The king sent a messenger back with a bowl full to the brim with milk on a tray, explaining that his kingdom was as full as the bowl of milk and had no room for newcomers. The Parsis then stirred a spoonful of sugar into the milk, saying that they would enrich the kingdom and not be a burden on it. Impressed, the king allowed them to stay on the condition they learn the Gujarati language, that their women wear saris, and that they not try to convert anyone. The Parsis accepted these conditions and stayed.

The Parsis flourished in India, especially in western India and in Mumbai, formerly known as Bombay. There are many references to Parsis in the accounts of European travelers to India reaching as far back as the fourteenth century. However, the Parsis began to emerge as a force in India's history beyond the importance of their relatively tiny numbers with the arrival of the British East India Company in Surat, Gujarat, in the early seventeenth century. Many Parsis, having already been active in trade with the Portuguese and the Dutch, took up work with the British, and their sons were educated in British schools set up by the company. The Parsis' trading and business acumen, their fluency in English, their non-vegetarian cuisine, and the relative freedom enjoyed by Parsi women propelled them to roles of prominence under the emerging British regime. When the East India Company moved the center of its operations to Bombay, many Parsis followed, and Mumbai remains a center of Parsi life and culture.

The most famous Parsi family is the Tatas. Jamsetji Nusserwanji Tata created the humble beginnings of what would become the Tata Group of companies, one of India's largest business groups, in 1868. In 1903, Jamsetji Tata built the Taj Mahal hotel in Mumbai, still one of India's foremost luxury hotels. Legend has it that Tata built the hotel as an act of revenge against the British after he was refused accommodation as an Indian in the then-swank Watson Hotel. The Tata Group, after expanding into steel, information technology, consumer products and manufacturing of all types over the course of the last century, recently acquired the iconic British brands Rolls-Royce and Jaguar, and is now the largest industrial employer in Great Britain. If the story of the Taj Mahal hotel's founding is true, the business group Jamsetji founded has more than avenged any snub he may have experienced.

Parsis have contributed to Indian culture beyond the sphere of business. Sir Pherozeshah Mehta was an Indian independence leader and the first president of India's Congress Party. Filmmaker and photographer Sooni Taraporevala has documented the lives of Parsis, especially in Mumbai, in film and photographs, and Parsi writer Rohinton Mistry, who lives in Canada, is one of India's most celebrated novelists. Never numerous in India when compared with other religious groups, the Parsi population has dwindled to alarming levels in the past several decades, from 115,000 in 1941 to fewer than 69,000 by 2004. Strict patrilineal practices and rules about conversion are mostly blamed for this decline, along with intermarriage with non-Parsis. The community's future is uncertain.

2

THE BRITISH RAJ AND THE ROAD TO INDEPENDENCE

What was the East India Company?

On December 31, 1600, Queen Elizabeth I granted a royal charter giving a group of English adventurers a fifteen-year monopoly over England's trade with Asia. The first incarnation of the British East India Company was born. The British were a century late to the India trade. The Portuguese explorer Vasco Da Gama's ragged fleet had landed in Calicut, the city now known as Kozhikode, on the west coast of India in 1498. The Portuguese founded the first European coastal trading post in India in Cochin in 1500. A century later, following on the heels of the British, the Dutch, French, and even the Danes founded India trading companies. These companies established trading posts, called "factories," along India's coast and fought constantly over access to India's spices, cotton fabrics, indigo, and other prized merchandise. King James I renewed the East India Company's charter in 1609 for an indefinite period. In 1612, he instructed Sir Thomas Roe, ambassador to the Mughal court at Agra, to seek exclusive rights for the Company to set up trading factories in Surat, in the modern Indian state of Gujarat, and other localities. In an incredible boon for the Company, Emperor Jahangir, wary of Portuguese attempts at Catholic conversion in India, conferred these rights in 1615. British trading posts in Madras and Calcutta followed.

In 1661, the islands that would be transformed into the city of Bombay, now called Mumbai, came into the possession of the British crown as part of the Portuguese Catherine of Braganza's dowry when she wed Charles II. Along with access to this territory, Charles II gave the East India Company sweeping powers, including the power to mint money, acquire autonomous territories, establish courts and mete out justice, hire troops, and wage war. Thus began the transformation of the British East India Company from a small joint-stock trading operation run by a handful of hardy, seafaring speculators into an instrument of empire.

This transformation continued through the end of the Seven Years' War in 1763, when the British defeated the French in India and in North America. Taking advantage of the disintegration of the Mughal Empire after Aurangzeb, Joseph François Dupleix, head of the French East India Company in India, formed alliances with disgruntled local princes and successfully routed the British from Madras, today's Chennai. But Robert Clive, the British Company commander, bribed Mir Jafar, commander of the Indian troops on which the French counted, to stay out of the decisive battle between the French and the British at Plassey, a small village near Kolkata in today's West Bengal, in 1757. The French were defeated.

What was Company Rule?

Once the French were out of the way, Robert Clive faced little opposition to expanding the British East India Company in India. Under Clive, the Company seized control of Bengal. The ensuing plunder made Clive a very wealthy man. But the East India Company was badly administered, and in 1773 the British Parliament held debates on the Company's affairs. The British government agreed to extend a loan to the Company in exchange for formal recognition that the British state, and not the East India Company, had ultimate authority over India. In 1765, the Company acquired the right of *diwani*, or the administration of justice and the collection of revenue, in Bengal and Bihar: "Company Rule," or the dominion of India by the British East Asia Company, was born. Its goal was to extract a maximum amount of revenue from India. Intent on maximizing profits, the East India Company callously raised taxes on lands it controlled, and it prevented merchants from putting aside grain reserves following severe drought, provoking a great famine in Bengal between 1769 and 1773. Some 10 million Indians are believed to have perished during these years from starvation or disease, including outbreaks of cholera and smallpox.

In 1773, the Company established its capital in Calcutta, known today as Kolkata, and Warren Hastings was named Governor-General of Bengal. Hastings believed that if the British were to govern India, they must know its history, its customs, and its religion, and he lent his support to the creation of the Bengal Asiatic Society, one of several centers of scholarship on Indian languages, literature, and culture. In 1780, he established the Madrasah-e-Aliah, now known as Aliah University, to educate young Muslim men. But Hastings was also ruthless in his pursuit of profits for the East India Company, caring little for the British crown or Parliament's interests.

In 1788, Britain's parliament, appalled by the excesses of the East India Company, attempted to impeach Hastings, charging him with a list of "high crimes" so numerous it took two days to read them out. Many of the details shared with the British public during the trial—rape, torture, and the systematic murder and starvation of Indians committed in the name of profits—were hardly exclusive to the Company's behavior under Warren Hastings: Robert Clive had been guilty of similar and even worse offenses. The trial proceeded in fits and starts over the course of more than seven years. Hastings was ultimately acquitted, but the trial set the stage for a series of reforms in the East India Company's administration of India, bringing India more tightly under the control of the crown and Parliament.

The beginning of the nineteenth century saw a dramatic expansion of Indian territory under British rule, either through military conquest and direct annexation or through subsidiary alliances with existing hereditary princes and rulers. By 1856, the British East India Company ruled, on behalf of the British government, most of the Indian subcontinent, as well as Burma, either directly or indirectly by affiliations with local rulers.

As dominion in India became an acknowledged fact, the British began to reflect on how they should rule. They did so with all the confidence of the Enlightenment and its accompanying revolutions in science and industry. The Whig politician and historian Thomas Macaulay famously declared in his 1835 "Minute on Indian Education" that there was no question that Western civilization and knowledge were superior to India's, that education should of course be provided in English, and that its goal should be to produce a class of learned natives who could serve as intermediaries between a relative handful of British administrators of empire in India and the millions of Indians they now governed. "We must at present," argued Macaulay, "do our best to form a class who may be interpreters between us and the millions whom we govern; a class of persons, Indian in blood and colour, but English in taste, in opinions, in morals, and in intellect."

What was the Indian Penal Code?

Thomas Macaulay also began drawing up a code of law to guide British administration of justice in India and to bolster British rule. The Indian Penal Code was adopted in 1862. In Macaulay's vision, Indian law under the British would embrace "uniformity when you can have it; diversity when you must have it; but, in all cases certainty." The code sought to usurp the authority of existing Muslim and Hindu law—about which Macaulay had only the most rudimentary understanding—and place all of Indian jurisprudence under a single, overarching British document. It was more or less adopted wholesale by the founders of the Republic of India, including Sardar Vallabhai Patel, Jawaharlal Nehru, and B. R. Ambedkar. Many laws laid down by the British in the mid-nineteenth century, including criminalizing homosexuality and limiting freedom of speech, remain in force today, though pressure is growing to strike a colonial-era law criminalizing homosexuality.

What was the Sepoy Rebellion?

Warren Hastings had made expanding the Company's army one of his priorities after assuming the new post of governor-general—the chief officer of Company Rule in India—in 1773. By 1857, the East India Company's army had swelled to 50,000 British troops and officers and some 300,000 Indian troops. Hastings meant to make the Indian troops—called sepoys, from the Persian word *sipahi*, meaning "soldier"—willing fighting men for their British masters. Part of Hastings's strategy lay in respecting Indian religious and caste sentiments. For example, separate dining facilities were instituted so that upper-caste Hindus did not have to eat with lower-caste Hindus. But in the decades following Hastings's departure from India in 1765, as the scope and reach of their power grew, the British had dwindling patience with what were viewed as ridiculous superstitions getting in the way of the empire's forward march.

British expansion across northern India destroyed much of the existing social and political fabric, severing millions of Indians from their ancestral lands and professions and stealing revenue rights from former landed gentry. One strategy for annexing territory and placing it under direct British rule was the refusal to recognize the traditional Indian inheritance practice whereby rulers could pass their kingdoms on to adopted children in the absence of a natural direct heir. Many of these, along with peasants who had few other options, ended up as pay-for-hire soldiers in the British army. Their salaries were a pittance compared to their British counterparts, and their orders came from British officers.

Under Company rule, justice was meted out with a clear double standard. The British were as unlikely to face punishment for abuses against Indians as Indians were to escape it if they crossed a British subject. At the same time, starting in the 1830s and 1840s, Christian missionaries increased proselytizing efforts in India. Believing that Christianity was superior to Hinduism, Sikhism, or Islam, the British used conversion as an instrument of a "civilizing mission" that justified their empire in India. By the mid-1850s, the rumor that the British were preparing a mass conversion of Hindus and Muslims to Christianity began to spread across India, raising tensions.

The introduction of the Enfield rifle, considered an improvement over previous rifles, was the spark that lit the conflagration. The cartridges for the new rifles were pre-greased, and soldiers needed to bite them before loading them. Rumor spread that the cartridges were greased with pork fat, abhorrent to Muslims, or beef tallow, abhorrent to Hindus. High-caste Hindus would immediately lose their status were they to bite into one. The British were aware that discontent was spreading among the sepoys. They suspected that chapatis, unleavened Indian bread, were being circulated as some kind of secret code for passing seditious information. In Barrackpore, on March 29, 1857, the first major incident of outright rebellion occurred when Mangal Pandey, an Indian soldier in the 34th Bengal Regiment, began pacing about, waving a loaded rifle in the air, yelling about the cartridges, calling for the other Indian soldiers to join him, and then firing on a British officer who had galloped up to subdue him. Pandey, injured when he attempted to shoot himself, was tried and sentenced to hanging. The name Mangal Pandey became a British epithet for all Indian "rebels." For Indians, Mangal Pandey is a national hero.

As revolt spread among Indian troops across northern India, the British found their scattered forces isolated, vulnerable, and woefully unprepared. The siege of the British Residency at Lucknow, which lasted from May 30 to November 27, 1857, was a pivotal event in the rebellion. Lucknow was the capital of the state of Oudh, which the British had annexed in 1856 in a way that had rankled the local population and former rulers. The attack on the British Residency was an attempt by Indian fighters to take back control of territory they felt had been unjustly taken from them. They nearly succeeded. A first relief attempt by the British failed. The second worked, however, and the British managed to break the siege.

During the course of the rebellion, British men, women, and children became targets of Indian fury, and many were killed in their homes or while attempting to flee. But the British riposted even more viciously, murdering thousands of unarmed civilians when they finally retook Delhi in September 1857. Indians—whether involved in the rebellion or not—were made to perform humiliating, soul-crushing punishments, such as licking floors covered with the blood of massacred English women and children in Cawnpore, before being hanged.

Bahadur Zafar Shah II, the last Indian Mughal emperor, had already been deprived of any real power by the Company Raj. His court in Delhi was looted and trashed, as was the city, where soldiers under British command went house to house, murdering the inhabitants and stealing anything of value they could get their hands on. Bahadur Shah, a poet, calligrapher, and patron of the arts, was exiled to Burma, where he died in a British prison in 1862. So ended Mughal rule in India.

On November 1, 1858, in Allahabad, Lord Canning, who presided over the transfer of India from the East India Company to the British crown and was India's first viceroy, read out a proclamation from Queen Victoria in which she asserted her direct rule over India. In 1876, Britain's Parliament gave Queen Victoria the title "Empress of India."

Crown colonies were territories of the British Empire administered by a governor appointed by the monarch. India was, by far, the most valuable and populous British colony. Benjamin Disraeli, who became prime minister of England at Queen Victoria's invitation in 1868, called India "the brightest jewel in the British crown."

Who was the Rani of Jhansi?

The British used what they called the Doctrine of Lapse to seize control of territory under Indian rule. Basically, if a ruler lacked a natural male heir, his kingdom was considered up for grabs. British refusal to recognize the adopted son of the king of Jhansi as his legitimate heir led to a revolt by the queen of Jhansi, Rani Lakshmibai. The British believed the rani had aided and funded sepoy rebels who had massacred British soldiers and their families at Jhansi. They refused to come to her aid to resist a run against her kingdom by neighboring rulers allied with the British Company. But when the British marched on Jhansi in 1858 and demanded the queen surrender, she refused. The image of Rani Lakshmibai of Jhansi on horseback, raised sword in hand, became an icon of India's first major fight against British rule. What the British called the Sepoy Rebellion, Indians call their first war for independence.

Who were the maharajahs?

In fact, the British cannily coopted many Indian royals by pledging to come to their aid against rival Indian rulers and by preserving their privileges and titles. In return, the royals were expected to provide a steady flow of revenue to the British through the payment of taxes and to help defend British interests. India's hereditary rulers—called *rajas*, meaning "kings," or *maharajahs*, "great kings"—were celebrated for their lavish lifestyles and fabulous jewels, as were their wives, called *ranis*, meaning "queens," or maharanis, "great queens." When India's *maharajahs* agreed to integrate their kingdoms into independent India in 1947, the new nation maintained the privy purses—payments made to them by their former subjects—that financed their luxurious lifestyles. India's parliament passed an amendment to India's constitution in 1971 abolishing the princely privy purses.

Who were the coolies?

At a far remove from the luxurious lives of the maharajahs were the coolies. A creation of British colonialism, "coolie" was a British term for indentured Indian laborers. The word derives from the Tamil word for wages, *kuli*. When a British law abolishing slavery went into effect in 1834, thousands of Indian coolies were sent to work on plantations in Mauritius, British Guiana, Fiji, the West Indies, and elsewhere. In India today, the word refers to a luggage porter, easily identifiable at India's railway stations by their red shirts and official "porter coolie" brass badges.

Who was Rabindranath Tagore?

Rabindranath Tagore (1861–1941) was an Indian poet, painter, novelist, essayist, philosopher, and educational reformer. An eminent member of the mid-nineteenth-century flowering of culture and religious revivalism in Bengal that is known as the Bengali Renaissance, Tagore was awarded the Nobel Prize for Literature in 1913—the first Asian to win the prize—for his series of poems *Gitanjali* (Song Offerings). Rabindranath Tagore was born into a highly cultured, landowning family in Bengal. His grandfather, Dwarkanath Tagore, was one of the first Indian Hindus to travel to England. His father, Debendranath, was active in the Indian nationalist and cultural movement called Brahmo Samaj (Society of Brahma) and founded an ashram 150 miles north of Kolkata that welcomed people of all castes and religions who wished to meditate there on the universal spirit of the divine. Tagore, who studied at the University of London, was well versed in Indian and English literatures. In 1901, he and his wife, Mrinalini, moved to his father's ashram, where he founded a school named Shantiniketan, the Abode of Peace, at which students were educated in a holistic, humanist spirit. Classes were often conducted outside, under the shade of a tree, with students and teacher sitting in a circle. Tagore was a product of, and believed strongly in, the synthesis of Asian and Western philosophies and aesthetics. He traveled to Japan and the European continent, where his work was well known, and from whose artistic traditions he freely borrowed. Tagore was deeply saddened by the communal violence, or violence between Hindus and Muslims, that gripped India in the years prior to independence. India's first prime minister, Jawaharlal Nehru, wrote after Tagore's death in 1941: "Perhaps it is as well that [Tagore] died now and did not see the many horrors that are likely to descend in increasing measure on the world and on India. He had seen enough and he was infinitely sad and unhappy."

Who was Subhas Chandra Bose?

Subhas Chandra Bose (1897–1945) was an Indian nationalist and freedom fighter who parted ways with the Indian National Congress in 1939 after he became convinced India's independence from Britain could not be won by the nonviolent methods advocated by Mahatma Gandhi. During World War II, Bose sought help for India's independence struggle from Britain's enemies Japan and Germany. He traveled to Germany in 1941, where he founded the *Free India* radio broadcast, known in Hindi as *Azad Hind*, and conscripted a battalion of 3,000 Indian soldiers who were prisoners of war in Germany. The Indian soldiers had fought for the British and been captured in Libya by the Nazis. Named the Legion Freies Indien, or Indian Free Legion, the force saw little action, though a small contingent was sent to defend the Atlantic Wall in France toward the end of the war. The uniformed men sported a shoulder badge featuring a leaping tiger over the Indian orange, white, and green tricolor.

In 1943, Bose traveled from Germany to Japan. Japan had captured some 40,000 Indian troops fighting under British command in Singapore and Malaysia. With support from the Japanese, the first Indian National Army was formed from these captured troops as well as Indians living in Southeast Asia. On October 21, 1943, Bose proclaimed the creation of a provisional government of a free India. His Indian National Army fought on the side of Japan against the British in Burma. It had a Youth Wing, known as the Tokyo Boys, and a women's brigade named for the Rani of Jhansi.

After the defeat of the Axis powers in 1945, soldiers from the Indian National Army and the Legion Freies Indien in Europe were repatriated to India to be tried for treason. The trials in 1945 and 1946 provoked massive demonstrations across India. Quick to recognize the value of harnessing these emotions, Jawaharlal Nehru and the Indian National Congress adeptly assimilated their own freedom struggle to that of the Indian National Army, taking up the defense of the first three Indian National Army officers facing court-martial. The three officers were convicted of "waging war against the King"—and then released, public support for them being too strong to be ignored. On August 15, 1947, the day India became independent from British rule, the remaining eleven Indian National Army prisoners were released under the historic occasion's general amnesty.

Subhas Chandra Bose did not live to see the final rehabilitation of the Indian National Army or India's independence. He is believed to have died from injuries sustained in the crash of a Japanese plane on August 18, 1945.

Who was Mahatma Gandhi?

Mahatma Gandhi, the most emblematic figure in India's independence movement, transcends India. His philosophy of nonviolent political resistance, known as *satyagraha*, not only played a key role in India's independence but inspired revolts against oppression across the globe, from America's civil rights movement to South Africa's struggle against apartheid. An original, self-critical thinker, Mahatma Gandhi was a communications genius, adept at using the media to further his cause.

Born Mohandas Karamchand Gandhi in Porbander, Gujarat, India on October 2, 1869, Gandhi was married as a teenager and had already started a family by the time he left for London in 1888 to study law. It was there that he began his transformation from a law student who tried to learn ballroom dancing, speak French, and play the violin into the ascetic political leader known as the Mahatma, or Great Soul. In London, Gandhi read Madame Helena Blavatsky's *The Key to Theosophy* and Henry Salt's *Plea for Vegetarianism*. He joined the London Vegetarian Society and wrote a series of articles on vegetarianism in India.

When Gandhi returned to India after being received at—passing, in other words—the bar, he had trouble finding employment as a lawyer. Debilitating shyness in public speaking made it impossible for him to argue cases. An opportunity to represent an Indian merchant in South Africa took him to Durban in 1893. He spent most of the next twenty years in South Africa, returning briefly to India in 1896 to fetch his family. It was in South Africa that Gandhi forged his political and personal philosophy. An early indication of Gandhi's resistance to injustice was a challenge to the strict racial segregation that barred Indians from traveling in first-class rail coaches reserved for whites. Gandhi won the challenge, successfully buying a first-class ticket and stubbornly staying in his seat when a stationmaster ordered him to move to the third-class compartment. Gandhi's work defending the elite Indians of South Africa from discriminatory laws that lumped them in with the "coolie class" of Indian workers led him to take on the issue of injustice against Indians generally. He founded the Natal Indian Congress in 1894 and began publishing political pamphlets. In 1903, he founded a weekly newspaper, *Indian Opinion*, where he expressed his evolving views on everything from labor strikes to the healthful effect of mud baths.

Gandhi transformed himself in South Africa. He read Tolstoy's 1893 philosophical magnum opus, *The Kingdom of God Is Within You*, a book whose meditations on nonviolence marked him profoundly. He corresponded with a friend, the Jain scholar Shrimad Rajchandra, on spiritual questions and read the books Rajchandra sent from India. He experimented with his vegetarian diet. He took a vow of *brahmacharya*, celibacy, to turn himself into a better instrument for his spiritual and political work. He forged friendships with Europeans who dabbled in the esoteric and alternative philosophies of the West, among them Herbert Kallenbach, a South African architect, and Henry Polak, a Dutch unionist. Gandhi was so inspired by his reading of a book Polak lent him, John Ruskin's *Unto This Last*, that in 1904 he decided to found a utopian community to put into practice an experiment in communal, self-sufficient living, Phoenix Settlement. It was the first of several utopian communities that Gandhi would found over his lifetime. In 1910, his friend Kallenbach offered him a tract of 1,100 acres on which he and Gandhi established another communal settlement, Tolstoy Farm.

Gandhi forged his method and philosophy of nonviolent, mass political resistance in South Africa. The turning point was the merging of his spiritual and political efforts in the form of what he called *satyagraha*, the firm hold on truth. *Satyagraha* involved mass nonviolent protest against injustice on the part of individuals ready to sacrifice their lives, if need be, to force the oppressor to admit moral failure. It was forged when Gandhi leapt to the defense of indentured laborers in South Africa in 1913 with a mass walkout. For the first time, Gandhi, who had dressed carefully for his role as an English-trained barrister, appeared at the laborers' side in Indian dress, his head shaved like a Hindu holy man. The Mahatma was born.

When Gandhi returned to India from South Africa in 1915, he moved to a new ashram on the banks of the Sabarmati River near Ahmedabad in the Indian state of Gujarat. From that point, the cause of Indian independence and alleviating the plight of India's poor millions was Gandhi's mission. In 1918, he led a campaign on behalf of the millworkers in Ahmedabad. In 1919, he called for a national *satyagraha* to protest the Rowlatt Act—about which we shall learn more later—and in 1921 he called for another national *satyagraha* over the killings in the Punjab. His goal for India, as for himself and his acolytes, became *swaraj*, meaning both self-rule but also control of the self. In 1909, he wrote *Hind Swaraj*, his clearest call for India's independence, both from Britain and from Western modernity. In 1926, his *Autobiography, or My Experiments with Truth* was serialized in his magazine *Young India*, published in both English and Gujarati.

Gandhi clashed with other Indian independence leaders almost as much as he did with the British. His belief that Indians were best off living in villages and that until the poorest man could afford better true nationalists should live, as Gandhi did, as spartanly as possible was not shared by leaders such as Jawaharlal Nehru, who envisioned a modernized, industrialized India after independence. B. R. Ambedkar strongly opposed Gandhi's belief that the Hindu caste system could be reformed yet left intact. Ambedkar ultimately came to see Hinduism as irredeemable on the issue of caste and the oppression of Dalits, and renounced it. Gandhi's pleas for communal harmony fell on deaf ears as Hindus and Muslims slaughtered each other in Bengal in 1946–47. Mohammad Ali Jinnah, head of the Muslim League and Pakistan's first leader, rejected Gandhi's opposition to the partition of India to create Pakistan.

On January 30, 1948, Naturam Godse, a Hindu extremist, shot and killed Gandhi as he walked to his regular evening prayers. In the speech he gave to the people of India after Mahatma

Gandhi's death, Jawaharlal Nehru said: Gandhi "lives in the hearts of millions and he will live for immemorial ages."

What happened at Jallianwala Bagh?

Toward the end of World War I—a war in which thousands of Indian soldiers fought under the British flag—Indian patience with the indignities of colonial rule was wearing thin, and there was growing agitation for independence. Alarmed, and with no intention of giving up India, the British charged lawyer Sidney Rowlatt to head a Sedition Committee to look into what could be done to quash "the revolutionary movement in India." The Rowlatt Committee issued a report in 1918 calling for national newspapers to be banned and for Indians suspected of fomenting revolt to be imprisoned indefinitely without trial. Based on that report, the Rowlatt Act, which criminalized sedition and recommended appropriately severe punishments, was passed on March 21, 1919, by the Imperial Legislative Council, the legislative body of British colonial India. Mahatma Gandhi immediately called for a *hartal*, or strike, in protest.

In Punjab, there was already a simmering independence movement under way. On April 10, a British schoolteacher named Marcella Sherwood, who was in charge of the mission schools in Amritsar, was attacked and injured by a mob as she rode through the town on her bicycle. On April 12, Michael O'Dwyer, Governor of Punjab, issued an order banning public assemblies. On April 13, 1919, a group of people, who may not have been aware of the order, assembled in peaceful protest at an enclosed public garden called the Jallianwala Bagh. British officer Reginald Dyer, who had come to Amritsar to quell resistance in the wake of the attack on Sherwood, ordered troops to fire, without warning, on the protesters, who had no avenue of escape. The hail of bullets killed 379 people and wounded 1,500. In panic, some tried to save themselves by jumping into an open well in the garden. One hundred and twenty bodies were pulled out of the well after the incident was over.

Dyer also ordered all Indians who passed on the lane where the attack on Sherwood had taken place to crawl its length on their bellies. Though Dyer was dismissed from the Army after an inquiry into the massacre, many British viewed him as a national hero who had defended the honor of a British woman and put down an insurrection that reminded too many of the Sepoy Rebellion.

The massacre at Jallianwala Bagh and Dyer's humiliating crawling order cemented many Indians' view that British rule had lost all legitimacy, and it marked an important turning point in India's struggle for independence. Rabindranath Tagore, Asia's first Nobel laureate, wrote to the British viceroy Lord Chelmsford after the events at Jallianwala Bagh on May 30, 1919, to renounce the knighthood conferred upon him by the British crown in 1915. In his letter, Tagore wrote: "The time has come when badges of honour make our shame glaring in the incongruous context of humiliation, and I for my part, wish to stand, shorn, of all special distinctions, by the side of those of my countrymen who, for their so called insignificance, are liable to suffer degradation not fit for human beings."

What was the Salt March?

On December 29, 1929, the All-India Congress Committee, under the presidency of Jawaharlal Nehru and comprising the leadership of the nationalist Indian National Congress party, approved a resolution in favor of India's complete independence—*purna swaraj*—from Britain. The committee acted in frustration over British flip-flopping on the granting of dominion status to India. The question of dominion status, a step toward independence, was to have been discussed at a roundtable conference, but the issue became hostage to a domestic British political tussle, and Lord Irwin, viceroy of India, was finally unable to promise the Indian nationalist leadership that a roundtable conference to discuss the matter would happen.

The Congress leadership knew that political action needed to follow the December 29 independence resolution if it was to make any impression on the British. On March 2, 1930, Gandhi sent a letter to Lord Irwin explaining that British rule was a curse under which Indians could no longer live, and that he intended to engage in a mass act of civil disobedience to make the British people "see the wrong they have done to India." On March 12, Gandhi set out on foot from Sabarmati Ashram at the head of a line of seventy-eight dedicated followers. Their destination was Dandi, on the southern coast of the state of Gujarat, where they intended to make free salt in defiance of British taxes on Indian salt designed to favor the import to India of British salt. The names of the participants in the protest march were published for the benefit of the police. Gandhi invited the British to dare to stop them. After walking two hundred miles in twenty-four days, the marchers arrived at Dandi. There on the beach, Gandhi picked up a bit of salt deposited by the waves.

The image of Gandhi—whose photograph was snapped by foreign reporters and quickly appeared in newspapers around the world—wrapped in a white dhoti and shawl, wearing simple sandals and resolutely marching forward with a long bamboo walking stick in hand, became the most iconic image of India's independence struggle. Following Gandhi's example, people began going to India's shores to make salt out of seawater. Mass arrests, exactly as Gandhi had hoped for, began. Gandhi's son Ramdas and other followers were arrested. The police began to use violence, beating and kicking protestors. Gandhi himself was arrested in the early hours of May 5, 1930. On May 21, the poet and nationalist leader Sarojini Naidu led a march of 2,500 white-clad participants in what became known as the "salt *satyagraha*" in a nonviolent protest against the Dharasana Salt Works. Groups of protestors resolutely walked forward toward the entrance to the salt works.

What happened when they refused to stop made instant world news, thanks to the presence of Webb Miller, an

American reporter for the United Press. Miller's eyewitness account of line after line of white-clad protestors walking unflinchingly toward the entrance of the salt works only to be brutally whacked down by Indian police under British orders wielding steel-clad lathis shocked the world and ended any moral pretense for British rule in India. "Although everyone knew that within a few minutes he would be beaten down, perhaps killed," wrote Webb, "I could detect no signs of wavering or fear. They marched steadily, with heads up, without the encouragement of music or cheering or any possibility that they might escape serious injury or death. The police rushed out and methodically and mechanically beat down the second column. There was no fight, no struggle; the marchers simply walked forward till struck down."

What was Quit India?

On August 8, 1942, frustrated with Britain's refusal to take steps to give India its independence until after the war—whose outcome at that point was very much in doubt—the Indian National Congress convened in Mumbai and ratified a call Gandhi had made earlier in the year for the British to "quit India" voluntarily. Gandhi rallied the Indian people with the slogan "Do or die." The British immediately took harsh steps against both Gandhi and the Congress leaders, arresting them and banning several Congress committees as unlawful associations. This crackdown united the Indian people behind the independence movement, provoking mass demonstrations across the country. Though Britain managed to contain public unrest by violently suppressing demonstrators, a turning point had been reached, and the end of British rule in India loomed.

What role did women play in India's independence?

Indian women were especially active in their nation's struggle for independence. Many responded to Gandhi's call to wear *khadi*, or homespun cotton cloth, and to donate their jewelry to the cause. They participated in strikes and peaceful demonstrations. India's independence movement offered Indian women, most of whom led lives strictly confined to the home under the tutelage of fathers or husbands, an avenue to assert themselves in public life. For privileged Indian women from liberal, educated backgrounds, the independence movement provided a path to political leadership.

Among women leaders in India's independence movement was Sarojini Naidu, a poet known as the "Nightingale of India." She was elected the first woman president of the Indian National Congress party—the party that led India's independence struggle—in 1925. In 1930, she led the Salt Satyagraha nonviolent protest, mentioned earlier, against the Dharasana Salt Works. She traveled to London with Gandhi in September 1931 to attend the Second Roundtable Conference to discuss independence for India. After India's independence, she became the first woman governor of the state of Uttar Pradesh.

Another was Anasuya Sarabhai, sister of the textile mill owner and Gandhi supporter Ambalal Sarabhai. She organized workers in Ahmedabad, Gujarat, beginning in 1914. In 1920, Gandhi put his support behind striking millworkers in Ahmedabad, initiating a fast on their behalf. The workers eventually received a pay increase, and Gandhi discovered the power of fasting as a political strategy. Anasuya's niece and Ambalal Sarabhai's daughter, Mridula, was jailed for her role in the Salt Satyagraha in 1930. She traveled to Punjab during the 1947 Partition of India and Pakistan to try to stop the slaughter and help refugees caught up in the deadly mayhem.

Vijaya Lakshmi Pandit, Jawaharlal Nehru's sister, was closely involved in the Indian Congress Party's independence struggle. The British imprisoned her three times for her efforts. In the 1930s, she was elected a member of the Legislative Assembly of the United Provinces (former Indian royal territories that would later become the Indian state of Uttar Pradesh) and was made minister for local self-government and public health. She was reelected in 1946. After India's independence, she served as India's chief delegate to the United Nations.

Who was Mohammad Ali Jinnah?

Mohammad Ali Jinnah was the founder of Pakistan. A brilliant barrister active in the Indian National Congress, Jinnah was the leader of the All-India Muslim League, founded in 1906 to represent the interests of India's Muslims in a Hindu-majority country. During the late 1930s and the 1940s, friction rose between the Indian National Congress and the Muslim League, and violent rioting between Hindus and Muslims tore the country apart. The British adroitly played one group off against the other. Jinnah came to view the partition of India and the creation of a separate state for India's Muslims as inevitable, a step Gandhi fervently opposed. Despite such opposition, however, Pakistan was formed and Jinnah became Pakistan's first governor general and first president of its constituent assembly. He died of tuberculosis just a year after India's independence and the founding of Pakistan in 1948, having left an indelible impact on both countries.

What was Partition?

Partition refers to the division of India to create the new state of Pakistan as a homeland for India's Muslims. There were two partitions. To India's east, Bengal was divided into what is now the Indian state of West Bengal and what was originally East Pakistan, now Bangladesh. To India's west, Punjab was divided into what are now the Indian state of Punjab and Pakistani Punjab. The lines of these divisions are known as the Radcliffe Line after Lord Cyril Radcliffe, chairman of the commission charged with drawing the new boundaries. As independence on August 15, 1947, loomed, the Indian National Congress and Muslim League representatives on the commission couldn't agree on exactly where to set those boundaries. On August 17, 1947, Lord Radcliffe made the final determination, to the satisfaction of neither the Indian nor the Pakistan sides.

Sporadic convulsions of violence between Hindus and Muslims in India throughout the early decades of the twentieth century grew in scope and frequency as independence for India became inevitable. The British bear blame for encouraging politically organized identities around religion. Lord Mountbatten, the last British Viceroy of India, charged with managing the transfer of power, rushed independence along, moving the anticipated date up by ten months. This created a kind of panic. The clash of personalities between Mahatma Gandhi and Mohammed Ali Jinnah didn't help matters. It is an irony of history that the secular, whiskey-drinking Jinnah ultimately became the father of the Muslim state of Pakistan, and that the spiritually minded Gandhi opposed to his last the division of India along religious lines.

So it was that when Pakistan and independent India came into existence in August 1947, millions of people scrambled to cross the new borders. Hindus and Sikhs headed to India, and Muslims fled to Pakistan. A mutual slaughter of nearly incomprehensible proportions accompanied terrified people on the move. By 1948, some 15 million people had migrated from one side to the other. Between 1 and 2 million were killed. Some 75,000 women were raped. The savagery was shocking: people were massacred by the thousands, in their villages, on the roads choked with refugees, and even in trains.

Neither India nor Pakistan has recovered from the trauma of Partition. The two countries have fought several wars, and Indian Kashmir remains the site of rancorous contestation between the Muslim-majority Kashmiri people and the Indian state. In 1971, East Pakistan fought a bitter war against West Pakistan for independence, a war that created the country of Bangladesh. The syncretic culture that had flourished in

Delhi and in Lahore for centuries was profoundly shaken by Partition, and the trauma still feeds a deep antipathy between Indians who hew to the idea of India as a secular republic where all faiths can live in harmony, on one hand, and champions of Hindu majoritarianism, on the other.

3

A NEW REPUBLIC

What challenges did India face at independence?

When India achieved independence from Britain on August 15, 1947, it faced a daunting situation. Its population of 345 million was largely poor and uneducated. Average life expectancy was just thirty-two years. Ninety-two percent of India's people were illiterate. Eight million refugees had poured into India from the Pakistani side of the new border separating the two countries. In addition to coping with the great trauma of Partition, which saw between 1 and 2 million people slaughtered in an orgy of sectarian violence, the refugees needs homes and jobs.

In 1947, India was still reeling from the aftermath of World War II and the Bengal famine of 1943, in which grain hoarding and profiteering—and the diversion of grain by the British away from hungry Indians to its troops around the world—caused the starvation deaths of 3 million Indians. Dependent on fickle monsoon rains, Indian agriculture could not expect to produce enough food to feed the new nation immediately, especially given that vast grain-producing areas that used to provide for an undivided India now lay in Pakistan.

A new democratic framework needed to be established, and a new constitution adopted that would bring together into a united polity a diverse nation of people who spoke different languages, held different religious beliefs, ate different food, and belonged to different castes. Many were the pessimists who believed democracy could never work in India, a staggeringly diverse country, with a largely poor and uneducated population. Yet India's leaders opted for universal suffrage, and though India's democracy, like all democracies, has its warts and has taken its knocks, the naysayers were proved wrong: Democracy in India flourished.

There was also the matter of 565 Indian princely states over which Britain did not have sovereignty. Most were cajoled into joining the new nation by the payment of privy purses—annual payments from the new government of India—in exchange for accession. Several of India's major linguistic groups had expectations that independence would create newly defined states based on language. The process of reorganizing India's states to integrate the former princely states while reflecting the aspirations of different linguistic groups began immediately. This process has continued in fits and starts throughout the Republic of India's seventy-odd-year history. The Republic of India began with fourteen states; it now has twenty-eight, with the most recent, Telangana, coming into existence in 2014. Likely it will have more in the future.

At independence, India badly needed development. A predominantly agricultural economy, India sorely lacked basic infrastructure. It needed power plants, roads, new industries, educational institutions, healthcare facilities—and jobs for its young and growing population. India's first government, led by Jawaharlal Nehru, opted for a program of state-planned development. A Planning Commission, charged with plotting a rapid rise in the country's development, was established with the founding of India's Republic in 1950. Until Prime Minister Narendra Modi dissolved the Planning Commission in January 2015, India's development was charted in a series of government-directed five-year plans.

There was also the problem of defending the new borders of the country. Pakistan's invasion of Kashmir in October 1947, in which it succeeded in wresting a portion of the region from

India, gave rise not only to ongoing enmity between India and Pakistan but also to endless Indian anxiety over maintaining sovereignty over its territory.

When was the Republic of India founded?

Though India gained its independence in August 1947, the country's new constitution was adopted on November 6, 1949, and the Republic of India was born on January 26, 1950. India's constitution established independent India as a "sovereign democratic republic." It guaranteed all Indian citizens justice, liberty, equality, and fraternity. It sought to promote communal harmony. And it set out the judicial and legislative bases for the new republic. India's constitution is one of the world's longest: including all amendments, appendices, an annexure, and an index, it weighs in at 467 pages.

Jawaharlal Nehru was named India's first prime minister and Sardar Vallabhai Patel the country's first deputy prime minister. Rajendra Prasad was India's first president. B. R. Ambedkar was minister of law. There was only one woman in the first cabinet: minister of health Amrit Kaur.

India celebrates August 15 as Independence Day and January 26 as Republic Day.

Who was Jawaharlal Nehru?

Jawaharlal Nehru was a core leader of India's independence movement. He became India's first prime minister after the country gained its independence in 1947. The son of a wealthy family originally from Kashmir who became a lawyer, Nehru was deeply influenced by Mahatma Gandhi, though he did not share Gandhi's vision of India as a nation of self-sufficient villages, nor Gandhi's rejection of technology and the trappings of a modern economy. The British arrested Nehru several times during the 1920s and the 1930s for his activities. He wrote his books *An Autobiography: Toward Freedom*

(1936) and *The Discovery of India* (1946) during two of his prison spells.

On August 15, 1947, Nehru gave a remarkably eloquent speech to mark the occasion of India's freedom with these memorable lines: "At the stroke of the midnight hour, when the world sleeps, India will awake to life and freedom. A moment comes, which comes but rarely in history, when we step out from the old to the new, when an age ends, and when the soul of a nation, long suppressed, finds utterance."

As prime minister, Nehru set India on a socialist-inspired course of industrialization managed under Soviet-type government-directed five-year plans. Under his leadership, India became a key member of the Non-Aligned Movement, a group of developing countries created in 1961 that refused to align with either the United States or the former Soviet Union during the Cold War. The 1962 defeat of India by China in a war over the two countries' disputed border—more fully discussed later—was a blow to Nehru, who had woefully miscalculated China's intentions.

One of the giants who conceived of and ushered in independent India, Jawaharlal Nehru won India's first election in 1952, and subsequent elections in 1957 and 1962. He died of a stroke in 1964. But his legacy lived on for decades, as first his daughter, Indira Gandhi, and then his grandson Rajiv Gandhi each became prime minister, perpetuating a family dynasty that dominated India's Congress Party and its hold on power into the twenty-first century. Both were ultimately assassinated. Severely weakened after India's current prime minister and member of the Hindu nationalist Bharatiya Janata Party (BJP), Narendra Modi, swept into power in the 2014 elections, the Nehru family, in the persons of Rajiv Gandhi's widow, Sonia Gandhi, and his son, Rahul Gandhi, soldiers on as legacy trustees of the Congress Party. But that party, the fabled architect of India's independence, now lies in political tatters, and much of Nehru's legacy—his belief that socialism was the only solution for a country as poor as India, his commitment to an idea of India as a diverse democracy where people of all faiths could live in harmony, a political and social vision steeped in the ideas and institutions of the West—is now being undone as India tacks steadily toward a Hindu majoritarian concept of nationhood.

Who was B. R. Ambedkar?

Bhimrao Ramji Ambedkar was the main architect of the Republic of India's Constitution and its first minister of law. Born into the Mahar caste of untouchables—now known as Dalits—in the Indian state of Maharashtra, Ambedkar led a remarkable life. His father used his job with the British army to get his children enrolled in the local school, though they were not allowed to sit inside the classroom with the higher-caste students. After the family moved to Bombay, Ambedkar was the first person of his caste to be admitted to that city's Elphinstone College. He received a scholarship from the princely state of Baroda to study at Columbia University in New York, where he earned a doctorate in economics. He then left for London, where he passed the bar examination and earned another doctorate from the London School of Economics.

Ambedkar was, as we've seen, a lifelong crusader for the rights of Dalits. He disseminated his views in periodicals he founded and he led marches against anti-Dalit discrimination, demanding they have access to Hindu temples and public wells. Ambedkar clashed with Mahatma Gandhi on the issue of Dalit rights, believing that Dalits could protect their interests only by electing their own leaders through separate electorates. He also believed in the affirmative power of being well dressed, and that Dalit liberation could be achieved only by fleeing the stifling social strictures of India's villages for the dynamism of cities. Ambedkar denounced the ancient Hindu law code, the Laws of Manu, for their rigid enforcement of the caste system. Convinced that Hinduism could never accommodate Dalits as equals, Ambedkar converted to Buddhism, along with some 400,000 Dalit followers, in a public ceremony in Nagpur, India in 1956.

Today, Ambedkar remains a source of inspiration and political vindication for members of India's lowest castes. Statues of Ambedkar, bespectacled and dressed in a three-piece suit, grace Dalit villages and neighborhoods throughout India. Yet, as we will see in Part II, Dalits in India continue to struggle against cruel, systemic discrimination. In July 2017, India's electoral college elected a Dalit, Ram Nath Kovind, as president of India, a largely ceremonial post in India's parliamentary democracy, where the prime minister is the seat of real power. Kovind is a stalwart of the governing Hindu nationalist Bharatiya Janata Party, and his election is widely viewed as a political calculation by the party to boost its support among low-caste Hindus in the 2019 general elections. While the election of a Dalit to India's presidency is significant, it remains to be seen if this will help change entrenched prejudice among India's upper castes, too many of whom continue to view Dalits as social outcasts.

What happened in Kashmir?

When India gained its independence and Pakistan was created in August 1947, the future of Kashmir—a princely state ruled by the Hindu maharajah Hari Singh but with a Muslim-majority population—was unclear. Neither Nehru nor Jinnah would accept independence for Kashmir. Nehru's view was that India, as a secular republic, could accommodate citizens of all faiths. Jinnah's view was that Kashmir, with its Muslim-majority population, belonged with Pakistan. However, Sheikh Mohammed Abdullah, who led the secular, democratic Kashmir National Congress, was not in favor of acceding to Pakistan.

On October 22, 1947, Pakistan invaded Kashmir. Kashmir's Maharajah Singh asked the Indian government for help, to which Nehru agreed after consulting with Sheikh Mohammed Abdullah, the leader of Kashmir's largest secular party, if

Kashmir acceded to India. The maharajah agreed, and Indian troops were sent to Kashmir, where they successfully halted the Pakistani advance. Pakistan remained, however, in possession of territory in northwestern Kashmir.

The United Nations brokered a cease-fire that took effect on January 1, 1949. Both sides agreed the Kashmiris should hold a plebiscite to express their wish to join either India or Pakistan. But India insisted Pakistan withdraw first. Pakistan demurred. The plebiscite was never held.

In 1965, Pakistani troops again invaded Kashmir, but they were repelled by India. In 1971, India and Pakistan went to war again when India came to Bangladesh's aid in its successful bid for independence from Pakistan. In 1972, India and Pakistan signed the Simla Pact, in which they agreed to recognize the 1971 line of control separating the two countries in Kashmir as the de facto border.

But the question of independence has never completely died in Kashmir. Nor has Pakistan's hope of one day seizing all of Kashmir. On top of this, a series of events during the 1970s set the stage for a popular insurgency in Indian Kashmir whose tragic effects roil the region to this day. In 1977, an alliance between the Congress Party and the Kashmiri state government of Sheikh Abdullah collapsed. In 1979, Pakistani prime minister Zulfikar Ali Bhutto pledged to fight for the cause of oppressed Kashmiri Muslims. The 1980s saw increased Islamization in the Kashmir valley, with madrassas springing up and young Kashmiri men, inspired by the successful ouster of the Soviet Union by the Taliban during the Afghanistan war, crossing the border to train as militants in Pakistan. What was widely perceived as a rigged election in 1986—which gave an alliance of the Congress Party with the National Conference party a landslide victory and left the Muslim United Front co-alition parties a mere four seats in the state's legislature—was a tipping point.

In July 1988, the Jammu and Kashmir Liberation Front (JKLF) exploded a bomb in Srinagar, marking the beginning of a full-blown insurgency waged by several militant groups, including Pakistan-based Lashkar-e-Taiba, Hizbul Mujahideen, and Harkatul Mujahideen. The insurgency, which would last through the 1990s, fed on frustration with the inability of the democratic process to deliver change and it thrived on Islamist ideology. It attracted many educated Kashmiri youth who had dim prospects for employment, and it was actively supported by Pakistan, which effectively waged a proxy war on India in Kashmir.

In January 1990, violent attacks by insurgents reached a fever pitch. Hindu Kashmiri Pandits were targeted, and thousands fled the Kashmir Valley. The Indian government, determined to put down the insurgency, imposed direct rule on Kashmir and sent in the army. Fighting between Kashmiri militants and Indian forces intensified throughout the 1990s, with both sides committing atrocities. But the Indian army's impunity for crimes against Kashmiri civilians—including disappearances, torture, and executions committed in the name of putting down the insurgency—alienated many Kashmiris, who chafed under the brutal occupation of what grew to some 700,000 Indian troops.

In 1999, India and Pakistan engaged in cross-border shelling in Kashmir in what is known as the Kargil War after the name of the district in which it took place. Fighting between Indian army troops and militants crossing over from Pakistan intensified. Between 1990 and 2011, more than 43,000 people were killed in Kashmir. As we will see in Part II, Kashmir remains a restive territory, and violence continues.

When did India become a nuclear power?

On August 15, 1948, the first anniversary of India's independence, India's parliament passed the Atomic Energy Act, which created the Indian Atomic Energy Commission. The purpose of the commission was to develop India's nuclear capacity for "peaceful purposes," though Prime Minister Nehru was clear from the beginning that should India need to deploy nuclear weapons, it would not hesitate to do so. In 1954, India set up the Atomic Energy Establishment at Tromblay (AEET), located near Mumbai. Homi J. Bhabha was made the director of the AEET and led India's early nuclear efforts. These received a boost in 1955 when Canada agreed to supply India with a research reactor and the United States, under the Atoms for Peace program, agreed to supply India with heavy water for the reactor. India began to manufacture natural uranium and weapons-grade plutonium.

In 1958, Nehru launched Project Phoenix to build a 20-ton-capacity plutonium plant. India then launched its nuclear weapons program in 1966 after the great powers refused to provide a nuclear guarantee following China's first nuclear test in 1964. On May 18, 1974, India tested a nuclear device. That day was the anniversary of the Buddha's birth, and the test was code-named Operation Buddha.

While domestic reaction to the test was positive, the international community was appalled. The Nuclear Suppliers Group was formed in reaction to India's 1974 nuclear test in an effort to thwart nuclear proliferation. Canada cut off nuclear assistance to India. In 1978, the US Congress passed an amendment to the 1955 Atomic Energy Act that effectively prohibited US participation in India's nuclear program.

But India was well on its way to further developing its nuclear capability on its own. On May 15, 1998, under the government of Atal Behari Vajpayee, India successfully set off a series of nuclear devices in the desert in the state of Rajasthan. Pakistan immediately followed with its own successful test, setting off a nuclear arms race in South Asia that continues to this day.

Who was Vikram Sarabhai?

Vikram Ambalal Sarabhai was the father of India's space program and founded a number of Indian scientific research and educational institutions that were considered essential to India's development. Despite the strength of mathematics, metallurgy, and other sciences in ancient India, the new Republic of India was woefully lacking in the institutions it needed to advance knowledge critical to protecting its independence and bettering the lives of its citizens. The son of Ahmedabad textile mill owner and independence supporter Ambalal Sarabhai, Vikram Sarabhai earned a PhD from Cambridge University in 1947 with a thesis on cosmic rays. Upon his return to India, he founded, with family financial support, the Physical Research Laboratory in Ahmedabad. In 1962, Nehru asked Sarabhai to chair the new Indian National Committee for Space Research. Under Sarabhai's chairmanship, India's space program literally took off when India launched its first rocket in 1963.

After the death of Homi J. Bhabha, who headed India's nuclear program, Nehru asked Sarabhai to take over the direction of the Indian Atomic Energy Commission as well. In addition to continuing his duties as professor of cosmic rays physics at the Physical Research Laboratory, Sarabhai headed both India's space program and India's nuclear program until his death in 1971.

Sarabhai, an inveterate institution-builder, also set up the Indian Institute of Management in Ahmedabad, the Vikram Sarabhai Space Centre in Thiruvananthapuram, the Variable Energy Cyclotron Centre in Calcutta, the Electronics Corporation of India in Hyderabad, the Uranium Corporation of India in Bihar, and the Faster Breeder Reactor in Kalpakkam. With his wife, Mrinalini Sarabhai, an innovative dancer and choreographer who infused her work with social themes, ranging from the oppressive lives of young Indian brides to the plight of India's Dalits, he cofounded the Darpana Academy of Performing Arts in Ahmedabad.

Following the rise to national power of the Hindu nationalist Bharatiya Janata Party in 2014, there has been a strong move—as we will explore in Part II—by members of India's government and its ruling party to shift scientific inquiry in

India away from Western norms and toward interpretations of science that draw from often literal readings of India's ancient Hindu texts, and to place Hindu-nationalist ideologues at the helm of India's research and educational institutions. Whether these efforts will undo the work of Vikram Sarabhai and others who contributed so much to advancing science and education in India remains to be seen.

What are the IITs?

Vikram Sarabhai wasn't the only person committed to building the educational and research institutions the new Indian republic needed. Ardeshir Dalal, a Parsi businessman associated with the Tata group of companies in Mumbai, first came up with the idea of creating institutes in India that would train a new generation of technological experts to help drive development after India's independence. In 1945, a committee headed by Nalini Ranjan Sarkar, a Bengali politician and insurance executive, proposed four such institutes. Nehru envisioned the institutes as a system that would "provide scientists and technologists of the highest caliber who would engage in research, design and development to help [in] building the nation towards self-reliance in her technological needs." In 1951, the first Indian Institute of Technology (IIT) was inaugurated in Kharagpur. Over the next decades, four more IITs were set up in Bombay, Madras, Kanpur, and Delhi.

In 2016, there were a total of twenty-three IITs in India. The IITs are among the world's premier institutions of higher education, and the most competitive in the world: only about 2 percent of applicants are admitted. Of these, less than 10 percent are women. Leading Indian and international companies routinely snap up IIT graduates, and IIT alumni can be counted among the top ranks of global business leaders, including Vinod Khosla, a cofounder of Sun Microsystems; Sundar Pichai, the CEO of Google; Nandan Nilekani, one of the founders of Infosys and the creator of India's Aadhaar unique identification system; and Satya Nadella, the CEO of Microsoft.

What was the impact of the Green Revolution on India?

Science and technology were also brought to bear on India's millennia-old agricultural practices. One of the major challenges of independent India was feeding its poor—and growing—population. During its first decades, the country was forced to import food grains, much from the United States, to stave off mass hunger. The Green Revolution—the dramatic increase in crop yields that resulted from the use of new hybrid seeds coupled with irrigation, mechanized farming, and chemical fertilizers and pesticides, an initiative pioneered by American agronomist Norman Borlaug—promised to make India self-sufficient in food grains and end its dependency on food handouts. In 1963, at the Indian government's request, Borlaug traveled to India, bringing with him hybrid wheat seeds. By 1968, India's wheat yield was so great, schools had to be used as granaries. The Indian Council for Agricultural Research went on to develop new hybrid cereal seeds, including wheat, rice, millet, and corn. Between 1961 and 2001, India's population more than doubled, from 450 million to more than 1 billion, but its grain production nearly tripled.

But the impressive increases in food production came at a price. The Green Revolution's reliance on irrigation, chemical fertilizers, and pesticides had severe negative effects on India's environment and on human health, particularly in Punjab, the breadbasket of India. The water table dropped precipitously, as irrigation sucked water out of aquifers faster than it could be replenished. Soils became saline—an effect of overirrigation. Pesticide use in India increased from 2,000 tons in 1960 to 75,000 tons in 1985. Cancer rates in Punjab rose alarmingly.

Who was Raj Kapoor?

India's rapid development during the first decades following independence was also evident in the arts. No single Indian was perhaps better known or loved, in India and around the world, than actor, film director, and producer Raj Kapoor, whose films captured the hopes and travails of millions of Indians as their country went through major economic and social changes. Called the "Charlie Chaplin of India," Kapoor produced and directed the 1955 film *Shree 420*, in which Kapoor also starred as an Indian everyman who confronts the cynical greed of the big city with a pure heart and a ready song on his lips. The song "Mera Joota Hai Japani" captured the pride and aspiration of a generation of Indians coming of age in the post-independence era, with lyrics that just about every Indian alive today still knows by heart: "My shoes are Japanese, these trousers are English, the red cap on my head is Russian, but my heart is Indian."

Who was Satyajit Ray?

Satyajit Ray was a Bengali film director who is widely considered to be India's greatest filmmaker. Far from the commercial dream machine of Bollywood, Ray grew up in the lap of the Bengali cultural ferment of the early twentieth century. Born in Calcutta in 1921, he studied drawing and calligraphy at Shantiniketan, the innovative school founded by Rabindranath Tagore. Ray was avidly interested in music, theater, and film and collected newspaper and magazine clippings on Hollywood movies and stars.

In 1950, Ray was commissioned to illustrate a children's edition of the story *Pather Panchali* (Song of the Road), by Bengali author Bibhutibhushan Bandopadhyay. *Pather Panchali* is the story of a poor Bengali Brahmin family, told through the eyes of the family's son, Apu. The illustrations Ray produced became the basis for his first film, *Pather Panchali*, released in

1955. The film won instant acclaim, garnering the Best Human Document prize at the 1956 Cannes Film Festival. Ray went on to complete a trilogy of films around the character of Apu as he grows into a young man and moves from a small village to the big city. He completed the Apu trilogy in 1959.

By the time of his death in 1992, Satyajit Ray had directed thirty-seven films, including *Charulata*, a 1964 movie based on Rabindranath Tagore's novella *Broken Nest*, about the frustrated wife of a newspaper editor, and *The Home and the World*, a 1984 movie, based on another story by Tagore, about a woman torn between an enlightened, humanist husband who wishes her fulfillment and a self-centered young radical in Bengal's swadeshi, or self-reliance, movement. The story reflects the political upheaval of 1920s Calcutta and captures the clash between a vision of India as an open society where individuals may freely choose their paths and one where political correctness in the name of the nation trumps all.

What was Doordarshan?

While independent India's film industry was blossoming on cinema's big screen, the new nation saw the smaller television screen as a means of transmitting national news and an appreciation of national culture to a still largely illiterate population. Television arrived in India in 1959 with help from UNESCO, and Doordarshan, India's state-run public-service television network, played an important role in shaping the new nation. The first presenter of a weekly broadcast was President Rajendra Prasad, reflecting the national importance of television to India yet distancing the new medium from the seat of real political power in India's parliamentary democracy, the prime minister. Doordarshan's purpose was to unify and uplift a diverse and largely poor population. Doordarshan means "seen from afar" in Hindi, a fair translation of the word "television."

The first imported color televisions arrived in India in 1982, the same year India's Insat-1A satellite made national broadcasting popular. Viewership soared. In 1983, television reached just 28 percent of Indians. That doubled to 56 percent by 1986, and rose to 90 percent by 1990. In 1984, Doordarshan launched its first serial show, *Hum Log* (We People), which depicted the everyday life of a middle-class Indian family and tackled social issues such as marriage dowries, the status of women, and family planning.

Hum Log was immensely popular, and it prepared Indian audiences for a 1987 broadcast that marked an important inflection point in the history of television and politics in India: the made-for-television serialization of the Hindu epic *Ramayana*. Millions of Indians tuned in for the weekly Sunday morning broadcasts. The show was a departure from the accepted taboo of religious partisanship in television broadcasting, and it helped set the stage for the rise to power of Hindu nationalists in the early 1990s.

Today, Doordarshan (DD), one of the world's largest terrestrial television networks, operates thirty channels in twenty-two languages.

What was the Hindu Code Bill?

Independent India's new constitution conferred rights on individuals, not on religious groups. With the goal of harmonizing new constitutional rights with existing religious personal law, Prime Minister Jawaharlal Nehru moved in 1948 to introduce a bill to create a Hindu civil code of law intended to codify and reform Hindu personal law. The goal was ultimately to create a uniform civil code on personal law matters. But the bill sparked such outrage among Hindu nationalists, it had to be withdrawn. Then Law Minister B. R. Ambedkar introduced new legislation in India's parliament in 1951. After much debate—and vigorous opposition again by Hindu nationalists—the Hindu Civil Code was adopted by India's parliament in the mid-1950s. The Hindu Civil Code included a new Hindu Marriage Law, which outlawed polygamy and dealt with divorce and intercaste marriages; the Hindu Adoption and Maintenance Bill, which dealt with the adoption of Hindu girls; and the Hindu Succession Law, which put daughters on the same footing as sons and widows with regard to inheritance. A uniform civil code was never adopted, and conflicts between constitutional guarantees of individual rights and the dictates of religious personal law remain a contentious issue in India today, especially as regards the treatment of Muslim women under Muslim personal law, as we shall see later.

What was India's role in the Non-Aligned Movement?

Mentioned earlier, the Non-Aligned Movement was born when twenty-nine leaders of newly independent former European colonies in Africa and India met in Bandung, Indonesia, in 1955. In 1960, four of these leaders—Nehru; Egypt's president, Gamal Abdel Nasser; Ghana's prime minister, Kwame Nkrumah; and Josip Tito, of Yugoslavia—played a key role in the admission of seventeen newly independent African and Asian nations to the United Nations General Assembly. These leaders are considered to be the founding fathers of the Non-Aligned Movement, which sought to preserve political space outside the global division of power between the United States and the Soviet Union during the Cold War. The Non-Aligned Movement defended newly independent states' right to national sovereignty and opposed apartheid, racism, colonialism, neocolonialism, and imperialism. As the global balance of power evolved, the Non-Aligned Movement's focus shifted from the East-West issues of the Cold War to North-South issues.

Why did China attack India?

Dashing Jawaharlal Nehru's hopes for transnational unity between India and China, the two countries engaged in border skirmishes in the high-altitude mountains of the Aksai Chin beginning in 1959. At issue was territory China believed belonged to it and India believed was part of Indian Kashmir. On October 20, 1962, China launched a fresh attack on Indian forces in the disputed area and seized control of the territory in two days. As we have seen, it was a humiliating defeat for Jawaharlal Nehru, who was accused of being too complacent in the face of Chinese aggression. China and India continue to dispute parts of the border that divides the two countries.

What was the Dravidian Movement?

The Dravidian Movement was a politically progressive movement rooted in Tamil language, culture, and identity in South India. It began with the Justice Party, founded in 1916, and the Self-Respect Movement, founded by Periyar E. V. Ramasamy in 1925. These parties, focused on social justice, evolved into today's Dravida Munnetra Kazhagam (DMK), or Dravidian Progress Federation, founded in 1949, and the All India Anna Dravida Munnetra Kazhagam (AIDMK), which broke away from the DMK in 1972. During the 1960s, agitation in the Tamil-speaking state against Hindi—which India's Congress Party founders, sitting in New Delhi, had made the national language of independent India—helped the DMK rout the Congress Party from power in the Tamil Nadu in 1967.

Tamil Nadu's political leadership has been closely associated with the Tamil film industry in a way politics in the north of India have not. The scriptwriter Muthuvelu Karunanidhi and the film stars Jayaram Jayalalithaa and Ramachandran all served as chief ministers of the state. Jayalalithaa was elected in May 2016 to her sixth term as chief minister of Tamil Nadu, which ended abruptly with her death in December of that year. Thousands of grieving fans and supporters thronged the streets of the state to pay her a final tribute.

Who were the Naxalites?

The Naxalite movement was a revolutionary movement that began in 1967 with an uprising in the village of Naxalbari in the state of West Bengal. The revolt was triggered by an attack on an Adivasi farmer by goons hired by a local landlord. Local Adivasis, considered indigenous inhabitants of India, retaliated, forcibly taking back land they considered theirs. The Communist Party of India (Marxist)–led government of West Bengal cracked down on the rebellion, and nine Adivasis were killed. The incident reverberated throughout India's so-called tribal belt in eastern India, where many Adivasis live.

By the 1970s, the Naxalites had become a guerrilla movement controlling several districts in India, and radical groups had formed in the states of Andra Pradesh and Bihar. The movement, dominated by Maoists, eventually spread to a large area known as the "Red Corridor," which stretches across a swath of the states of Andra Pradesh, Jharkand, Orissa, West Bengal, and Chhattisgarh. In 2010, Prime Minister Manmohan Singh called the movement India's "greatest internal security challenge."

Who was Indira Gandhi?

The Naxalite movement was just one challenge to India's unity during the tenure of Indira Gandhi as prime minister. The only child of Jawaharlal Nehru, India's first prime minister, and Kamala Kaul, Indira Priyadarshini Gandhi was born in 1917 in Allahabad. Her parents were often in jail or otherwise occupied by India's independence movement, and Indira was reportedly a lonely child. After her mother died in 1936, young Indira, fluent in English and French, assumed the role of hostess for her father. She married Feroze Gandhi (no relation to Mahatma Gandhi), a Parsi newspaperman she had met while a student at Somerville College, Oxford, in the early 1940s. The couple had two sons, Rajiv, born in 1944, and Sanjay, born in 1946.

Though Feroze Gandhi went on to become a member of India's Parliament, the couple became estranged and lived separately. Elected to the Congress Party Working Committee in 1955, Indira Gandhi accepted a Cabinet post in the government of Lal Bahadur Shastri after her father died of a stroke in 1964. In 1966, Shastri died, and Gandhi was chosen to be prime minister by Congress Party leaders who thought she would be pliable. She was not.

Indira Gandhi proved herself to be a canny, tough, and strong-willed politician, determined to hold the reins of power. In 1969, she faced down a split in the Congress Party, winning a narrow victory against a mutiny by the party's old guard. She promptly moved to nationalize India's banks and eliminate the princely purses of the country's maharajahs. In 1971, her party won a decisive victory in national elections. Her popularity soared after India's victory over Pakistan in the Bangladesh war. But this high was to be short-lived, as we shall see in the following series of events under Gandhi's leadership.

What was India's role in the Bangladesh War?

When Pakistan was created in 1947, it was a country divided in two, with the entire breadth of India separating West Pakistan from East Pakistan, located in the former Indian province of East Bengal. Though a majority of East Pakistanis were Muslim, they spoke Bengali, not Urdu, the language of West Pakistan. East Pakistanis resented being ruled from faraway Islamabad. In 1970, the Awami League party, which advocated autonomy for East Pakistan, won an overwhelming majority of seats in East Pakistan and a majority of seats overall in Pakistan's first general elections. By rights, Awami League party leader Sheikh Mujibur Rahman should have been named Pakistan's first elected prime minister, but this was simply not acceptable to West Pakistan–based General Yaya Khan, Pakistan's martial law administrator. In March 1971, West Pakistan launched a massacre in Dhaka, targeting the city's intelligentsia. Thus began an orgy of unspeakable atrocities committed against East Pakistanis. Some 30 million people were displaced, and 10 million Hindus fled to safety in India.

Under the leadership of Indira Gandhi, India supported Bangladesh's bid for independence by providing arms and training for East Pakistani forces. As tensions grew between India and Pakistan, Pakistan launched preemptive air strikes on Indian air bases on December 3, 1971, kicking off a thirteen-day war. On December 16, Pakistan surrendered, conceding the liberation of East Pakistan, which became the new country of Bangladesh. The number of Bangladeshis who were killed during the upheaval is the subject of great controversy. The official number accepted by the government of Bangladesh is 3 million.

What was the Emergency?

In 1973, India was gripped by runaway inflation. Prime Minister Indira Gandhi faced riots in the streets and a re-volt among the Congress Party senior guard, whom she had sidelined from power. Morarji Desai and Jaya Prakash (J. P.) Narayan led a *janata* (people's) movement whose slogan was "Oust Indira!" By 1975, Gandhi's hold on power had become tenuous. A court in Allahabad—her birthplace—convicted her of electoral malpractice and banned her from politics for six years. With encouragement from her son Sanjay, Gandhi declared a national state of emergency on June 25, 1975. Opposition political leaders were rounded up. Phone lines were cut. The press was censored. All opposition parties were banned. More than 100,000 people were jailed. Forced sterili-zation was introduced to curb India's rapidly growing pop-ulation. All this was shocking behavior from a democratic government.

In 1977, Gandhi released Morarji Desai, the elderly and ailing J. P. Narayan, and other political prisoners from jail, and called for new elections. The new Janata Dal party swept to power, and Morarji Desai was made prime minister.

Indira Gandhi was out, but not for long. The Janata Dal government was hobbled by petty infighting among its members. By 1979, Desai, facing a no-confidence vote in parliament he knew he would lose, submitted his resignation. Gandhi swept back to power in 1980 in a landslide victory.

What was the Khalistan movement?

India was shaken in the 1980s by a Punjabi Sikh secessionist movement. The movement sought to create an independent state called Khalistan (Land of the Pure) as a homeland for the Sikhs.

The Khalistan movement had its roots in the aftermath of the Partition of India in 1947, which cut through the region of Punjab, where many Sikhs lived. With no provision for a separate state for the Sikhs, many Sikhs on the Pakistani side of the new border fled to the Indian side. In the 1950s, the Akali Dal Party led a movement to create a Punjabi-language majority state in East Punjab. This was rejected by India's central government, but in 1966, following a war between India and Pakistan in 1965, the state of Punjab was finally created, with Hindi-speaking majority areas forming the new separate state of Haryana.

The Green Revolution had a profoundly disruptive impact on Punjabi farmers. Larger farmers were in a better position to adopt the new techniques than smaller ones were. Many Punjabi Sikhs migrated to Britain and Canada. The issue of Sikh identity gained new prominence, and a man named Jarnail Singh Bhindranwale emerged as a spiritual leader of Sikh revival that was at once religious and political.

In 1980, the Congress Party, already in power in New Delhi, won power in the state of Punjab. In 1982, Bhindranwale joined the Akali party to militate against the policies of the central Congress Party government. The Sikh militant movement became increasingly violent. In 1983, terrorist attacks by Khalistan-inspired militants killed at least 175 people. Bhindranwale, whose authority derived as much from his religious fervor as from his political militancy, set up his headquarters in the Golden Temple complex, Sikhism's most holy site. In June 1984, Gandhi ordered Indian soldiers to storm the complex, in an attack that was dubbed Operation Blue Star. Bhindranwale and other militants were killed, but so were many civilians—493, according to a government of India white paper, though other sources cite civilian casualties in the thousands.

What was the Sikh massacre of 1984?

On October 31, 1984, Indira Gandhi was assassinated by two of her Sikh bodyguards in revenge for the attack she had ordered on the Golden Temple. It was a shockingly violent end for someone who was born to power, who had held India's highest office four times, and who had led the country through years of turbulent contestation as India grappled with regional conflicts and the perennial problems of poverty, hunger, population growth, and chronic caste and religious strife.

In response to news of her death, an anti-Sikh rampage broke out in New Delhi. Some 3,000 Sikhs were murdered. Men, women, and children were dragged from their homes or their cars and slaughtered by angry Hindu mobs. According to eyewitness accounts, law enforcement officers and government officials incited the violence, and senior Congress Party officials aided and abetted the slaughter. The killing went on for three days, with no interference from authorities.

The government of India has as yet failed to bring the authors of the carnage to justice, and it has never conducted a truth-and-reconciliation process to heal a shattered community. The political careers of many of the Congress Party officials implicated in the massacre rose in its wake. No reforms of police conduct during communal violence were ever undertaken.

Such was the violent end of independent India's founding titan Jawaharlal Nehru's daughter, Indira. India's first and, as yet, only woman prime minister, Indira Gandhi was a towering figure who did much to shape the contours of modern India.

Who was Rajiv Gandhi?

Born in 1944, Rajiv Gandhi was the elder son of Indira and Feroze Gandhi. He was more interested in flying than in politics, and became a pilot with Indian Airlines after studying at Cambridge. At Cambridge, he met an Italian student, Sonia Maino, whom he married in 1968. The couple lived in Indira Gandhi's residence with their two children, Rahul and Priyanka.

When Rajiv's brother Sanjay—who was being groomed by his mother for political succession—was killed in a plane crash in 1980, Rajiv Gandhi was inducted into the family vocation of Indian politics. He ran for, and won, his brother's seat representing Amethi, Uttar Pradesh, in Parliament. When his mother was assassinated in 1984, he took office as prime minister. Only forty years old, he was India's youngest prime minister.

Determined to break with the Congress Party's socialist past, Rajiv Gandhi introduced measures to unfetter India's economy from state-imposed taxes, quotas, and tariffs many in India's business community found too constricting, surrounding himself with a new coterie of advisors drawn from free-market economic and business circles, including Manmohan Singh, Montek Ahluwalia Singh, Abid Hussain, Arun Jha, and Arun Nehru. India's economy had, since the era of his grandfather Jawaharlal Nehru, followed a policy of import substitution—the replacement of foreign goods with domestic production—in an attempt to stimulate Indian industry and make the country self-sufficient. Rajiv Gandhi eased import duties and barriers on selected items, lowered corporate and personal income taxes, and relieved industry of some state controls. The reaction was swift. By 1986, perceived now as being anti-poor, the Congress Party began losing in state polls. Rajiv Gandhi saw his popularity plummet and faced opposition from the rank and file of his own party. Some of that opposition is detailed in what follows.

What was the Shah Bano controversy?

In 1985, India's Supreme Court, in a unanimous decision, awarded alimony payments to Shah Bano Begum, who had been divorced by her husband, Mohamed Ahmed Khan, in 1978 by Muslim *talaq*—reciting three times the phrase "I divorce you." The couple had been married in 1932 and had five children. When Shah Bano was sixty-two years old, her husband, who had taken a second wife, threw her and their five children out. He subsequently stopped paying a modest 200 rupees monthly maintenance to Shah Bano. In 1978, she took him to court to get the maintenance restored. In response, he divorced her, saying that under Muslim personal law, as she was no longer his wife, he had no obligation to her. After lower courts upheld Shah Bano's right to support, Khan filed a case with the Supreme Court, which ruled in favor of Shah Bano.

Muslims in India hit the streets in protest, saying the ruling was a violation of Muslim personal law. Panicked by the prospect of losing the support of Muslim voters in the 1986 national elections, the Congress Party government, led by Rajiv Gandhi, enacted legislation in 1986 that gave Muslim women the right to alimony for only three months following divorce, after which responsibility for maintenance shifted to the Muslim Wakf Board, which administers properties and funds for pious purposes. The Bharatiya Janata Party condemned the 1986 Muslim Women (Protection of Rights on Divorce) Act as appeasement toward India's Muslims. Others pointed out the inherent discrimination in a law that gave Muslim women lesser rights than other women in India.

In August 2017, India's Supreme Court struck down the legal provision that allowed Muslim men to divorce their wives simply by uttering the Arabic word *talaq*, meaning "divorce," three times.

What was the Bofors scandal?

In 1986, the Rajiv Gandhi government was also hit by a corruption scandal involving kickbacks to Indian politicians from the Swedish arms manufacturer Bofors. The Congress Party lost the 1989 general elections, ceding power to a National Front coalition government (which included the Hindu nationalist BJP)—led by V. P. Singh.

Who assassinated Rajiv Gandhi?

The Liberation Tigers of Tamil Eelam (LTTE), a Sri Lankan ethnic Tamil revolutionary group involved in a guerrilla war against the Singhalese-dominated Sri Lankan state, decided in 1991 to target Gandhi for assassination while he was campaigning for reelection in South India. The motive was retaliation for Tamils killed in Sri Lanka by Indian troops when they intervened in the conflict between 1987 and 1990. The leadership of the LTTE feared that if Gandhi was reelected, he would send Indian troops to attack them in Sri Lanka again.

On May 21, 1991, a flower-garlanded LTTE militant detonated a body bomb as Gandhi bent to greet her at a campaign stop in a village near Chennai, blowing up both herself and the heir to the Nehru-Gandhi dynasty. It was a horrific end for a man who had political power thrust upon him, a tragedy for his young family, and a blow to the Congress Party. Though his widow, Sonia Gandhi, would take up the reins of power of the Congress Party, and her and Rajiv's son, Rahul, would make several attempts to run for political office, Rajiv Gandhi was the last —so far—of the three-generation Nehru-Gandhi dynasty that governed for most of the first forty-six years of independent India.

What happened in Bhopal?

One of the most tragic—and callous—events in independent India's history happened shortly after Rajiv Gandhi assumed the office of prime minister after his mother's assassination. In the early morning hours of December 3, 1984, a leak of toxic gas from a pesticide factory in Bhopal killed at least 15,000 people and sickened thousands more. Up to 600,000 people were ultimately affected. Even today, decades later, the site remains polluted with chemical waste that had been dumped near the factory for years before the deadly leak, in addition to pollution from the leak itself.

The factory was owned by the Indian subsidiary of the American chemical giant Union Carbide. In 1989, Union Carbide paid the Indian government $470 million in compensation for the victims. This worked out to average payments of $2,200 to families of the dead and $550 to the injured. Many people in Bhopal complained they received little or no compensation. Investigations linking residual health effects, such as birth defects and cancer, to the 1984 leak have been tepidly pursued.

Under a deal brokered by India's Supreme Court, all pending civil and criminal cases against Union Carbide were dropped in return for its 1989 payment. By the time eight Indian Union Carbide executives were finally convicted of negligence by Indian courts in 2010, one had died. For years the Indian government tried, in vain, to have Warren Anderson, the CEO of Union Carbide at the time of the accident, extradited. Anderson died in the United States in 2014 of natural causes at the age of ninety-two. In 1999, the Dow Chemical Company purchased Union Carbide. Dow denies any responsibility for Bhopal.

The Bhopal gas leak did prompt some action in India against industrial polluters. In 1986, India passed an Environmental Protection Act, and in 1989, the government handed down

Hazardous Waste Management and Handling Rules to help ensure the safe management and handling of toxic industrial waste. These rules are routinely flouted by industry in India.

What was the Mandal Commission?

In 1979, the government led by Morarji Desai commissioned a report on India's Backward Classes—lower-caste, disadvantaged citizens. Bindeshwari Prasad Mandal, a former chief minister of the state of Bihar, was tasked with leading the report. In 1980, the Mandal Commission duly submitted its report, but it was considered too hot politically and likely to spark anger among India's upper castes, so it was quietly shelved. It was not released until 1990, when the United Front government, led by V. P. Singh, informed India's parliament that it had accepted the report's recommendation that 27 percent of all government service positions should be reserved for citizens belonging to historically disadvantaged castes categorized under the rubric "Other Backward Class." These disadvantaged castes actually made up about 52 percent of the population, but as 22.5 percent of government service jobs were already held by members of these castes and India's Supreme Court had ruled that caste-based reservations could not exceed 50 percent, the Mandal Commission settled on 27 percent, a number aimed at bringing the total number of government service jobs held by disadvantaged castes to just under 50 percent.

The Mandal Commission report provoked uproar among upper-caste Indians, who felt the new reservations would unfairly block their access to government services, including public universities. One month after the report's recommendation was made public, Delhi University student Rajiv Goswamy set himself on fire in protest. He survived, but several other students across India subsequently also set themselves on fire, and demonstrators took to the streets to protest the Mandal Commission's recommendation. The government was forced to shelve the report, but the political damage was done: the BJP withdrew its support from Singh's United Front government, which promptly fell.

The Mandal Commission's recommendation was finally implemented in 1993, but the issue of affirmative action to redress historic caste discrimination continues to be politically charged.

What was the Permit-Quota-License Raj?

As confident in the state's ability to direct development as he was in its ability to reform religious personal law—all in the name of modernizing India—Jawaharlal Nehru was determined to guide India forward on a path to industrialization. He was impressed with the rapid industrialization achieved by the former Soviet Union, and he was convinced government planning was the key to India's development, placing great faith in large-scale, state-managed projects. He famously referred to massive new concrete dams as the "temples" of modern India. And so India began a series of five-year plans overseen by a new Planning Commission.

C. "Rajaji" Rajagopalachari—a lawyer who, frustrated with Nehru's socialism, founded the more free market–friendly Swantantra Party in 1959—is credited with coining the phrase "permit-quota-licence Raj" to describe India's government planning regime. The regime required businesses to obtain permits or licenses from various government agencies before pursuing projects. Initially, the system worked fairly well, but by the 1980s India's economy was seen by many to be hamstrung by what had become a heavily government-regulated, and often corrupt, business environment.

What was the balance of payments crisis?

As India prepared to enter the twenty-first century, no single event affected the country's economic fortunes more than the balance of payments crisis of 1991 and its aftermath. Under the government of Rajiv Gandhi in the 1980s, India began to shift its economy away from import substitution to export-led growth, easing some import restrictions and licensing requirements. But the value of imports, especially of petroleum, grew faster than the value of exports. Events in the Middle East in 1990 caused oil prices to rise sharply but foreign exchange remittances from Indian workers in the Gulf to fall. Meanwhile, exports to the United States, India's largest export market, also fell on weakening demand. Between 1985 and 1991, India's current-account deficits doubled. Political instability in India—coalition government leader Singh was forced to resign in December 1990—also contributed to a downgrade of India by international credit rating agencies, increasing the cost of borrowing money. The Indian rupee went into free fall, and India rapidly depleted its foreign currency reserves.

The result of all this was that in 1991 India was forced to accept structural adjustment measures imposed by the International Monetary Fund—including easing import restrictions, tax reform, and reform of the financial sector—in exchange for emergency funding. Under the new government of Narasimha Rao, Finance Minister Manmohan Singh oversaw a series of economic reforms: 80 percent of India's industries were taken out of the licensing regime, the private sector was allowed to play a larger role in India's economy, large companies were allowed to diversify and expand capacity without prior government approval, and the foreign equity ceiling in some Indian business sectors was raised from 40 percent to 51 percent.

The 1991 balance of payments crisis ushered in a new, more business- and investment-friendly economic era in India. It marked the beginning of the end of the Nehruvian socialism that had defined India's economic and social policies since 1950.

What was Ram Janmabhoomi?

Meanwhile, on the political front, Hindu nationalist political parties and groups steadily rose in power and popularity during the 1980s. A rallying point for these groups also emerged: the call to raze the Babri Masjid, a sixteenth-century mosque in Ayodhya, Uttar Pradesh that had been built over the ruins of a Hindu temple ordered destroyed by the Mughal emperor Babur, and rebuild a Hindu temple dedicated to the god Ram on the site. Hindu nationalists identified Ayodhya as the location of Ram's birth.

In 1984, the Hindu nationalist group Vishwa Hindu Parishad (VHP) launched a Ram Janmabhoomi—"country of Ram's birth"—movement to destroy the Babri Masjid. In the summer of 1989, the VHP organized worship sessions featuring bricks printed with Ram's name that would be used to build the new Hindu temple on the site of the mosque. The Hindu nationalist Bharatiya Janata Party rallied to the Ram Janmabhoomi cause, organizing processions throughout India. The strategy paid off: the BJP increased its seats in India's parliament from two to eighty-eight. The BJP joined other opposition political parties in a coalition to oust the Congress Party government led by Rajiv Gandhi.

In September 1990, BJP leader Lal Kishen Advani launched a 10,000-kilometer chariot-led procession (Ram Yath Rastra) to Ayodhya. This marked an important turning point in the fortunes of Hindu nationalists. On October 30, police prevented *kar sevaks*—devotees to the cause of rebuilding the Ram temple—from attacking the Babri Masjid. But the Ram Yath Rastra proved to be a brilliant public relations move, rallying Hindu voters to the Hindu nationalist cause. In the 1991 general elections, the BJP increased its number of seats in parliament yet again, to 120.

On December 2, 1992, *kar sevaks* stormed the Babri Masjid and demolished it. Violent clashes between Hindus and Muslims immediately broke out across India. Some 1,200 people were killed in just the first few days following the mosque's destruction. In the city of Mumbai, Muslims were hunted down and killed in the streets or in their homes. Some Hindus were also killed, but the slaughter of Muslims was systematic: The city's government, led by Bal Thackery and his regionalist Maharashtrian Shiv Sena party, identified Muslim homes and businesses and ensured that police gave roving mobs of Hindu attackers a free hand. Then, on March 12, 1993, bombs went off in the heart of Mumbai's commercial district, killing hundreds of people. This was revenge by Islamist terrorists based in Pakistan—aided by Muslim Mumbai criminal kingpin Dawood Ibrahim—for the destruction of the Babri Masjid and the killings of Muslims in India.

The events following the destruction of the Babri Masjid shocked the nation. In response, the BJP adopted a more moderate political line and forged a coalition with regional political parties to form the National Democratic Alliance (NDA). After elections in 1998 and 1999, the NDA was able to form a government led by BJP politician Atal Behari Vajpayee and set about implementing a program to shift India toward its goal of a Hindu state. Prominent members of the overarching Hindu nationalist movement, called Sangh Parivar, were appointed to head educational and cultural institutions. School textbooks were rewritten to reflect Hindu nationalist views.

In the run-up to the 2004 general elections, the NDA campaigned with the slogan "India Shining" and images of sweeping modern highways, India's road to the future. But most Indians didn't own cars, and many were alarmed by the NDA government's Hindu nationalist program. The NDA was handily defeated by the United Progressive Alliance (UPA) coalition of parties, led by the Congress Party.

How did India's democracy evolve after independence?

As the party that brought freedom to India, the Indian National Congress party was the natural leader of newly independent India. It was the party that gave India its constitution and created a republic that unified a diverse nation into a single polity.

The Congress Party built a powerful patronage system that favored local elites: the wealthy, the educated, and the high-caste. But India's new democratic politics began to mobilize the country's poor, who also became better educated and dared to aspire to a more empowered life. India's new citizens had regional and caste-based allegiances as well as national ones. Regional parties began to emerge in the 1960s. And the Congress Party began to fray. After Indira Gandhi was expelled from the party in 1969 on charges of indiscipline, the Congress Party split into two factions: Congress (O), for "Organization," and Congress (I), for "Indira." And while Indira Gandhi's 1971 promise to alleviate poverty with the slogan "Garibi hatao" (end poverty) helped her win a landslide victory and increased her personal power, that concentrated power sucked sustenance from the party's grassroots.

The state of emergency Gandhi declared in 1975 deeply shocked many of her supporters. The Janata Dal, or People's Party, formed by an alliance of parties alarmed by the Emergency, won the 1977 election and formed the first non-Congress coalition government in India's independent history. The Janata government collapsed in 1979 due to infighting, and Indira Gandhi swept back into power in 1980, but seeds of discontent had been planted and began to grow. Her assassination in 1984, followed by her son's assassination in 1991, left the Congress Party—wedded now to a dynastic politics that had given India three generations of leaders—bereft of a Gandhi-family candidate. Though Rajiv Gandhi's widow, Sonia Gandhi, assumed the leadership of the Congress Party after her husband's death, her Italian birth made her a target of xenophobic politics by the Hindu right: running for office was not a viable option, had she wanted to run.

Following India's independence, agitation for the recognition of new states based on language groups evolved into new regional parties. These regional parties went hand in hand with caste identities. In Tamil Nadu, strong regional parties imbued with Tamil language and culture and marked by opposition to Brahmanism emerged early on. In 1982, the Telugu Desam Party was founded on the twin promises of defending the Telugu language and looking after the interests of the Kamma caste.

During the 1990s, three strong regional leaders who championed the lower castes emerged: Mulayam Singh Yadav, Laloo Prasad Yadav, and Bahan Kumari Mayawati. Mulayam Singh Yadav founded the Samajwadi Party in Lucknow, Uttar Pradesh, in 1992. The party "speaks for the upliftment and economic progress of the minorities, especially the Other Backward Classes (OBCs) and the Muslims." The Samajwadi Party won state assembly elections in 2012, unseating four-term chief minister Bahan Kumari Mayawati, the head of the Bahujan Samaj Party. Founded in 1989 by Kanshi Ram, a follower of Dalit leader B. R. Ambedkar, the Bahujan Samaj Party is dedicated to the "missionary cause and cherished goal" of the social transformation and economic emancipation of all Backwards Classes. In 1997, Laloo Prasad Yadav, chief minister of the state of Bihar in 1990, founded the Rashtriya Janata Dal Party. The party billed itself as the voice of the "socially and economically downtrodden sections of society."

Various regional parties represent India's Muslims, including the Indian Union Muslim League in Kerala, the Majlis-e-Ittehadul Muslimeen in Andra Pradesh, and the All India Ulema Council, based in Uttar Pradesh. Kashmir, of course, has its own specific political history. In 1998, Mufti Mohammed Sayeed founded the Kashmir People's Democratic Party (PDP), dedicated to self-rule in Kashmir. In April 2016, the PDP formed a coalition government with the BJP. Mehbooba Mufti Sayeed, Mufti Mohammed Sayeed's daughter, is chief minister of the state of Jammu and Kashmir.

Like the Congress Party, the Communist Party of India traces its roots to the early years of India's independence movement. In 1977, the Communist Party led a left-wing government to victory in assembly elections in West Bengal, which it governed for the next thirty years. The Communist Party of India also had deep roots in Kerala, where it won assembly elections in 1957, and remained in power until 2011. In 1964, the Communist Party split, and the Communist Party of India (Marxist) emerged in West Bengal, where it too remained in power until 2011. By that time, India's economy was posting strong growth following economic reforms undertaken after the balance of payments crisis in 1991, and in West Bengal, maverick leader Mamata Banerjee swept to power with her All India Trinamool Congress Party, a party she created after breaking with the Congress Party in 1997.

During India's independence struggle, there were two competing visions for independent India. Leaders of the Congress Party, such as Mahatma Gandhi and Nehru, envisioned a secular republic inclusive of Indians of all faiths, whereas the thought leaders of Hindu nationalism, including Vinayak Damodar Savarkar and M. S. Golwalkar, envisioned the creation of a Hindu state. The assassination of Mahatma Gandhi in 1948 by Naturam Godse sharply discredited the Hindu right. Godse, a one-time member of the Rashtriya Swayamsevak Sangh (RSS), a militant Hindu organization, and a member of the Hindu Mahasabha, a right-wing Hindu nationalist party, said during his trial that he had no regrets, and that he killed Gandhi because he was emasculating Hindus and destroying the future of the Hindu nation. Nehru banned the RSS in 1948 and arrested the group's leader, M. S. Golwalkar. But the ban was lifted the following year. At no time did the RSS cease its activities.

The BJP emerged from this turmoil as the moderate political face of Hindu nationalism. Founded in 1980, the BJP was the successor to the earlier Bharatiya Jana Sangh. The BJP steadily increased its popularity during the 1980s, successfully using India's Muslims as a scapegoat for frustrations among urban, lower-middle-class Hindus in western and northern India. In 1990, the Mandal Commission's recommendations for quota-based affirmative action to redress historic discrimination against low-caste members of the Backward Classes caused upper-caste Hindus to turn to the Hindu right to defend their caste privileges.

The progressive emergence during the decades after India's independence of a host of new regional and caste-based parties—as well as the split in the Congress Party—resulted in the fracturing of an increasingly complex political landscape in India. The chances of any one party, including the Congress Party, governing India without the support of coalition partners ended in 1989. For the next twenty-five years, coalition governments ruled India. Two major coalitions emerged: the United Progressive Alliance, led by the Congress Party, was secular and progressive (at least in theory) socialist, while the National Democratic Alliance, led by the BJP, was Hindu nationalist with a penchant for neoliberal economics and technical solutions to social problems. The NDA was in power from 1999 to 2004 with Narasimha Rao as prime minister. The United Progressive Alliance, led by the Congress Party, was in power from 2004 to 2014 with Manmohan Singh as prime minister.

At the turn of this century, many observers believed coalition politics would continue to dominate India's democracy for a very long time. But in 2014, the BJP, with Narendra Modi as its candidate for prime minister, swept to power with enough seats to form a government on its own. After sixty years on the sidelines of power, or hobbled by coalition partners, the Hindu right was finally in control of India's destiny.

Part II

WILL THE TWENTY-FIRST CENTURY BE INDIA'S CENTURY?

4

SOCIETY

How large is India's population?

In 2017, India's population of 1.33 billion slipped past China's 1.29 billion, making India the most populous country in the world. India's population is expected to keep rising until it hits 1.7 billion people in 2050, after which it could stabilize or it could continue to grow to as many as 2 billion people.

It is important to bear in mind that, as with nearly everything else in India, population growth varies considerably from region to region, with the fastest growth occurring across India's northern third. According to India's 2011 census, the population of Indian states of Bihar, Meghalaya, and Arunachal Pradesh grew by more than 25 percent between 2001 and 2011, while during the same period, the state of Goa grew by a little over 8 percent and Kerala's population increased by less than 5 percent.

India also suffers from a disproportion of males to females, the result of patriarchal family structures that strongly favor male offspring. Selective abortion based on the sex of the fetus is illegal in India, but its use is widespread by families seeking male births. Neglect of female babies, such as feeding them less, skipping medical care, or even infanticide, also contributes to higher mortality rates for girls and a lopsided sex ratio in favor of males. The result is that there are 1.13 Indian males under the age of twenty-five for every Indian female under the age of twenty-five. As with almost every other statistic in India, this ratio is higher in some parts of the country and lower in others.

India's population is young: more than half of its 1.3 billion people are under the age of twenty-five. Fulfilling the aspirations of India's youth will be a major challenge for the nation as it struggles to educate its young people and create employment as successive generations reach adulthood. On the other hand, its "youth dividend" confers a potential competitive advantage over other aging economies, potentially making India both the world's largest source of labor and its largest consumer market.

India's population is living far longer and is better educated in the twenty-first century than it was when the country won its independence. Life expectancy rose in India from just thirty-two years in 1947 to sixty-nine years in 2014. Literacy rates rose from 16 percent in 1951, when the country's first census was conducted, to 74 percent by the 2011 census. However, though primary school enrollment is up, educational outcomes remain poor and, as we will see, too many Indians enter the job market lacking basic literacy and numeracy skills.

India has done less well on addressing poverty and health. Despite decades of poverty eradication efforts, about 30 percent of Indians live on less than $3 per day, and more than 20 percent get by on less than $2 per day. The country's infant mortality rate—50 deaths for every 1,000 live births—has hardly budged in seventy years. While the percentage of Indians who are malnourished fell between 1990 and 2016 from nearly 24 percent to about 15 percent, the number remains high: 194.6 million people in 2016 versus 210 million in 1990.

What are the major religions of India?

It is impossible to understand the dynamics of twenty-first-century India without some sense of the country's religious landscape. As we saw in Part I, the vast majority of Indians, nearly 80 percent, are Hindus. A little over 14 percent of Indians are Muslims and 2.3 percent are Christians, while Sikhs make up 1.7 percent of Indians. The remaining about 2 percent of Indians are Jains, Buddhists, animists, atheists, or Jews.

How many languages are spoken in India?

India's constitution recognizes twenty-two languages. In alphabetical order, these are Assamese, Bengali, Bodo, Dogri, Gujarati, Hindi, Kannada, Kashmiri, Konkani, Maithili, Malayalam, Manipuri, Marathi, Nepali, Odia, Punjabi, Sanskrit, Santhali, Sindhi, Tamil, Telugu, and Urdu. The constitution also designates Hindi as the official national language, while recognizing English as an additional official language. India's constitution allows individual Indian states to designate their own official state language. Beyond India's officially recognized languages, a 2013 survey identified 780 languages spoken in India, though some are spoken by fewer than 10,000 people. Bhojpuri, a language most people outside India do not know exists, is spoken by more than 33 million people, according to India's 2001 census.

Language is a contentious issue in India. Most Indian states were created along linguistic lines. One of the concerns of the architects of independent India was to choose an official language for the conduct of government distinct from English, the language of the British Raj. They chose Hindi, the language spoken by the largest number of Indians. Non-Hindi-speakers in India, particularly in the southern state of Tamil Nadu, have chafed at an official language with roots in India's north. While all Indians learn Hindi in school, in practice many outside the area where Hindi is spoken use English as a means to communicate with Indians who don't speak their regional language. English is also the passport to highly paid jobs, to study abroad, to work in tourism, or even to jobs in India's call centers, providing customer service for clients in the United States and other English-language countries. Indian parents put a high premium on their children learning English. At the same time, the Hindu nationalist government of Prime Minister Narendra Modi is actively seeking to move the conduct of official business away from English and into Hindi. India's major languages boast their own literatures, press, broadcast media, and film industries, contributing to the rich cultural diversity of the country.

What is a joint family?

Despite differences in religion, language, and regional culture, the so-called joint family, where multiple generations live together under one roof, is the typical family structure in India. The Indian joint family is patrilineal: sons stay in the parental home, where their wives join them and where they raise their children along with the children of any brothers in the family. Daughters leave their parental home upon marriage, joining their husband's family. The nuclear family, consisting of husband, wife, and their children is becoming more common in India's cities, but the joint family remains dominant in India. Indians point to its advantages: incomes from several working sons are pooled and expenses are shared; women who work outside the home can confide childcare responsibilities to grandparents or the children's aunts, uncles, or cousins at home; children grow up with sibling-like relationships with their cousins. The terms "cousin-brother" and "cousin-sister" are common in India to describe these relationships.

But the joint family can also be a suffocating environment for young brides, who can be relegated to performing domestic chores under the command of their mother-in-law. The joint family also encourages the practice of dowry—cash, jewelry, and consumer durables given to the groom's family by the bride's parents upon her marriage—since the idea is the groom's family is taking the young woman off her parents' hands and deserves to be compensated for doing so. Unfortunately, as the appetite for consumer goods has risen, so too has the practice of dowries, and their amounts have increased. While the exact amount and composition of the dowry vary widely according to social standing, regional practices, and the family's means, parents routinely take on massive debt in order to cough up the dowry demanded by the groom's family and get their daughters married off. The dowry system—and even the entire joint family system—reinforces the status quo.

What is the status of women in India?

India's constitution guarantees equality for women and prohibits discrimination on the basis of sex. There are many powerful female politicians as well as business and opinion leaders. India's growing economy has created new opportunities for women to pursue professional careers. Female literacy is increasing, and more girls and young women are being educated than ever before.

Overall, however, Indian women still face widespread discrimination, and their low status contributes to high maternal and infant mortality rates, decreased levels of literacy and education for women, and high rates of sexual abuse and other crimes. In 2011, a Thomson Reuters Foundation–sponsored poll of 370 aid and development experts ranked India the worst place for women among all the Group of 20 nations, including Saudi Arabia.

Dowry is at the root of several injustices perpetrated against India's female population, from aborted female fetuses to the practice of "dowry deaths," where in-laws unhappy with the amount of dowry they've received kill newly married women. According to India's Crime Records Bureau, crimes against women in India steadily increased between 2009 and 2013. In every one of those years, more than 8,000 women, or nearly one per hour, were killed over dowry. Between 1970 and 2010, India chalked up a staggering total of 43 million "missing girls" due to prenatal sex-selective abortion as well as female infanticide and other forms of lethal gender discrimination, including feeding girls less and spending less on their medical care. Alarmed at the worsening sex ratio in India—from 945 girls to every 1,000 boys born in 1991 to 918 girls to every 1,000 boys born in 2011—the government of India launched a national campaign in January 2015 to encourage parents to value female children.

Rape is hardly a problem exclusive to India, but it exploded on India's national consciousness in 2012 after a twenty-eight-year-old college student died of injuries sustained during a brutal gang rape on a bus in New Delhi. The woman, whose parents had sacrificed to pay for her education, symbolized young, aspirational India. She and a male friend were attacked after they were lured onto a private bus by a group of young men. The attackers—poor, uneducated, and not able to mix easily with members of the opposite sex—were also very much a part of India's churning modernization: young, uneducated men pulled to India's burgeoning cities in search of work. News of the crime sent Indian citizens into the streets in protest. In response, India's government set up a special panel headed by a retired Supreme Court judge, Justice J. S. Verma, to look into strengthening legal remedies for crimes against women. The Verma Committee issued a wide-ranging report, recommending a slew of measures to better protect India's women. The government adopted many of the report's recommendations. Unfortunately, brutal rapes in India continue, with reports appearing almost daily in the country's newspapers and on television. The attitudes aired by some of India's politicians and by the lawyers for the attackers in the 2012 case, as well as by one of the attackers himself, included the outrageous notion that any woman out in the evening is "asking" for rape. This attitude is the biggest hurdle to reducing violence against women in India. Marital rape is not a crime in India.

Discrimination against women is also hurting India's economy. The Organisation for Economic Co-operation and

Development (OECD) pointed to the low economic contribution by Indian women as an important factor holding back economic growth in India. Less than one-third of the nation's women are in the paid workforce, and many are stuck in low-wage jobs. Workforce participation by women actually declines as incomes rise: a woman not working outside the home is often considered a sign of family affluence.

What about LGBT rights in India?

India, ever full of paradoxes, is a country where in 2014 its Supreme Court recognized transgender people as a third legal gender but where, as of January 2018, it remained a crime, according to a law that dates back to British colonial days— Section 377 of the Indian Penal Code (1861)—to engage in "carnal intercourse against the order of nature."

Thanks to the 2014 decision, Indians now have the option of selecting "T" in addition to "M" or "F" for their gender on official forms and may bear the gender "T" on their passports. In its decision, India's Supreme Court recognized the existence in India for centuries of transgender people and groups, including hijras, Aravanis, Jogtas, Kothis, and Shiv-Shakthis. It is common to see hijras, a traditional group of transgender people who are born men and usually undergo voluntary castration as boys, dressed in colorful saris in Indian cities. In 2015, India's first transgender college principal started work, and 2016 saw the first transgender modeling agency.

In 2013, India's Supreme Court voided a 2009 Delhi High Court ruling striking down Section 377. The law had rarely been enforced but was commonly used by police to harass and blackmail gay Indians. In February 2016, the Supreme Court, acknowledging the "constitutional importance" of the issues surrounding Section 377, agreed to hear a petition asking the court to reverse its 2013 decision. In 2017, the Supreme Court made a landmark ruling supporting Indians' right to privacy, which specifically singled out the private nature of sexual orientation, and as of January 2018, the Supreme Court was deliberating yet again the constitutionality of Section 377.

Meanwhile, there are online gay and lesbian dating sites, and prominent writers, such as Vikram Seth and Sandip Roy, whose 2015 novel *Don't Let Him Know* delves poignantly into the pain caused by cultural strictures against homosexuality, make no secret of the fact they are gay. Deep Mehta's 1996 film *Fire* tells a story about two women who fall in love, and lesbian writer Minat Hajratwala and publisher Shobhna Kumar published *Out! Stories from the New Queer India* with HarperCollins India in 2012.

Still, it is difficult for gay, lesbian, bisexual, and transgender people to live in a society where gay marriage is illegal, and yet where life as an unmarried adult is beyond the imaginary boundaries of most Indians. And as long as Section 377 remains on the books, the threat of criminal prosecution will hang over the lives of Indians—even in the country's booming cities—who are not heterosexual.

What is life like in India's cities?

In 2016, 429 million Indians lived in cities. The World Bank projects that number will double by 2050. New Delhi, with 25 million people, is India's largest city and the world's second most populous, after Tokyo. By 2030, the United Nations projects, New Delhi's population will swell to 36 million people. The population of India's financial, business, and entertainment capital, Mumbai, is projected to grow from 21 million in 2016 to 28 million by 2030. The Kolkata metropolitan area counts more than 14 million people, and Bengaluru and Chennai each have populations of over 8 million; the populations of these cities and others will also grow over the coming decades.

India's cities—cultural centers and hubs of connection to the world beyond—are expected to generate 75 percent of India's GDP by 2020. They are also, as most cities in the world, starkly divided between the rich and the poor. Rich urban dwellers can shop for any international luxury or mass-market brand at shopping malls that are equal to the best in the world, eat at restaurants that offer a dizzying array of domestic and international cuisines, and have themselves ferried to and from their air-conditioned homes in an air-conditioned, chauffeur-driven car. India's urban poor live in a parallel city of garbage- and sewage-choked lanes, slapped-together slum dwellings, long lines for drinking water, and open defecation or stinking public toilets. Poor urban Indians often spend hours commuting in packed trains and buses from the ever-expanding urban periphery to jobs in the city center.

Upgrading urban infrastructure and building for future growth is one of the major challenges India faces in the twenty-first century. Water shortages are common in cities, where the rich stock water in rooftop tanks to ensure water flows from taps throughout the day. Electricity demand in cities has also skyrocketed, and brownouts and blackouts are so frequent that any household that can afford it has a backup generator. Large luxury hotels, apartment complexes, and business office towers have underground diesel tanks to tap for electricity generation when the municipal power goes out, and water tanks to provide a constant flow of water.

India's major cities have begun to upgrade public transportation. The Delhi Metro is the country's largest network of subway and suburban trains. Other cities are following Delhi's lead, with metro rail systems started or planned for Kolkata, Chennai, Hyderabad, Kochi, and Ahmedabad. Mumbai plans to upgrade its famously crowded urban rail network with faster trains, renovated stations, and elevated corridors through clogged neighborhoods. The Maharashtra Maritime Board has also announced plans for an ambitious waterways transportation network around Mumbai.

Buses remain the most common public transportation option in India's cities, and efforts are being made to convert them into less polluting electric vehicles. While many of the urban poor get around on foot or by bicycle, there is virtually no public infrastructure for pedestrians or bicyclists. Instead, most cities have concentrated on building new infrastructure for automobile traffic, though not at a sufficient rate to keep up with the burgeoning numbers of new cars on India's roads. No visitor can escape the massive traffic jams in India's major cities.

Vehicular emissions, industrial pollution, dust, and smoke from refuse the poor burn to do their cooking or to warm themselves during winter and from fires set in fields to burn crop waste have helped make the air of India's cities among the most polluted in the world. In 2016, the World Health Organization ranked Delhi the most polluted of the world's megacities, with a population of more than 14 million inhabitants; the World Health Organization named thirteen Indian cities among the twenty worldwide with the worst air pollution. Mumbai and Kolkata also made the list, as did Gwalior, Allahabad, and Raipur.

Housing is another major problem in India's cities. Rents and sale prices in New Delhi and Mumbai easily rival those in New York or London. Entire families live in a single small room. In 2013, 17 percent of Indians lived in urban slums.

What is the plan for "smart cities" in India?

India's urban growth has been chaotic, with planning for basic amenities, such as sidewalks, schools, post offices, medical facilities, and fire departments, a long-delayed afterthought. Taking a cue from China, Prime Minister Modi intends to change that. Shortly after he was elected in 2014, his government kicked off the Smart Cities Mission, an initiative aimed at getting ahead of India's skyrocketing urban growth. According to the government's Smart Cities Mission website, "the objective is to promote cities that provide core infrastructure and give a decent quality of life to its citizens, a clean and sustainable environment and application of 'Smart' Solutions." Like the smart cities now being planned elsewhere in the world, India's smart cities would leverage information technology for e-governance and to improve the efficiency of traffic and the delivery of basic services. India's smart cities also promise something its current cities lack: decent infrastructure for water, power, education, and healthcare. India's government plans to build 100 brand-new cities and retrofit 500 existing cities. The consulting firm Deloitte estimates that India will need $150 billion for new smart cities alone. Eighty percent of this must come from the private sector. As a federation of states and a democracy, India faces far more hurdles than China, which has 193 smart cities in the works, in creating new smart cities: Appropriating privately owned land or clearing the slums where millions of urban Indians now live is no easy feat. The Chinese government can act quickly by fiat in these and other areas where India faces numerous local, state, and national hurdles that will no doubt slow down the process. How successful India's ambitious Smart Cities project is, and how inclusive and equitable it turns out to be, will determine much about the quality of urban life in India in the twenty-first century.

What is life like in rural India?

In 2016, some 70 percent of Indians lived in rural areas, and more than half of the country's workers were employed in agriculture. Many villages remain cut off from the country's power grid. In 2015, 300 million Indians lacked electricity, most of them rural poor. Children frequently have to walk long distances to schools, which often lack such basics as toilets. These two factors—accessibility and facilities—keep many girls at home. Rural schoolteachers may show up sporadically, or pocket their salary and hire a local youth on the cheap to substitute for them.

Life in India's villages is often circumscribed by social traditions that dictate what people can and can't do, according to caste and gender rules enforced by local *panchayats*, or village councils. As in the cities, inequality stalks India's countryside, where there are stark divides between landowners and tenant farmers. Often these divides fall along caste lines, with lower castes making up the bulk of the landless poor. Though women in India's villages have made strides—leading community water efforts to build and maintain small dams to catch rainwater runoff, for example, or using cell phones to manage microlending projects—most rural poor women are uneducated, married off at a young age, prone to poor maternal health, and subject to the dictates of their parents, their husbands, and their in-laws.

In many North Indian villages, *kap panchayats*—councils of elders from several neighboring villages that have no legal recognition—enforce strict codes of conduct regarding how women may dress and whom young people can love or marry. Punishment for rebellion can be severe, including banishment, rape, beatings, and even death. Honor killings of couples in defiance of caste rules are defended by *kap panchayats* as fitting punishment for those who dare to stray. The problem is so pervasive that India's Supreme Court weighed in on the matter in 2011, declaring *kap panchayats* illegal and calling the honor killings they order "shameful and barbaric." But *kap panchayats* continue to exist and to mete out their sometimes terrible judgments. Some village councils have banned all young women from owning cell phones, seen as devices that can be used for forbidden courtships. Other councils have imposed mass rape by village men to punish women, or even to punish the family of a woman who has done no wrong herself.

India's small-scale farmers are experiencing severe stress from high input costs (seeds, fertilizer, and pesticides), low market prices, unpredictable rainfall, and high levels of debt. Many are driven to seek work in cities as contract laborers in the country's booming construction business. In every city, rural Indians in colorful traditional dress can be seen ferrying cement in baskets on their heads and scaling rickety bamboo scaffolding. Others contract themselves—and even their young children—out to brick works, a largely unregulated industry that is entirely dependent on low-wage and indentured labor.

Falling procurement prices (the price farmers get for their crops) and rising input prices (for fertilizer, seeds, and pesticides) have driven millions of small-scale farmers into debilitating debt. While the government offers loans to farmers, these mostly go to larger-scale farmers. Most small farmers are forced to borrow from local lenders—often neighboring large landowners—at extortionate rates. When farmers cannot repay their debts because their crops fail, a family member falls ill, or a daughter needs a dowry to be married, too many commit suicide.

Distinguished Indian journalist P. Sainath has been tracking and writing about India's agricultural crisis for years. He has documented 300,000 farmer suicides in India between 1995 and 2013 alone. And the suicides continue: In the state of Maharashtra, which is comparatively wealthy, 2,568 farmers committed suicide in 2014. In 2015, 3,030 killed themselves—an 18 percent increase. Altogether, farmer suicides increased by 40 percent between 2014 and 2015, jumping from 5,650 farmers who took their lives to over 8,000.

In November 2016, thousands of farmers marched on New Delhi to demand relief. Farmers want the government to guarantee them a minimum income, lift the minimum support price the government guarantees farmers for their crops, and subsidize the cost of their seeds, fertilizers, and pest management. These demands run directly counter to international pressure for India to open its markets and end artificial price supports and subsidies. India's farmers are also up against the focus of successive governments on development, understood as industrialization and urbanization, which effectively means moving millions of farmers off their land and into cities, a wrenching process under the best of circumstances.

Agriculture contributes a pittance to India's storied economic growth. While the country's economy grew overall at a rate of 7.6 percent during the fiscal year 2015–16, its agricultural sector grew at a rate of only 1.2 percent. In the previous year, agriculture actually contracted by 0.2 percent, mostly due to debilitating drought. The fact that boosting agricultural growth would go a long way toward boosting India's economic growth overall is not lost on its leaders, who seek private sector investment to transform Indian agriculture along the industrial farming model of the West.

India's corporate sector has moved full-scale into farming, embracing a farm-to-fork vertical integration model for agricultural production in which a corporation owns and controls every step in the chain, from growing crops to food processing to selling packaged food to customers in grocery stores. For these powerful businesses, profits are made from adding "value" to raw basic food products. Farmers are encouraged to sell or lease their land so that a patchwork of small farms can be amalgamated into large fields and put into industrial production. They are then hired as laborers on the land they used to own.

On the brighter side, India is also home to many promising experiments in sustainable agriculture. Whole villages have become food-secure and debt-free by minimizing or eliminating costly chemical fertilizers and pesticides, saving seeds from one harvest to use in the next, and using natural pest control and fertilizers. Micro-irrigation—which India's government supports—is helping many farmers cope with water scarcity and has the potential to help many more as its use expands.

Small-scale solar, wind, biomass, and methane gas projects have brought power and cleaner-burning fuels to areas that lacked them until just a few years ago. Indoor air pollution, mostly in the form of primitive stoves that burn cow dung or wood in rural homes, is the leading cause of respiratory illness and death in Indian children under the age of five. In 2016, Prime Minister Modi promised to electrify all of India's villages still without power within two years. Electricity means power for irrigation pumps, but it also means light for children to study after dark, and power to connect to the world beyond the village via computers, televisions, and rechargeable mobile devices.

India will change dramatically over the next several decades. Whether prosperity for all will accompany that change remains to be seen. How rural India copes with climate change, and whether deeply ingrained inequalities due to caste and gender discrimination will abate, are open questions.

What is the state of education in India?

In 2009, the Indian government passed a landmark act called the Right of Children to Free and Compulsory Education Act. Known as the Right to Education (RTE) Act, this legislation constitutionally guarantees the right of all Indian children ages six to fourteen years to a basic education. Since then, the country has made remarkable progress in boosting primary school enrollment. As of 2014, more than 96 percent of India's nearly 200 million primary-school-age children were enrolled in school. Everyone is aware that educating India's massive youth population holds the key to a brighter future for hundreds of millions.

Unfortunately, serious problems remain, including poor infrastructure, irregular student attendance, a lack of competent teachers, poor learning outcomes, and a growing divide between private and public education. In its 2014 Annual Status of Education Report for rural India, Pratham, a nonprofit group dedicated to improving education in India, reported that more than half of children in Standard V (fifth grade) had reading levels stuck at Standard II (second grade) levels. Too many children are going through their early schooling years without acquiring the basic reading and math skills they need to pursue secondary-school studies or to get even halfway decent jobs.

This contrast between improved access to schooling and a lack of improvement in the quality of the education children receive continues at India's secondary school level. In 2009, the government launched the Rashtriya Madhyamik Shiksha Abhiyan, or National Mission for Secondary Education, a program aimed at achieving 90 percent enrollment in India's lower secondary schools (grades 9 and 10) and 75 percent enrollment in higher secondary schools (grades 11 and 12). Since the launch of the program, an additional 10 million students have enrolled in more than 200,000 secondary schools. The number of female students is nearly on par with male students—real progress in India. However, there are still way too few students getting a secondary school education in India: in 2013, only 66 percent of eligible boys and 62 percent of eligible girls were enrolled in secondary school. For those who do enroll, poor infrastructure, too few teachers, and poorly trained teachers are the norm for most. Meanwhile, the very privileged enjoy access—for a price—to world-class private schools.

To address the woeful disconnect between the skills needed for a twenty-first-century workforce and the underpreparedness of India's youth, the government is expanding vocational education beginning in Class IX (ninth grade). Vocational training is being offered in industries as diverse as information technology, automotive manufacturing, and beauty and wellness. Industry in India routinely complains about the lack of skilled workers. The government's National Skills Development Corporation, started in 2009, was working with seventy-one private skills institutes in India in 2013, with the goal of training 150 million people by 2022. But there were only 11,000 vocational schools in India in 2013, versus 500,000 in China.

In March 2016, Modi pledged to include 800 vocational courses on secondary school syllabi. But as noted, India's government schools lack basic equipment and qualified teachers to provide hands-on learning of vocational skills. Clearly, more funds for equipment and teacher training are needed. In 2016, India signed a pact with Germany worth over $3 million to boost vocational training, especially for skills needed in automobile manufacturing.

With nearly 26 million students enrolled in more than 45,000 institutions, India boasts the third-largest higher-education system in the world after the United States and China. Over 60 percent of those schools are private—an astonishing ratio for a developing country when one considers the dominance of public higher education institutions in Europe and even in the United States, where private institutions also thrive. But, as at the secondary school level, the gap between the high quality of a handful of institutions, such as the world-famous Indian Institutes of Technology, and a large number of mid- to poor-quality colleges, universities, and institutes is huge. By and large, despite historically controversial efforts to reserve a certain number of places for lower-caste and other disadvantaged students, access to the top universities and institutes in India remains the privilege of higher-caste students. This inequity carries over into the job market, where upper-caste Indians occupy the lion's share of high-level jobs. Other students travel abroad for university education: nearly 300,000 in 2014, of which a little over one-third went to the United States—a number second only to China's more than 650,000 university students studying abroad.

What about healthcare?

India is home to private medical centers and hospitals that, for a price, deliver excellent medical care to India's wealthier citizens and foreign patients. India has become an attractive medical tourism destination for Western patients who can fly to India, undergo a surgical procedure, recuperate, and visit the Taj Mahal—all for less than the procedure costs at home.

Public health is where India falls short. According to the World Bank, the Indian government spent just 1.3 percent of total expenditure in 2013 on healthcare. The vast majority of Indians lack access to even rudimentary care. Public health facilities are understaffed and underequipped. Despite successful public campaigns to fight tuberculosis or vaccinate against smallpox, preventive care is rarely an option for India's poor. Many are forced deeply into debt when a family member does need emergency treatment. Rural Indians may live miles from the nearest clinic or hospital.

In India's cities, public hospitals do provide care at a far more reasonable cost than private facilities, but hygiene is poor and wards are often little more than bare rooms with lines of steel cots, with some patients forced to lie on mats on the floor. In the absence of an affordable public health system, a lack of medical insurance puts treatment, including pain medication, even for terminally ill patients, out of the reach of the poor. A notable exception to this grim picture is the growing hospital chain Narayana Health. The chain aims to provide affordable, high-quality healthcare, including heart surgery, on a sliding scale.

Rather than increase public expenditure on healthcare, the Modi government is focusing on increasing health insurance coverage, to allow more Indians to access private care. India's 2016–17 annual budget includes funding for a new national health insurance plan that would cover medical expenses up to a value of 1 lakh Indian rupees (about $1,400) per family.

Poverty, pollution, and a lack of access to clean water and sanitation also contribute to the poor health of too many Indians. Many women are anemic and undernourished, resulting in underweight babies. More malnourished children live in India than in sub-Saharan Africa. Mosquito-transmitted diseases, such as malaria, dengue fever, and encephalitis, are endemic. India also suffers from high levels of pesticide residues on fruits and vegetables, in soil, and in the water, especially in areas of high agricultural production, such as the state of Punjab, where cancer levels are alarmingly high. Air pollution in the cities takes a toll on human health. The explosion of fast-food outlets, including many international chains—a growing trend among those who can afford to eat out—have contributed to a recent rise in obesity and heart disease among India's rising, urban middle class.

After his election in 2014, Modi set up a new ministry, the Ministry of AYUSH (Ayurveda, Yoga and Naturopathy, Unani, Siddha, and Homeopathy), dedicated to improving and advancing Indian traditional medicinal systems. Ayurveda (*ayur*, "life," and *veda*, "knowledge"), discussed in India's Vedic literature dating back more than 1,000 years, is based on the idea that a healthy person is one whose spirit, senses, mind, and physical functions, such as the digestive and immune systems, are in harmony. Ayurvedic treatment seeks to restore that harmony.

Ayurveda in a truncated form of relaxing warm-oil treatments and massages is the latest trend in wellness spas in the United States. A ninety-minute Ayurvedic treatment at the Surya Spa at the Four Seasons Hotel in Beverly Hills, California, will set you back $395—if you can get a slot in between the legions of Hollywood stars booking sessions.

Is mosquito-borne disease on the rise in India?

Some certainly are. The mosquito-borne diseases malaria, dengue fever, chikungunya, Japanese encephalitis, and lymphatic filariasis (commonly known as elephantiasis for the swelling the disease can cause in victims' legs) are all present in India. While the country has made good progress, halving the number of malaria cases between 2010 and 2013, the World Health Organization warned in 2016 that one in seven Indians was still at risk of contracting the disease. A 2010 report published in the *Lancet* indicated that some 200,000 Indians die of malaria every year. Accurate numbers are difficult to obtain: many of the rural poor do not have a means of accurately reporting cause of death.

Dengue fever and chikungunya, both viral diseases for which there are as yet no cure or preventive vaccine, have become endemic in India, striking the country's capital, New Delhi, particularly hard. In 2015, hospital wards in Delhi were overwhelmed with cases of both. The culprit is the *Aedes aegypti* mosquito, which has found an ideal breeding ground in puddles of standing water, a problem exacerbated by widespread building construction, annual monsoon rains, and open drains.

Unless India's cities make a concerted effort to cover open drains and eliminate standing water, mosquito-borne diseases will remain a serious problem. Improving access to basic healthcare in rural areas would reduce the number of deaths from malaria. Visitors to India are advised to take precautions, such as wearing long-sleeved shirts and trousers and using insect repellents, to prevent being bitten by mosquitos.

What about science? Do Indians really believe ancient Indians flew airplanes?

India produces some of the world's top scientists and mathematicians, is home to several world-renowned research institutions, and has a successful space program that has reached Mars. Yet despite solid achievements in the sciences and India's technological ambitions for the future, beliefs about the scientific achievements of Indians in the Vedic period—circa 1500 to 500 BCE—abound. These beliefs are central to the project of Hindutva: restoring India—or Bharat, as Hindu nationalists prefer to call it—to a former glory.

In late 2015, Prime Minister Modi voiced some of his own views on ancient Indian scientific achievements. At the dedication ceremony of a Mumbai hospital, Modi claimed that "genetic science" was present during the days of the *Mahabharata*. He similarly argued that the elephant-headed Hindu god Lord Ganesha was proof of the existence of ancient plastic surgeons. "There must have been some plastic surgeon at that time who got an elephant's head on the body of a human being and began the practice of plastic surgery," he said. "If we talk about space science, our ancestors, at some point, displayed great strengths in space science. What people like Aryabhata said centuries ago is being recognized by science today."

Modi went further, writing the foreword to a textbook used in Gujarati schools that teaches Indian children that ancient Indians had mastered stem-cell technology and that the god Ram flew the first airplane. These, and claims that ancient Indians had nuclear weapons technology and automobiles, are being taught in schools in India as historical fact, thanks to the efforts of Hindu-nationalist ideologues such as Dina Nath Batra, the author of textbooks used in the state of Gujarat and an educational advisor to the government of the state of Haryana. Batra told the *Times of India* in November 2015 that his goal is the "saffronization of education of the whole country." By "saffronization"—a reference to the yellow-orange color Hindus hold sacred—Batra means coloring education with the ideology of the Hindu right. India's scientists are aghast. "We are giving a young, aspirational generation a wrong idea of science," lamented D. Raghunandan, president of the All People's Scientific Network, after a January 2015 conference in Mumbai on Vedic science.

These forays into ideological fantasy discredit India's very real scientific achievements, both ancient and modern. They also distract from the investment India must make in basic and applied scientific education and research to make the country competitive internationally and to give Indians the knowledge they need to tackle the country's problems and prepare its future. While India's top institutions, such as the Indian Institute of Science and the Jawaharlal Nehru Center for Advanced Scientific Research, in the city of Bengaluru, are top-notch, far too many of the country's scientific education and research institutions, starved for government funding, lack such basics as qualified professors and decent lab equipment. The result is that India is lagging behind some other developing countries in the sciences when it should be leading them.

How is information technology changing India?

Only a little more than one-third of Indians had access to the Internet in 2015. But that's more than 400 million people, which means more Indians are online than Americans. India's information technology trade group, NASSCOM, predicts that there will be 730 million Internet users in India by 2020. Significantly, NASSCOM says 75 percent of new Internet users in India will be from rural areas, and that 75 percent of new internet users will access data in local languages. Most Internet access will be via smartphones, far less expensive than computers.

And thanks to cheaper smartphones, the Internet is changing everything: how Indians receive services, how they communicate, how they get information, how political parties court them as voters, and how they advocate for social change. Doctors are using the Internet to deliver healthcare services to a greater number of remote patients. Students are using it to take courses, and farmers are using it to check commodity prices and track monsoon rains. E-governance is gradually replacing government paper forms, circulars, and records. Indians can now make train and airplane reservations online.

Prime Minister Modi has great hopes that information technology can solve some of the country's most vexing problems, create jobs, and develop vital services aimed at the poor, such as mobile bank accounts where they can receive government subsidies. But not all of India's problems—including pollution, crumbling and inadequate infrastructure, rising inequality, and communal and caste conflicts– can be solved by the Internet. And a failure to meet expectations raised by greater access to news and services on the Internet could increase citizens' frustration as the gap between what they see on the Internet and the reality of their daily lives grows.

What about social media?

Social media is booming in India, with 143 million users as of April 2015. Rural users accounted for 25 million of these. Over one-third of Indians on social media are college students. Sixty-one percent of Indians access social media on mobile devices, an astonishing percentage given high levels of poverty. Indians spent, on average, about the same amount of time as Americans do—between one and two hours daily—on social media in 2016, accessing the globally popular platforms Facebook, Twitter, WhatsApp, and Instagram. And, as it is doing globally, social media is changing how Indians construct identities, how they communicate, how they mobilize politically, and how they respond to disasters. Social media has become one of the most important ways for marketers of products and services, but also for government and for politicians, to reach Indian citizens, and for citizens to connect with each other.

How have cell phones changed India?

No technology has transformed more Indians' lives in recent years than cellular phones. There were more than 1 billion Indian cellular phone subscribers in 2015. The low cost of entry-level phones and rate plans has made it possible for everyone from housemaids to young professionals to buy and use one. Cellular phones have provided connectivity to hundreds of millions of Indians who had no hope of obtaining a landline. They have been a boon to informal workers across a wide range of sectors—from farmers and fishermen to chauffeurs and laundrymen—allowing them to interact in real time with customers and suppliers.

As of 2015, a very small portion of Indians—some 160 million—used the more expensive smartphones common in richer countries: Few Indians can afford a new iPhone, for example. But there are a number of cheaper smartphones hitting the Indian market. These may have fewer bells and whistles and less capacity for data, but they do allow access to the Internet. By 2020 India is expected to count more than 700 million smartphone users. Smartphones are affordable, portable, all-in-one communication, entertainment, and information devices that are far less expensive than laptop computers.

What is Aadhaar?

India is embracing information technology in other domains as well. Aadhaar, a Hindi word meaning "foundation" or "base," is India's unique biometric national identity plan. Launched by the Unique Identification Authority of India (UIDAI) under the United Progressive Alliance government led by Prime Minister Manmohan Singh in 2009, Aadhaar seeks to provide every Indian citizen with a permanent, unique twelve-digit identification number, much like an American's Social Security number. Nandan Nilekani, former CEO of Indian tech giant Infosys, headed up the effort. The idea behind Aadhaar was to eliminate corruption by ensuring that only those who are eligible get their fair share of government subsidies and services, and to offer a transportable, official identity to millions of India's poor who may not be able to produce other forms of identity and may not have a fixed address.

But Aadhaar has been criticized for opening the door to government surveillance and data collection on a massive scale, as well as to breaches of citizens' privacy through hacking or accidental leaks of government data. These concerns are well founded: the Bengaluru-based Centre for Internet and Society charged in May 2017 that private data on 130 million Aadhaar-holders had been leaked from just four government websites. In August 2015, India's Supreme Court ruled that enrollment must be strictly voluntary: "The production of an Aadhaar card will not be a condition for obtaining any benefits otherwise due to a citizen." Yet the Modi government has largely ignored the Court's decision, and enrollment in Aadhaar is increasingly becoming mandatory for access to basic financial and government services. In November 2016, Modi announced that Aadhaar would be integrated into Umang, its new mobile application for accessing government services. In July 2017, the government made it mandatory for income tax filers to link their Aadhaar number to their tax identification number in order to file their taxes.

Meanwhile, India's airports are beginning to perform biometric screening on Indian passengers holding Aadhaar cards. Hyderabad's airport began screening of this nature in 2015, followed by Bengaluru's. There is a major push to have Indian travelers use Aadhaar screening coupled with e-boarding passes at all of India's airports. By the end of 2016, more than 1 billion Indian citizens had enrolled in Aadhaar.

The 2017 ruling by India's Supreme Court that privacy is a fundamental right, which we looked at earlier in the context of gay rights, could bolster the arguments of critics who say Aadhaar violates Indians' right to privacy. This issue is sure to be debated in subsequent legal hearings.

What is curry?

While Indians are increasingly identified by their Aadhaar numbers, nothing says India more to the rest of the world than curry. With its varied climate—alpine to tropical—and topography and its many different religious, linguistic, and ethnic groups, India boasts a vast array of distinct cuisines. From the rich biryanis of Hyderabad and the crispy dosas of Tamil Nadu to the fish dishes of West Bengal and the vegetarian cuisine of Gujarat, India is one of the world's great culinary cultures.

So, what is curry? The English word *curry* comes from the Tamil *cari*, meaning a sauce flavored by a mix of spices. Different Indian dishes call for different mixtures, with the spices freshly roasted and ground before being tempered in hot oil to release their flavors. The Hindi word for "mixture of spices" is *masala*. Turmeric gives curries their yellow color, while chilies, garlic, ginger, and onions give Indian food its punch. Other typical spices include black mustard seeds, cumin and coriander seeds, cinnamon, cloves, and black pepper.

While the staple food in South India is rice, in North India it is wheat. Unleavened whole-wheat chapatis and rotis, or fluffy naans baked in a traditional tandoor clay oven, are torn into bite-size pieces to scoop up different dishes often served in small bowls or simply arrayed in little mounds on a large round metal tray called a *thali*. Many Indians are vegetarian, either by religious conviction (because they are Jains or vegetarian Hindus) or because they cannot afford to eat meat, poultry, or fish. The main vegetable protein in Indian cuisine comes from dried beans, chickpeas, and lentils of many varieties. These form the basis of dals, thick soups that are a ubiquitous feature of many Indians' daily fare. Plain yogurt is also a common part of meals.

Many Indian sweets are based on milk, boiled with sugar into thick custards or reduced further to form little cakes. Rice or noodle milk-based puddings are popular, as are nut brittles, halwas made from sweetened grated carrots, and ice cream made from frozen milk custard called kulfi. There are jalebis, golden curlicues of fried pastry soaked in saffron-infused sugar syrup, and gulab jamuns, spongy fried milk balls the size of donut holes soaked in rose-flavored syrup. Saffron is a prized ingredient in many Indian sweets, as are almonds, pistachios, and cashews. For special occasions, sweets may be decorated with paper-thin sheets of edible silver.

Indian cuisine is changing. The opening up of the nation's economy to foreign brands following the 1991 balance of payments crisis, discussed in Chapter 3 of Part I, and the subsequent emergence of a thriving consumer culture have brought global fast-food brands to India and sparked a boom in Indian packaged snack foods and chain restaurants. More and more, those who can afford it are purchasing processed foods that used to be prepared at home from scratch. Mass-produced brands, such as Lays snack products or Maggi noodles—ubiquitous in India—are quickly replacing salty snacks and sweets made locally by mom-and-pop enterprises.

In the wake of these changes in Indians' diet, obesity is on the rise among the privileged and middle classes. Meanwhile, too many Indians remain malnourished, unable to afford to buy enough food for a normal daily caloric intake, much less fresh vegetables, fruit, dried beans and lentils, milk, or eggs for a healthy, balanced diet. Chronic malnutrition leading to stunted growth affects nearly 39 percent of India's children. Only Yemen, Pakistan, and the Democratic Republic of Congo report higher levels of children stunted.

What is traditional Indian dress?

While Western clothes are common in India, especially among the urban young, traditional Indian clothing remains popular and visible. Most male politicians wear traditional clothing, including long tunics and vests over fitted or loose drawstring trousers for men. Female politicians tend to wear a sari, which consists of six yards of fabric draped around the body to form a long gown, with one end flung over the left shoulder. In fact, there are many different ways to drape a sari. While most urban young women now dress in Western clothes or wear Indian-inspired tunics over jeans for every day, opting for traditional Indian dress on special occasions, older women tend to wear traditional Indian dress on a daily basis. Saris remain the primary form of women's dress across large swathes of rural India.

In Punjab and elsewhere in India, especially in the north, many women also wear *salwar kameez* or *churidar kameez*, long tunics over loose or tight-around-the-calf drawstring trousers, often with a long scarf, called a *dupatta*, either draped across the chest or, sometimes, used to loosely cover the head.

India's woven and printed silks and cottons have been the envy of the world for centuries, and originally drove the expansion of the British East India Company into India during the eighteenth and nineteenth centuries. Traditional Indian printing, dyeing, and weaving techniques vary from region to region: a handwoven sari from Orissa is nothing like one from Gujarat. Embroidery, beadwork, mirror work, and other labor-intensive textile arts are still important industries in

India, used to embellish Indian contemporary clothing as well as textiles for export.

Choosing to wear Indian clothing has been a way to express national pride since the days of the independence movement. The backlash among India's Hindu conservatives against what they see as permissive Western values has politicized the issue of what young women wear, and it has even prompted bans on young women wearing jeans—let alone skirts or shorts—on some university campuses.

What is bharat natyam?

Traditional Indian dress is incorporated into the costumes of both India's ancient classical dance forms and newer contemporary dance. India's best-known dance form—with its costumes of brilliant pleated silks, golden jewelry, and tinkling ankle bells—is *bharat natyam*. This dance form originated in Tamil Nadu centuries ago where it was performed by female temple dancers. Despite its popularity now, *bharat natyam* remains at its core a devotional dance form that retells episodes from India's Hindu epic tales. *Bharat natyam* is a highly codified art: each gesture and each glance has meaning. Other major Indian dance forms include *odissi, kuchipudi,* and *kathakali.* Popular dance styles, originally performed by community members at festivals, include *garba* (from Gujarat) and *bhangra* (from Punjab). Both these popular dances, especially *bhangra,* have been taken up by the Indian diaspora, notably in the United States and in Britain, and transformed into elaborate stage productions and contests where teams of costumed dancers compete against one another.

Contemporary dancers and choreographers, such as Mallika Sarabhai, Anita Ratnam, Rajika Puri (based in New York), and even Bangladesh-born Akram Khan (based in London), have brought innovative themes and staging to traditional Indian dance forms and opened new horizons for contemporary dance.

What is Bollywood?

It's impossible to imagine a Bollywood movie without a number of highly choreographed dance scenes. Indian cinema was born when Harishchandra Bhatavdekar produced his first movie in Bombay in 1899. Bollywood, the name of India's Hindi-language commercial film industry, is a neologism invented by combining the words *Hollywood* and *Bombay*, the longtime name for the city, now called Mumbai, where the industry is based. Bollywood conjures images of curvaceous leading ladies and hulking male stars, impossible love stories, and lavishly produced dance scenes. The classic Bollywood film, while it may grapple with social issues, generally concentrates on escapism and fantasy, offering dreams that rarely come true in real life amid settings of a luxury lifestyle very few Indians can afford. Music is an essential component of Bollywood films, and the success of a movie on release can often be gauged by the success of its songs, and whether they are widely played on the radio and available to download as ringtones for fans' cell phones. Celebrated Bollywood filmmakers include Guru Dutt, Raj Kapoor, and Yash Chopra.

Beyond the glitz and the perpetual rumors about the stars' love lives, the Bollywood film industry is big business. At some 1,000 films per year, Bollywood is the world's most prolific film industry, with distribution stretching from the Middle East through Southeast Asia and to the Indian diaspora around the world. Bollywood movies are popular in Russia, Japan, and Peru—not to mention in India's neighbor, Pakistan. By 2020, the industry is projected to generate revenues of $3.7 billion annually. Male stars, such as global megastar Shah Rukh Khan, command salaries per film comparable to Hollywood stars; female stars earn far less. Still, the glamour of Bollywood stars is the source of much of the mystique that clings to the city of Mumbai, a hardscrabble place for most.

But Indian filmmaking is much more than Bollywood. There is Tollywood, for example, the Tamil-language film industry. And there is a strong tradition in India of auteur or art films. Satyajit Ray remains the best known of India's noncommercial filmmakers, but others in the auteur tradition include Mani Kaul, Shyam Benegal, Ritwik Ghatak, and Aparna Sen. New York–based Mira Nair and Toronto-based Deepa Mehta have tackled the experience of the Indian diaspora—or made movies with no overt India link at all.

Bollywood became the target of a culture war between India and Pakistan following an attack on Indian soldiers in Kashmir by Pakistan-based militants in September 2016. After director Karan Johar was criticized for featuring Pakistani film star Fawad Khan in his movie *Ae Dil Hai Mushkil* ("Oh the Heart Is Difficult") and a Hindu nationalist group threatened violence at theaters screening the movie, Johar produced a video apology and vowed never to hire Pakistani actors again.

How is television changing India?

Television has an enormous impact on the social and political dynamics of India, as it does everywhere in the world. The arrival of satellite television in India in the 1990s marked a point of no return for a medium that had been controlled since its advent on the subcontinent in 1959 by the government. Satellite television brought the world—a world most had never seen before—into Indians' homes. The arrival of a host of international brands after economic liberalization in 1991 spurred advertising as companies both Indian and foreign vied for the Indian consumer's wallet. Television advertising has since played a key role in transforming India into a consumer society.

In 2015, India counted 832 television channels, with more than 200 new channels waiting for licensing from the country's Ministry of Information and Broadcasting. These numbers are less surprising than one would think when one considers Indians speak 22 different recognized regional languages and that 78 percent prefer watching broadcast media in their mother tongue.

Indian television offers a full range of programming, including soap operas, dramatic series, game shows, reality shows, and 24/7 news channels. Indian versions of popular international shows, such as *Kaun Banega Crorepati?* (based on *Who Wants to Be a Millionaire?*), *MasterChef India, Indian Idol,* and *Big Boss* (the Indian version of *Big Brother*), are all popular. Indian television news networks compete fiercely for viewers, often veering into sensationalism.

After the election of Prime Minister Narendra Modi, Indian television embraced hypernationalism, with news networks vying to be the most fervent in their support of India's government and military. Critics charge that a combination of concentrated corporate ownership, ownership by politicians, and a growing temptation by India's government to censor television news by threatening to pull licenses or ordering networks off the air is making it harder to find unbiased news reporting on Indian television.

Who are the best-known Indian writers?

The Indian writers best known outside the country are those who write in English. (There are many authors who write in Indian languages but whose work is not well known beyond those who can read them in the original.) The publication of Salman Rushdie's *Midnight's Children* in 1981 thrust Indian fiction onto the global stage. This fictional parable of independent India, written in a startlingly original form of magical realism, won the Man Booker Prize. In 1989, Rushdie's fame reached a new high when Iran's Ayatollah Khomeini issued a fatwa calling for Muslims to murder him after his book *The Satanic Verses* provoked a firestorm of protest in Pakistan on the grounds that it insulted the Prophet Muhammad. Rushdie's prolific literary career was not derailed by the controversy, and he has gone on to publish many more books.

Other Indian authors who have won international recognition and fame—many of whom live outside India or who divide their time between India and Britain, the United States, or Canada—include Amitav Ghosh, whose book *The Sea of Poppies*, the first in a trilogy, was short-listed for the 2015 Man Booker Prize; Arundhati Roy, whose novel *The God of Small Things* won the Man Booker Prize in 1997; Jhumpa Lahiri, whose short-story collection *Interpreter of Maladies* won the Pulitzer Prize in 2000; and Aravind Adiga, whose novel *White Tiger* won the Man Booker Prize in 2008. These are just a very few of a long—and growing—list of successful Indian authors in English.

Indian writers and readers have benefitted from a boom in bookstores and literary festivals in India. The best-known festival is the Jaipur Literary Festival, now known as the Zee Jaipur Literary Festival after one of its sponsors, Zee Entertainment. Founded in 2006 and directed by author Namita Gokhale and historian William Dalrymple, the festival brings writers from all over the world to an eager Indian and international audience in the Indian city of Jaipur. Goa, Kolkata, and Mumbai also boast thriving literary festivals.

What about contemporary art in India?

Indian contemporary art can trace its beginnings to the founding of the Progressive Artists' Group in 1947 by the painters Francis Newton Souza and Fida Maqbool Husain. These were the first Indian artists to bring international modern art forms and abstraction to work that was vibrant with Indian themes and colors. In 1956, a group of artists, including Jyoti Bhatt, N. S. Bendre, and K. G. Subramanyan, founded the Baroda Group, based at the Faculty of Fine Arts in Vadodara, where artists Gulam Mohammed Sheikh, Bhupen Khakhar, and Haku Shah were also based. The 1970s saw the emergence of painters Ganesh Pyne, Tyeb Mehta, and Gieve Patel. In 1992, a group of artists in Delhi founded Raqs Art Collective, a multifunctional group engaged in making and curating diverse artistic works and events. Toward the end of the twentieth century, Indian artists began to attract international attention, with the work of such artists as Atul Dodiya, Subodh Gupta, and Bharti Kher commanding high prices in international galleries and art auctions.

Photography is another medium where Indian artists—including Dayanita Singh, Pablo Bartholomew, Ram Rahman, Gauri Gill, and Pushpamala N.—have made their mark. Many artists are also producing multimedia works that blur the boundaries between painting, sculpture, photography, installation, and video. Outside India, such contemporary artists of Indian origin as Natvar Bhavsar in New York and Anish Kapoor in London have infused their work with vivid colors and pure pigments that have deep roots in India. Indian women artists have also come into their own. In addition to those already named here, Rina Chatterjee, Shilpa Gupta, Nalini Malani, and Hema Upadhyay (tragically murdered in 2015) are among those whose work is internationally recognized.

India's major cities are home to thriving contemporary art scenes. But Indian contemporary art has also been a lightning rod for censorship and even vicious attacks by Hindu nationalist groups ever alert for any work they consider an insult to their beliefs. Fida Maqbool Husain, known as the "Picasso of India," was shamefully hounded out of India in 2006 after receiving death threats from such groups for depicting the Hindu goddess Saraswati in the nude in a 1996 painting. Forced to leave India for exile in Dubai, he died at Brompton Hospital in London in 2011.

How important is cricket in India?

Art and culture pale in importance to the average Indian compared to the game of cricket. Cricket is a national obsession in India. Whatever may separate Indians—religion, politics, language—cricket is a passion shared by all. Legend has it that cricket arrived in India in 1721, when a group of merchant sailors played the first game on Indian soil. The Calcutta Cricket Club—restricted to European players—was established in 1792. Indians began playing the game in Mumbai in the nineteenth century. By 1877, a group of Parsi players was good enough to beat a European team. In 1932, a national team was recognized, and in 1952, India beat England at a game held in Chennai. Children can be seen across India playing cricket with improvised equipment on any patch of bare ground.

Cricket in India changed radically in 2008 with the creation of the Indian Premier League, a franchise system modeled on the English Premier League and the American National Basketball Association. Whereas traditional cricket matches, including Test (international) cricket matches, can last between three and five days, the Indian Premier League plays Twenty20 cricket, in which matches generally last about three hours, making the game suitable for television. Viewership of Premier League games has skyrocketed, reaching 191 million screens in 2014.

Professional players from around the world play on India's eight Premier League teams. They are wooed like professional athletes in other major world sports. In 2016, the Royal Challengers Bangalore team paid $1.4 million for cricketer Shane Watson; while perhaps modest compared to the sky-high sums paid for soccer players in Europe or professional American baseball players in the United States, that's big money for cricket in India. And Indian Premier League cricket is big business, contributing $182 million to India's GDP in 2015.

With big money have come allegations of corruption and cronyism leveled at the Indian Premier League and at the game's regulating body, the Board of Control for Cricket in India. Responding to these allegations, India's Supreme Court directed a panel, chaired by former Indian chief justice R. M. Lodha, to investigate a 2013 price-fixing and betting scandal. The court ruled on a series of reforms in July 2016, but a year later the Board of Control was still resisting implementing the court's order.

Legendary cricket players include Sunil Gavaskar, who played professionally from 1971 to 1987, and Kapil Dev, an all-round player whose record of more than 5,000 runs and 400 wickets in Test cricket remains unbeaten in India. Rahul Dravid was one of the top five Wisden Cricketers of the Year. Finally, there is Sachin Tendulkar, who retired in 2013 from One Day International playing, ending a twenty-four-year career. His name is known to cricket fans around the world.

5

ECONOMY

What is the size of India's economy and how fast is it growing?

In terms of purchasing power parity, India's $2.3 trillion economy ranked third in the world after the United States and China in 2016. Purchasing power parity means a comparison of economies in terms of the relative cost of basic goods and services. A pound of rice, for example, costs less in India than it does in the United States. In 2016, India was the world's fastest-growing economy, with an annual growth rate of 7.6 percent. At that rate, India's economy would double in size by 2025 and grow to five times its current size by 2040. But India's economic growth rate slowed in 2017 to 5.7 percent. A demonetization move in November 2016 that rendered 500- and 1,000-rupee notes in circulation worthless and forced their exchange for new notes hit India's economy hard. And India still lags far behind China. While India's economic growth drove 10 percent of the increase in global economic activity during the decade from 2005 to 2015, China weighed in at up to 30 percent of that increase.

In any case, high economic growth is a deceptive indicator of progress in the living standards or the purchasing power of India's still largely poor population. Growth is also unequal across different sectors of the economy. Services, which make up 55 percent of India's economy, grew by 8.9 percent in 2015–16, and industry (including manufacturing and construction) grew by 7.4 percent. Thanks to the government's Make in India initiative—which we will explore in a separate question further on—manufacturing alone, which makes up 16 percent of India's economy, grew at a rate of 9.3 percent in 2015–16. However, that rate fell to 7.4 percent in 2016–17 and to just 5.2 percent in 2017–18, a worrisome trend. Meanwhile, agriculture—which employs half of India's workforce and on which some 60 percent of Indians depend for their livelihood—only grew at a rate of 4.1 percent in 2016–17, contributing 17 percent to India's GDP.

How large is India's middle class?

According to a 2015 study by the Pew Research Organization on the global middle class—defined for India as people earning between $10 and $20 per day, an amount adjusted to reflect purchasing power parity—India's middle class increased from 1 percent to 3 percent of its total population between 2001 and 2011. While this is a 300 percent increase, India's middle class remains a tiny proportion of the country's total population. During the same decade, China's middle class rose from 3 percent to 18 percent of total population, a remarkable achievement. Still, a 2011 Brookings study indicated that India's middle class could grow to 20 percent of India's population by 2030, and number 1 billion people by 2039.

But a detailed look at income levels in 2016 by economists Joydeep Bhattacharya and Shyam Unnikrishnan revealed that while India did succeed in moving millions of people out of poverty since economic liberalization began in 1991, only 20 percent of its people now have an annual income of over $10,000, whereas in China half of the population earn over $10,000. Most of the Indians who escaped dire poverty in recent years now make between $5,000 and $10,000 per year and remain vulnerable to unexpected shocks such as job loss or major illness. Job growth, urbanization, and Internet penetration among India's youth combined with an increasingly digital economy should drive middle-class growth in the coming decades. But how many Indians will be members of a solid middle class and how many will hover somewhere between poverty and the lower middle class is not clear.

The percentage is important because it is the middle class that drives consumption. A middle class of 1 billion would make India the global economy's biggest market for consumer products and services.

What about poverty in India?

Every government since 1947 has promised to improve the lot of India's poor. Indira Gandhi's 1971 election slogan was "Garibi hatao"—"Abolish poverty." The mantra of the United Progressive Alliance government led by Manmohan Singh between 2004 and 2014 was "inclusive growth." Prime Minister Modi, elected in 2014, promises "saabka saath, saabka vikas"— "all together, development for all."

India has made progress. Between 2001 and 2011, India's poor—defined as people earning less than $2 per day—fell from 35 percent to 20 percent of the country's total population. Yet some 300 million Indians still live in extreme poverty, the highest number in the world. Moreover, the decline in the proportion of Indians living in extreme poverty has not been equaled by an equivalent rise in India's middle class. Instead, the ranks of the lower middle class—people earning between $2 and $10 per day—have swelled.

This means that many who did move out of poverty between 2001 and 2011 have barely moved up. Consider that someone earning $10 per day, or $300 per month, earns five times more than someone who is considered poor. But that person would be hard pressed to afford to rent a decent apartment in Mumbai or New Delhi; to buy a car, an air conditioner, or a laptop computer; or to afford major medical care or tuition at India's elite private schools. In 2014, India's government considered raising its national poverty line from $1.90 to the equivalent of $2.50 per day, but even at that level of income, food alone would take up about half a person's budget. In the end, India's official poverty line was left at $1.90 per day, which means that millions of Indians who are not counted among the poor are, in fact, quite poor.

One of the most effective anti-poverty programs in India is the Mahatma Gandhi National Rural Employment Guarantee Act of 2005, which guarantees 100 days of employment to one member of a poor rural family. This social safety net has helped millions of rural families make it through the lean months between harvests. But in 2015, the Modi government called the program, a product of the previous, more left-leaning administration, a "living monument of failures." It argued that economic growth, stimulated by improved infrastructure and education, would be more effective in poverty alleviation than government handouts. The next year, forced by a rural farming crisis in 2015–16 that left millions of poor Indian families in dire straits, Modi's government reversed course, calling the program the "nation's pride." The reality is that the Rural Employment Guarantee program provides an essential safety net to rural Indians—and these Indians vote.

India's most important task in the twenty-first century is to create economic opportunity for its massive poor population by creating mass employment at decent minimum salaries, giving youth the education and skills they need to qualify for these new jobs, and providing a strong social safety net to those who are not benefiting from economic growth. If it fails at this task, mass unemployment and underemployment, and a growing population of young people who come of age without the skills and opportunities for a chance at a better life, will lead to social friction and political upheaval.

Is India creating enough jobs?

The short answer is no. India's high economic growth is not translating into enough new jobs, a major problem in a country where 41 percent of the population—about 530 million people—is under the age of twenty, and many live in poverty. In fact, since Prime Minister Modi was elected, the rate of new jobs being created has actually fallen, despite robust economic growth. In 2015, a mere 135,000 new jobs were created in India, according to the country's Labour Bureau. That number compares to 490,000 jobs created in 2014 and 1,250,000 in 2009. In the last quarter of 2015, India actually lost jobs: an analysis of India's Labor Bureau statistics by the nonprofit group Prahar indicated that India lost an average of 550 jobs per day between 2010 and 2015.

This is highly worrisome in a country that is adding more than 1 million new people to its workforce each year. India's economy is on track to double in size by 2025 but is expected to create only 30 million new jobs, the vast majority in the informal, low-wage sector. Clearly, this is far from sufficient.

A whopping 92 percent of Indians work in informal jobs—meaning jobs that are not salaried, taxed, or protected. Half of Indians work in agriculture, and while that proportion has come down from 60 percent just a few years ago, most of the movement of people out of agriculture has been into India's booming construction business to work as contract laborers. These workers fall into the 40 percent of Indians who work in "small and medium-sized enterprises." In addition to construction workers, this category includes everything from a guy with a coal-heated iron on a street corner who does ironing for families in the neighborhood to a food-cart vendor, from a housemaid to a small brickworks or auto-repair business, from a restaurant worker or owner to a family that works rolling beedies—popular cigarettes of tobacco tightly rolled up in a leaf—in their home.

According to a 2016 report by the International Labour Organization's India office, manufacturing employed 12 percent of India's workers in 2010. The US Bureau of Labor Statistics reported that 40 percent of India's manufacturing workers were employed in the comparatively low-wage sectors of food, beverage, tobacco, leather, textiles, and apparel in 2010, and that the average hourly compensation paid to an Indian worker in manufacturing was $1.46. In October 2016, India's government set the minimum wage for agricultural workers at 360 rupees per day, or about $5.40, a major increase from the prior rate of 160 rupees, or about $2.40, per day. But even with this increase, having a job in India is no guarantee of escaping poverty.

Those who work in higher-wage manufacturing sectors fare better. Striking workers at a Renault-Nissan automobile plant near Chennai won a 57 percent increase of 19,100 rupees, or about $286, on average monthly salaries of 33,000 rupees, or about $494, raising their average monthly salaries to $780. Hyundai, Maruti, and Ford also gave workers hefty wage increases in 2016.

It is unclear how many jobs manufacturing will create in India going forward. Optimistic projections count a potential 65 million new jobs in the booming automobile industry alone. But modern factories increasingly rely on automation and robotization, resulting in greater efficiency with fewer workers—exactly the opposite of what India needs. In 2016, the government of India launched a $1.5 billion start-up fund in the hope of generating new businesses and more employment.

Youth unemployment is a problem even in advanced economies. In India, where half the population is under the age of twenty-five, it poses an especially daunting challenge. Unfortunately, India is not creating enough jobs for its young people nor giving them the skills they need for the jobs that are being created.

In February 2016, members of the Jat caste—a community with roots in farming—went on a violent rampage in the state of Haryana that included murder, rape, and cutting off part of New Delhi's water supply to demand their recognition as a "backward" caste eligible for quotas of government jobs reserved for those who historically struggle with discrimination. This followed mass demonstrations in the state of Gujarat in 2015 by Patidars—a traditionally prosperous farming community—demanding the same. These incidents indicate that the lack of jobs is beginning to chafe. If India's economy cannot generate mass employment, there will be more social and political friction ahead.

India's economy must also deliver improved wages and working conditions to those who have jobs. In September 2016, in what was billed the largest labor strike in history, 140 million public-sector workers went on strike. While less than 4 percent of India's workers are unionized, in a country of 1.3 billion that's still a lot of people. Workers complained they were not being paid their salaries on time. Among the unions' demands were a minimum daily wage of 692 rupees (about $10), universal social security, and a ban on foreign investment in public sector industries such as the country's railroads, the defense industry, and the insurance industry. Striking workers were concerned that attracting foreign investment would involve promises of weaker worker protections. Indeed, many investors and champions of economic liberalization point to India's inflexible labor laws—it is difficult to fire workers in businesses employing more than 100 people—as a brake on foreign investment. But given the fact that 92 percent of India's workers enjoy no benefits or employment protection at all and that only 4 percent are unionized, this concern seems exaggerated.

What are India's major industries?

Services, including hospitality, insurance, financial services, and information technology, make up the lion's share of India's economy—65 percent in 2015. While some 70 percent of India's people live in rural areas, agriculture only accounts for 17 percent of India's GDP. Manufacturing accounts for 18 percent.

Major industries include pharmaceuticals, automobile and automobile parts manufacturing, biotechnology, oil refining, textiles and apparel, leather goods, information and communications technologies, and media and entertainment. India's research and development companies accounted for over 20 percent of the global market for such services in 2016. India's pharmaceutical market was the world's third largest in 2016, and it is one of the world's most important suppliers of generic drugs. By 2020, the industry will be worth $45 billion. Biotechnology, another strong growth area in India, is expected to be worth $100 billion in 2025.

India's auto industry generated $74 billion in revenue in 2017, and the Society of Indian Automotive Manufacturers projected the industry would generate $300 billion by 2026. Two-wheeled motorcycles and scooters accounted for over 80 percent of India's domestic automobile market in 2016. India produces 97 percent of the components needed to make a domestic passenger car.

Healthcare, currently valued at $100 billion, is expected to grow to $280 billion by 2020. Given how underserved most Indians are by healthcare, the potential for growth in this area is enormous. India will need up to 700,000 additional hospital beds within the next five years alone. A woeful lack of public healthcare services, international demand for relatively low-cost medical care, and government policies now favoring the private sector have sparked a boom in India's private healthcare sector. Foreign medical tourism was a $3 billion business in India in 2015.

How important is information technology to India's economy?

Information technology services helped launch India's entry into the global economy. In the late 1990s, Indian companies such as Tata Consulting, Wipro, and Infosys, taking advantage of new communications technologies, offered cost-effective back-office processing services to international clients, mainly in the West. India's young, English-speaking workforce found ready employment in call centers, where they worked all night handling customer calls in the United States, where it was daytime. India is well on its way to shifting from a major outsourcing destination to a major hub of research and to an incubator of new technologies and applications. India's information technology sector is expected to be worth some $330 billion by 2020.

India is the world's leading destination for high-technology outsourcing, accounting for 67 percent of the US outsourcing market alone. Its high-tech industry is concentrated in the Indian cities of Bengaluru, Hyderabad, Chennai, and Pune. In 2017, India's high-tech industries employed 3.9 million people. But while India's high-tech sector is expected to continue to grow—by 2018, India's Internet economy will be valued at more than $150 trillion and India's information technology market will be the second largest in the Asia-Pacific region after China's—employment in this area is stalling. In 2017, India's top Internet technology firms were expected to lay off nearly 60,000 workers. This is disappointing news for thousands of educated young Indians pinning their hopes on new high-tech jobs.

India is now the largest market for smartphones, and second only to the United States in the number of Facebook users on mobile application. As smartphone usage in India grows, so too does the ability of Indians—especially those who do not have access to the Internet via computers—to access social media with their phones. More Indians will access Facebook via mobile application in 2017 than Americans will: 145 million in India versus 138 million in the United States. Yet, in 2016, the Telecom Regulatory Authority of India rejected Facebook's Free Basics program to offer Internet access to rural Indians over concerns the free platform unfairly limited what applications Indians could access.

With the launch of its Digital India program, a bid to transform India into a digitally empowered country, the government of India spent nearly $7 billion in 2015 on information technology, pushing for the electronic delivery of government services to citizens. Some of that spending is earmarked to launch 100 "smart cities"—which, as we have seen, use technology to function efficiently—by 2020.

What is "Make in India"?

In 2015, Prime Minister Modi introduced a program called Make in India to encourage foreign investment in India's manufacturing sector. Manufacturing is seen to be essential to boost economic growth and to create mass employment. India's government wants to expand manufacturing from a 16 percent share of GDP in 2015 to a 25 percent share by 2025, hoping to add 90 million jobs along the way. These targets are ambitious: increased automation in manufacturing is already putting downward pressure on employment in skilled manufacturing industries. In any case, most of the job growth will likely be in low-wage, low-skilled industries, such as leather goods, textiles, and apparel.

What are the biggest companies in India?

The biggest companies in India in 2016 by revenue were, in descending order, the Indian Oil Corporation, with revenues of $61 billion; the diversified conglomerate Reliance Industries, with revenues of $44 billion; auto giant Tata Motors and State Bank of India (tied), with revenues of $42 billion; Bharat Petroleum, with revenues of $36 billion; Hindustan Petroleum, with revenues of $32 billion; Oil and Natural Gas Corporation, with revenues of $21 billion; Tata Steel, with revenues of $20 billion; metals and mining company Hindalco Industries, with revenues of $17 billion; and information technology company Tata Consultancy Services, with revenues of over $16 billion. Other giants include Bharti Airtel, Larsen & Toubro, ICICI Bank, Essar Oil, NTPC (National Thermal Power Corporation), Coal

India, Vedanta, Mahindra & Mahindra, Adani Enterprises, and GAIL (Gas Authority of India Limited).

Employment numbers tell a different story. The top employers were Tata Consultancy Services, with more than 370,000 employees, while nearly 300,000 people worked for State Bank of India. None of the other ten largest companies broke the six-digit ceiling in number of employees. Reliance Industries employed fewer than 25,000 people, and Hindustan Petroleum fewer than 12,000 people.

What are India's major exports?

India's major exported products in 2016 were, in descending order, petroleum products, precious stones, automobiles and automobile parts, heavy machinery, biochemicals, pharmaceuticals, cereals, iron and steel, textiles, and electronics. But India's exports of what the World Bank calls modern services—services that can be digitally stored and do not require face-to-face interaction—grew to over a third of total exports. The total value of India's exports in 2015 was a little over $260 billion. Europe was the destination for more than 17 percent of India's exports. Fifteen percent of India's exports went to the United States, and a little more the 3.5 percent went to China. Meanwhile, the share of India's exports to developing countries is growing, with the Middle East and East Asia the top two destinations for India's exports. That trend is expected to continue as these emerging markets post higher demand than mature markets do. How India's export mix of services versus manufactured goods changes will depend on how successful the country is at expanding manufacturing—the goal, as we have seen, of Prime Minister Narendra Modi's Make in India effort—and what the impact of a growing pushback against globalization and outsourcing (evident in US president Donald Trump's Make America Great Again politics) is on India.

What does India import?

By far the biggest import item for India is crude petroleum—over $116 billion worth in 2015. Gold was next at more than $34 billion, followed by gems, petroleum products, coal, telecommunications instruments, iron and steel, organic chemicals, vegetable oils, and raw materials for plastics. The total value of India's 2015 imports was a little over $379 billion. China was the top country for imports to India. India consistently imports more than it exports, making for a trade deficit in 2015 of more than $118 billion.

A successful transition away from petroleum would reduce India's dependency on imported oil. In 2017, India's minister for power, Piyush Goyal, suggested a target for India of 100 percent electric cars by 2030. That would go a long way toward reducing India's dependence on foreign oil, as well as its greenhouse gas emissions. India imported more than 5 million tons of wheat between June 2016 and March 2017, and it was expected to import 2 to 3 million more tons during the 2017–18 fiscal year. Wheat imports were needed because of poor harvests due to drought in 2015–16. As for future food imports, much will depend on the vagaries of weather during a period when the effects of global warming are expected to increase, and on how successful India is in reforming its agricultural sector to make it more resilient to climate change and more productive.

What about agriculture in India?

India is the world's largest producer of milk, the largest producer (and consumer) of spices, and the second-largest producer of sugar. Agricultural products constitute 10 percent of India's exports. Rising demand and drought over two consecutive years in 2014 and 2015 forced India to import 5 million tons of wheat during the 2016–17 fiscal year—the highest amount of wheat imported in a decade.

India's farmers are suffering. In June 2017, thousands of farmers marched in India's capital, New Delhi, to demand relief from falling prices for onions and other vegetables. Farmers have been hit hard by a combination of factors, including erratic monsoons, drought, flooding, salinization of soils due to excessive irrigation, and the rising cost of inputs, including chemical fertilizers, pesticides, and patented hybrid or genetically modified seeds. Nearly 60 percent of Indians depend on agriculture for their livelihood, and many are struggling. Between 1995 and 2013, as we have seen, some 300,000 Indian farmers committed suicide. Debt farmers cannot repay, often to usurious private moneylenders, drives many to despair.

In its 2016–17 budget, the government gave a nod to the distress of India's farmers, budgeting public funding to make irrigation more efficient, to pay farmers for crop losses, and to extend institutional credit to farmers. Rural roads and electrification also got a boost. The budget even allocates funds to convert a modest 500,000 acres to organic farming over three years. In 2016, the government raised the minimum price guaranteed farmers for rice, legumes, oilseed, and cotton.

In order to maximize the food India does produce, the government is pushing for the creation of more cold-storage facilities to prevent the loss of produce after harvest, and to reform the country's wholesale markets, where many farmers sell their crops. The government also raised the minimum wage for farm laborers to 360 rupees per day, or about $5.40. But many Indian farmers who farm their own land—most small plots of less than five acres—earn far less.

India is home to many grassroots initiatives to embrace sustainable agricultural practices, including using traditional pest control and fertilization techniques, avoiding monocropping, planting more trees, using drip irrigation and constructing small-scale water catchment basins, planting traditional cereal and legume seeds that are better adapted to local conditions and soils, and saving a portion of that seed to avoid the expense of purchasing expensive patented seeds and the expensive chemical fertilizers and pesticides these seeds require to thrive.

The United Nations recommends agroecology—agriculture that gives back as much as it takes away from nature and that is part of an ecosystem that can be supported over the long term—as the only way forward for human survival. Agroecology has been proven to help Indian farmers free themselves from debt and produce more than enough to feed their families a healthy diet. But there is little value added to be wrung from this kind of approach to agriculture. Boosting economic growth in the agricultural sector and boosting farmers' incomes do not necessarily go hand in hand when agribusiness dictates the price of seeds and fertilizers and big-box retail stores set the wholesale price of what farmers produce ever lower.

How India manages agriculture and the welfare of farmers not only will determine to what extent India will be able to feed its growing population but also will have profound environmental, social, and political consequences.

What is India's monetary policy?

Food inflation has a major impact on India's monetary policy. When food prices rise, in addition to creating hardship for the millions of Indians who struggle to earn enough to feed their families, it drives up inflation overall, puts upward pressure on wages, and can inhibit economic growth. The Reserve Bank of India is responsible for India's monetary policy. The bank's goals are price stability (inflation control), exchange rate stability (value of the Indian rupee), and economic growth.

As part of reforms undertaken after the balance of payments crisis in 1991, the Reserve Bank of India, which had closely controlled currency exchange since 1947, instituted a Liberalized Exchange Rate Mechanism System (LERMS) with a dual exchange rate: foreign exchange earned by Indian exporters had to be surrendered to the bank, which converted 40 percent of the funds at a fixed rate and the remaining 60 percent at a market rate. In 1993, India moved to single market-rate conversion. In 2016, the Indian rupee was freely convertible in current accounts, and nonresidents could repatriate profits earned in India, but controls remained on currency exchanges by Indian residents, primarily as a guard against capital flight.

Between 1999 and 2015, the average daily turnover of India's foreign exchange market increased from $2.7 billion to $30 billion. In 2016, the government of Prime Minister Narendra Modi announced that it planned to seek an amendment to the 1934 Reserve Bank of India Act to create a Monetary Policy Committee tasked with setting inflation targets and the benchmark interest rate. It also said it wanted to amend Indian law to enable an Asset Reconstruction Company to help prop up banks that have invested in unrecoverable loans.

There is good reason to act. In July 2017, India's banks were holding a whopping $154 billion in bad loans, most of them to private companies. In an effort to address the problem, India's lower house of parliament passed a new bankruptcy law in May 2016 to speed the process of resolving bankruptcies, which can take up to fifteen years in India. The same year, India's Supreme Court ordered the Reserve Bank of India to assemble a list of corporate defaulters. In June 2017, the Reserve Bank of India ordered the top fourteen defaulters, whose debts represent a quarter of the total bad debt held by Indian banks, to bankruptcy court. That's a good start, but India still has a ways to go to solve its bad-loans problem. When banks hold too much bad debt, they are unable to lend, cutting off the flow of money that feeds economic growth.

Is corruption also hindering growth?

Bad bank loans aren't the only thing dragging India's economy down: corruption is also a serious problem. Corruption is pervasive in India, touching every aspect of people's lives, from the bottom to the top of the social pyramid. Corruption in India can be traced back at least as far as the days of the British East India Company, whose employees understood their posting to India as a license to loot. Corruption became tightly woven into the fabric of modern Indian society during the decades of the "permit-quota-licence Raj" when government permits and licenses were needed for companies to do just about anything. These prized permits could often be procured at a certain price, paid under the table, to the government official in charge.

One of the reasons government jobs in India are so sought after is that they are considered a lifelong opportunity to amass personal wealth through taking bribes. For a price, one can get just about anything in India done, and get it done faster. India's police and judiciary are highly corrupt, and laws on the books against graft are rarely enforced. Corruption also undermines Indians' faith in their elected representatives, assumed to be on the take.

That assumption is reinforced by the corruption scandals that periodically rock the government. As India's economic growth has accelerated, so have the opportunities for graft. In 2010, under the government of Prime Minister Manmohan Singh, there was a hemorrhage of money in the run-up to India hosting the Commonwealth Games. Corruption was estimated to have sponged up to $1.8 billion from a budget that ballooned to eighteen times its original estimate. But the Commonwealth Games corruption scandal paled in comparison with the telecom scam that closely followed it the same year, when an estimated $39 billion was raked off the sale of telecom spectrum at prices well below market value. That, in turn, was followed in 2012 by "Coalgate," a $34 billion corruption scam involving the sale of coal-mining licenses that reached all the way up to Prime Minister Singh himself.

Disgust with such mind-boggling larceny at the highest levels of government was one factor in the decisive election of Modi, who promised voters his would be a clean government. But even if Modi's government were free of corruption at the cabinet level, the system is so corrupt it will take time and considerable effort to convince salaried school teachers they cannot pocket their salaries and hire out their jobs for a pittance to a young villager to stand in their place, or state government officials that new mining ventures do not exist primarily to line their pockets with kickbacks. The conversion of farmland for urban or business development and the booming construction industry are other areas with rich pickings for the corrupt.

In addition to corruption, there is a huge problem in India with criminal gangs and organized crime networks that operate with impunity, engaging in illegal activities of every sort, from stripping beaches of sand for the cement industry and smuggling iron ore out of the country to trafficking girls and women into prostitution while police and government officials are paid to turn a blind eye.

One tactic aimed at eliminating corruption is the use of Aadhaar, the biometric-unique identity number discussed earlier. It is hoped that the use of Aadhaar—while, as we have seen, is problematic in other respects—will help ensure that only those who need and deserve government subsidies and antipoverty programs actually get their due, and that some of the leakage that percolates down from the moment funds are disbursed in Delhi until they are distributed at the village level is staunched. Technology has helped eliminate corruption in other areas, such as the sale of train tickets, now commonly done online. And farmers who can access commodity prices are better armed to insist on a fair price for their crops from middlemen.

The illicit financial flows watchdog organization Global Financial Integrity estimates there have been $54 billion in illicit outflows from India since 1991, when economic liberalization took off. The overseas assets of Indian residents held in banks abroad are estimated at between $100 and $150 billion. Unrealistic campaign finance rules are part of the problem: campaign costs across all parties and elections in India between 2010 and 2015 were estimated to be $5 billion. Reforming campaign financing would begin to address part of India's corruption problem, but since every politician is on the take, or at a minimum accepts illicit money to finance his or her campaign, there is little will to tackle this.

What was "demonetization"?

In November 2016, the Modi government made a dramatic move to curb so-called black money by suddenly withdrawing old 500- and 1,000-rupee notes (worth about $8 and $15, respectively). A new 2,000-rupee note was introduced. The idea was to obliterate the value of illegal cash hordes, cripple terrorist groups that deal in cash, encourage the poor to open bank accounts, facilitate the taxation of income less easily hidden from tax authorities, and move toward a cashless society.

This "demonetization" action removed 99 percent of the targeted bills circulating in India's economy. But it did little to eliminate so-called black money, and it disproportionately hit the poor and the lower middle class, who earn and spend in cash: 87 percent of transactions in India. Many rural Indians live far from banks and do not have bank accounts. There were scenes of chaos as long lines snaked in front of banks that ran out of smaller bills. The new 2,000-rupee notes didn't fit in existing ATM machines, which had to be retrofitted to accommodate them. By the end of the first week after the shock announcement, the Indian press was reporting that thirty-three people had died as a result of the change, some of heart attacks and some from suicide. Many poor saw their entire life savings erased.

A year later, the negative impact of demonetization on India's economy was clear, as India's economic growth rate fell to a three-year low of under 6 percent, down from over 7 percent the previous year. In an article titled "Modi's Money Madness" published on June 16, 2017, in *Foreign Affairs*, James Crabtree, at the time a visiting research fellow at the Lee Kuan Yew School of Public Policy in Singapore, called India's 2016 demonetization move "one of the most disruptive experiments in recent economic history."

Why do so few Indians pay taxes?

In May 2016, in an effort to bring transparency to India's budget, the government made tax data public for the first time. The data, provided in the Indian numbering system of lakhs (units of 100,000) and crores (units of 10 million, or 100 lakhs), showed that a mere 1 percent of Indians paid tax on income earned in 2012. Out of a population of 1.3 billion, 28.7 million Indians filed 2012 tax returns. Of these, 16.2 million owed no tax; 11.1 million who did owe income tax on 2012 income paid less than 1.5 lakh rupees, or less than about $2,800. Five thousand very rich Indians paid tax between 1 and 5 crore rupees, or between $189,000 and $943,000. Public tax data showed dramatic improvement in tax collection, which rose ninefold, from a total of 317.6 billion rupees, or about $4.7 billion, in 2001 to 2.8 trillion rupees, or about $420 billion.

In an effort to recover money from tax cheats, the government sent notices to about 700,000 suspected tax dodgers between June and September 2016, asking them to pay up. The cheaters would face penalties but would not be prosecuted for tax evasion. The result from 64,275 individuals who paid up was a $10 billion windfall.

In August 2016, the government also won passage of a constitutional amendment in India's upper house of parliament for a uniform national goods and services tax (GST) or value-added tax (VAT). In 2017, India's parliament passed legislation clearing the way for the new tax, which went into effect on July 1, 2017.

Taxes on goods and services had previously been the purview of India's states, resulting in an excruciating hodgepodge of different rates that slowed interstate commerce, facilitated tax evasion, and discouraged foreign investment. The GST was hailed as an important achievement toward fulfilling the promises of economic reform Modi made before his election. But the GST's roll-out was criticized for inflicting an overly complicated burden on small businesses, which were ill equipped to track multiple levels of taxation on different goods and services, that hurt economic growth.

What are India's infrastructure needs?

Crumbling and inadequate infrastructure, including for water and power, roads, air transport, and access to the Internet, is another big obstacle to India's development and economic growth. It may be hard to believe today, but during the 1980s India had better infrastructure than China did. Since then, China has moved far ahead of India in terms of both infrastructure and economic growth, created a sizable middle class, and built a profitable manufacturing base that is eight times larger than India's. Can India catch up with China during the next several decades? The odds are very long, and there is much work to be done.

The World Bank estimates that India will require $1.7 trillion in investment in infrastructure by 2020. The country needs just about everything: roads, ports, airports, public transportation, fiber-optic cable lines, power production, cleaner coal-burning plants, expansion of the electrical grid, sanitation and water treatment, housing, schools, hospitals, and more. Most of that money must come from the private sector. The 2016 budget allocated funds for the electrification of villages, new roads, and ports. Prime Minister Narendra Modi's Smart Cities program should also bring infrastructure improvement to India's cities.

But India's ability to attract the private investment it needs is hampered by regulations that can turn on a dime, contracts that some government-backed entities have refused to honor, and high levels of corporate debt. High economic growth during the late 1990s and early 2000s fueled property speculation and grand projects for luxury townships on the outskirts of India's major cities. But these townships depend on an ecosystem of public transportation and road connections, business parks, and shopping malls. If just one key piece of this interconnected web fails, the whole development project can grind to a halt, leaving investors holding the bag, unable to repay their bank loans.

To spur private investment in infrastructure, the World Bank recommends India "reduce the regulatory uncertainty" in the country and "ensure that public money earmarked for existing projects is well spent"—a clear allusion to India's corruption problem.

How much energy will India need?

India is currently the fourth-largest consumer of electricity in the world. On a per capita basis, however, India lags far behind advanced economies: 875 kilowatts per Indian compared to 6,600 per German and 11,900 per American. Another way of looking at it is this: India is home to 18 percent of the world's population but consumes just 5 percent of the world's energy. In 2015, 240 million Indians did not have access to electricity at all.

India will be the biggest contributor to the rising global demand for power in coming decades. By 2040, its economy will be five times larger than it is today, and its energy consumption will have more than doubled. How India satisfies its part of the growing global appetite for energy will have an enormous impact on global warming and on global energy markets. But India also has the potential to become a global leader in innovations that might lead to new energy technologies that are cleaner and less expensive.

Fossil fuels make up three-quarters of India's energy consumption, and coal supplies 70 percent of its electricity. India has become more efficient in its use of energy: it took 12 percent less energy to create a unit of GDP in 2013 than it did in 1990. But there are still gross inefficiencies in India's energy production, including inefficient coal-fired plants and poor distribution and transmission capacities. Currently India has some 290 gigawatts of installed power generation capacity. It is aiming to increase that to 850 gigawatts by 2030. Of that, the hope is that 390 gigawatts, or 40 percent, will come from renewable energy sources, primarily solar and wind.

In 2015, India was the world's third-largest oil importer, behind the United States and China. With more cars, better roads, and more industry, India's demand for crude petroleum will increase at a rate of 4 percent per year for the next quarter of a century, surpassing China's demand by 2040. Nearly all of that oil will be imported, as India has scant proven reserves.

Though it imports most of its crude oil, India is the world's fourth-largest petroleum refiner—behind the United States,

China, and Russia—and a major exporter of refined petroleum products, including diesel fuel to Europe and transport fuels to the Middle East and across the Asia-Pacific region. India's petroleum refining industry will also boost demand for crude petroleum.

Why do some Indian states perform better than others?

Each Indian state has its own rules on land acquisition, labor and environmental laws, and state taxes. Indian states also have historically made their own decisions on investing in education and health, reflecting their different demographics.

According to a report published by the Indian government in 2015, the states with the least onerous business regulations were Gujarat, Andra Pradesh, Madhya Pradesh, Rajasthan, Maharashtra, Karnataka, Uttar Pradesh, West Bengal, Tamil Nadu, and Bihar. But ease of doing business does not necessarily correlate with human development, including such benchmarks as literacy, health, and spending power. Within high-performing states, there is also considerable variance between living standards in cities versus in rural areas.

In 2011, India's Institute of Applied Manpower Research (now the National Institute of Labour Economics Research and Development) released a report on how India's states fared in terms of human development. Kerala, a state that made general literacy a priority decades ago, has long topped India's literacy charts, followed by Delhi (India's capital city counts as an Indian state), Himachal Pradesh, and Goa. The states with the lowest human development rankings were Bihar, Andra Pradesh, Chhattisgarh, Madhya Pradesh, Orissa, and Assam.

Why are so many Indian companies family-run?

Family-owned businesses account for two-thirds of India's GDP, 90 percent of India's industrial output, and 79 percent of organized private sector employment. Family business ownership is a natural extension of India's joint family structure, where brothers traditionally remain part of their father's household.

Some of India's largest business groups today began as family-run businesses, and many continue to be closely controlled or actively supervised by members of their founding families. India's top family-founded businesses include the Tata Group (founded in 1868), Reliance Industries (the Ambani family), the Birla Group, Mahindra & Mahindra, Bharti Airtel, Wipro, and the Jindal Group.

In 2016, the Tata Group summarily dismissed its chairman, Cyrus Mistry, the son of the company's largest shareholder, in circumstances that remain unclear. Former chairman Ratan Tata temporarily stepped back into the job. The incident highlighted the growing tension between the instinct of many of India's old family businesses to keep management tightly controlled by an inner circle of trusted stakeholders versus a more modern approach to corporate governance that puts accountability to shareholders first and seeks the best person for the job, even if that person is an outsider. Whether family control of India's big business houses will crimp economic development or provide stability in a world where big companies increasingly provide no guarantees of job security or career advancement remains to be seen.

What about the wealth gap in India?

The growing gap between a superrich minority, an embattled middle class, and the poor is a global phenomenon. Despite gains against poverty, India has not escaped this dynamic of early twenty-first-century capitalism. Inequality in India has grown apace with its economy, rising from a Gini coefficient (a widely used measure of inequality named for its inventor, Italian statistician Corrado Gini) of 45 in 1990 to 51 in 2013 when looking at income. In 2017, Forbes magazine counted 101 billionaires in India, making India the fourth largest home to billionaires in the world. Nearly half of all of India's wealth is in the hands of the top 1 percent, and the top 10 percent holds 74 percent of the country's wealth.

Meanwhile, the poorest 30 percent of Indians hold just 1.4 percent of India's wealth. India's 2015 Socioeconomic and Caste Census revealed that of 300 million poor households—73 percent located in rural areas—only 5 percent earned enough to pay income tax, only 2.5 percent owned a four-wheel vehicle, and only 10 percent had a salaried job.

What about women's participation in India's economy?

Nothing would boost India's economic growth more than having additional women in the paid labor force. Yet economic growth and improvements in women's education and literacy levels have not led to more women working. In fact, female labor force participation actually fell from nearly 43 percent in 2004 to 31 percent in 2011. Gender norms that laud female "purity" and extol the traditional roles of wife and mother are the main culprits, according to Rohini Pande and Charity Troyer Moore of Harvard's Evidence for Policy Design Initiative. Many Indian families regard being able to afford not to have to send women in the family outside the home to work as a sign of upward mobility.

Exceptions to India's dismal levels of female employment are the rise in the number of women working in the banking and financial sector and in aviation: nearly 12 percent of commercial pilots in India are women, compared with 3 percent worldwide. But these represent a tiny proportion of Indian women in the workforce.

McKinsey estimates that achieving gender equality in the workforce could boost India's projected 2025 GDP of $4.83 trillion by somewhere between 16 and 60 percent. Of course, for that to happen, India as a whole would also have to strive for gender parity, hardly an easy task given entrenched patriarchal family and social structures, and the low status of women overall.

6

POLITICS

What is India's political system?

The 1949 constitution established India as a "sovereign democratic republic." In 1976, under a state of emergency imposed by then Prime Minister Indira Gandhi that suspended many citizen rights and freedoms, a forty-second amendment to the original constitution added the words "socialist" and "secular" to this definition, making India a "sovereign, socialist, secular, democratic republic."

Today, the Republic of India is a federation of twenty-nine states and seven union territories, including the National Capital Territory of Delhi. Indian citizenship is acquired by descent—at least one parent must be an Indian citizen. India's chief executive is the president and its chief of state is the prime minister. The prime minister presides over a cabinet, called the Union Council of Ministers, recommended by the prime minister and appointed by the president.

India's president and prime minister are elected indirectly by an electoral college composed of members of both houses of parliament. India's upper house of parliament, the Council of States, or the Rajya Sabha, is composed of 245 seats. India's lower house of parliament, the People's House or the Lok Sabha, is composed of 545 seats. Rajya Sabha members are elected to six-year terms. Lok Sabha members are elected to five-year terms.

National elections for seats in India's lower house of parliament are held every five years; every six years for seats in the upper house. The party winning a majority of seats in the lower house, or cobbling together a coalition of parties to form a majority, names the prime minister. The prime minister names the president. In the 2014 general elections, 814 million Indians were eligible to vote. Due to India's large and still growing population, every election held in India is the largest in history. State legislative assembly elections are held every five years, but on a staggered schedule set by the Electoral Commission of India.

What is a panchayat?

Panchayati raj, or *panchayat* rule, is one of the oldest forms of political organization in South Asia. The word derives from the Sanskrit *panch,* meaning "five," and *ayatta,* meaning "dependent upon," and defines a council of five members. The *panchayat* is the basic unit of local government in India, recognized and defined in Part IX of India's constitution. A 1992 amendment to India's constitution set the term limit for *panchayat* seat holders at five years and mandated that in any given *panchayat* area no fewer than one-third of *panchayat* seats be held by women. The constitution of India further defines *gram panchayats,* or village councils; *panchayat samiti, panchayats* at the level of groups of villages; and *zila parishad,* or district-level *panchayats.*

What are the major political parties in India?

There are scores of registered political parties in India. The major national parties are the Indian National Congress Party, heir to the party that led India's independence movement, and the Bharatiya Janata Party, a Hindu nationalist party, which is currently in power. The Communist Party of India (Marxist) or CPI (M) is also a national party. The Aam Aadmi Party is a reformist party with an anticorruption platform founded in 2012. Major regional parties include the Biju Janata Dal, based in the state of Orissa; the Samajwadi Party, a secular, socialist party based in Bihar; and, in the south, the Dravida Munnetra Kazhagam (DMK), the All India Anna Dravida Munnetra Kazhagam (AIADMK), the Telugu Desam Party, and the Telegana Rastra Samiti. Major caste-based parties include the Bahujan Samaj Party (BSP), a party that seeks to represent Bahujans, or the lower castes, and Adivasis, the indigenous population; and the Rashtriya Janata Dal, based in Bihar, which has its major support base among Muslims and Yadavs, a community traditionally engaged in raising livestock and farming. The Shiv Sena Party, a regionalist party based in Maharashtra with its power base in the city of Mumbai, is a Hindu-nationalist party allied with the governing BJP.

How does India's judicial system work?

At the top of India's judicial hierarchy is the Supreme Court. Under the Supreme Court, each state has a High Court, under which there are session and district courts. Some states have local courts as well.

The Supreme Court listed twenty-five justices in 2016, including the chief justice. Supreme Court judges convene in benches of two, three, or five justices to hear cases brought before the court. Proceedings of the Supreme Court are conducted in English.

The attorney general of India is appointed by India's president. Indian law is a complex affair. India's constitution is the primary source. Criminal law is laid out in the Indian Penal Code. Parliament, state, and union territory legislatures also enact laws. Municipalities and *panchayats* can issue rules, regulations, and bylaws. India's judicial system also recognizes religious customary laws.

The whole judicial system is badly in need of reform. The wheels of Indian justice turn so slowly that some wonder if they turn at all. In 2013, there were more than 31 million open cases making their painful way through India's courts. One reason is needless litigation pursued by lawyers for no other reason than to pad their fees. Another is an absence of judges: thousands of judicial positions are unfilled. When positions are filled, they too often go to family members of current sitting judges. Many Indians don't even bother to file complaints: they know it may take thirty to forty years for their case to be heard.

India's judiciary is also plagued by corruption. The stellar exception has been the Supreme Court, for long a bastion of integrity in a country where corruption taints almost every other facet of life. High-profile cases have been moved quickly to the Supreme Court for a hearing when it is widely acknowledged the case cannot get a fair hearing in a lower court, where vested interests may prevail. Sadly, faith in India's Supreme Court was shaken in 2017 by allegations over the court's handling of a corruption case involving a medical college that caused leading academic Pratap Bhanu Mehta to warn the court was "facing its worst crisis of credibility since the Emergency" of 1975 to 1977. The Supreme Court's credibility was further undermined in January 2018 when four senior justices of the court went public with concerns over the preferential allocation of certain cases to specific benches of judges and over the court's response to the suspicious December 2014 death of Maharashtra judge Brijgopal Harkishan Loya while he was hearing a case involving an extrajudicial killing in which BJP party chief Amit Shah was accused. The status of the Supreme Court as chief guardian of Indian citizens' rights and chief defender of impartial justice is in serious crisis, posing alarming questions about the future of the rule of law in India.

In 2016, the Bar Council of India announced a crackdown on lawyers practicing with fake law degrees. The chairman of the Bar Council, Manan Kumar Mishra, estimated that 30 percent of India's lawyers are practicing law with fraudulent credentials. In February 2016 in New Delhi, lawyers closely associated with the Bharatiya Janata Party boasted they beat an arrested student leader for three hours inside the courtroom while police looked mutely on. India's dysfunctional judiciary is a problem for a country that prides itself on offering its own citizens and foreign investors the stability and the protection of the rule of law.

Aside from the constitution, the sovereign law of the land, Indian criminal law is laid out in the British imperial-era Indian Penal Code. Drafting of the Indian Penal Code began in 1833, but the code was not adopted until 1860. Though the code has been amended and augmented over the years, it remains astonishingly intact nearly two centuries after its conception. Some of India's most contentious contemporary legal battles—on the rights of homosexuals and the right to free speech, for example—are the direct result of colonial-era laws in the Indian Penal Code regarding "intercourse against the order of nature," defamation, or sedition. If many laws crafted in the nineteenth century to quell dissent or rebellion against British rule, and to guide the administration of a diverse country by a handful of British officials, continue to exist, it is because they continue to serve the powers that be.

What about the police in India?

The Indian Police Service is a national organization that was created by Article 312 of India's Constitution in 1949. India's Police Division is housed under the Ministry of Home Affairs. The Indian Police Service provides the bulk of senior officers to India's state police services. Policing is the responsibility of India's states, and each state has its own rules and regulations. The Director General of Police is the chief of the state police. Each state is divided into different police subdivisions, and each subdivision has a certain number of police stations.

Under Indian procedure, all crimes must be recorded at a police station. Police stations handle preventive, investigative, and law-and-order work.

Kiran Bedi became India's first female police officer after she joined the force in 1972. There are now more than 100,000 Indian women police officers out of a total of more than 1.7 million police in India. There are also special police stations where women can report crimes without fear of being molested or raped by male police officers.

India's police are famously corrupt, with everyone from the level of local constables on up open to bribes. Cases of police falsifying evidence, selectively pursuing people for arrest, looking the other way when crimes are being committed, and torturing detainees in jail—or even murdering them in extrajudicial killings known in India as "police encounters"—are dishearteningly common.

The issue of extrajudicial police killings gained a new level of notoriety in October 2016, after videos came to light of police in the state of Madhya Pradesh staging an "encounter" with eight accused militants of the banned group Students Islamic Movement of India (SIMI). Police said the men had escaped from jail and were armed and dangerous. The videos appeared to indicate they were not armed and were trying to surrender when they were killed. They were suspiciously dressed in fresh, identical shoes and clothing. Police were to receive a reward of 5 lakh rupees, or about $7,500—a hefty sum for an Indian police officer—per militant apprehended or killed. After the incident received attention in India and in the international media, an investigation was ordered.

The same month, police constables in the state of Chhattisgarh burned effigies of scholars, journalists, and activists who had reported on or defended the human rights of local Adivasis, punching and kicking the burning straw figures lined up as a gallery of "traitors." The police were angry after the Central Bureau of Investigation held local police responsible for acts of arson in three Adivasi villages in 2011. Inspector General of Police Shiv Ram Prasad Kalluri, who was senior superintendent when the arson took place, slammed journalists for reporting the story, complaining: "Creating an atmosphere of doubt and trying to break morale of the police who are taking care of internal security is unfair and anti-national." The absence of any accountability for police abuses and the tarring of journalists and social activists who would shed light on such abuses as "anti-national" bodes ill for democratic India's future.

Why is there a Maoist revolution in India?

In 2010, Prime Minister Manmohan Singh declared India's Maoist insurgency to be the "biggest internal security threat" to the country. The insurgency began in West Bengal in the 1960s. Known as "Naxalites" following a violent confrontation in the village of Naxalbari in 1967, India's Maoist insurgents are active across a region that includes the states of Jharkhand, Chhattisgarh, Orissa, Bihar, and Andra Pradesh. This region is often referred to as India's "Red Corridor."

Forty percent of India's coal reserves lie under the dense forests of the states of Jharkhand and Chhattisgarh, forests inhabited by Adivasis, many of whom live by exploiting forest products. A name coined from the Sanskrit word *adi*, meaning "the time of the beginning," and *vasi*, meaning "inhabitant," Adivasis, also referred to as "tribals," include, as we have seen, peoples considered indigenous to India. A highly diverse group comprising more than 100 distinct peoples who speak some 200 different languages or dialects, Adivasis have long been considered "primitive." Stigmatized and marginalized by mainstream Indian society, their communities have been upended by mining operations in recent years. India's government sees the mining of coal, bauxite, iron and other ores as vital to India's development. But mining, far from bringing prosperity to the region's poor, has resulted in environmental destruction and the forced displacement of people from land that had sustained them for generations.

The Maoists have staged spectacular attacks on Indian security forces and police over the years. India's Home Ministry maintains that 3,000 people have been killed in Maoist attacks since 2008. The movement feeds off local grievances and finances itself through raids on police stations, by exacting levies for passage through areas it controls, and by the extortion of protection money from mining companies.

The Indian government and state governments in the region have responded by deploying police and security forces. In their zeal to go after the Maoists, security forces routinely interrogate, beat, and torture local people. The Maoists, in turn, punish locals suspected of helping police and state security forces.

India's security apparatus also targets human rights activists and social workers in the region. Anyone extending a helping hand to the poor is liable to be charged with being a Maoist sympathizer. Such was the case with Dr. Binayak Sen, arrested in April 2007 and charged with ferrying messages to the Maoists. He was convicted of sedition and sentenced to life in prison. Finding no evidence to support this, India's Supreme Court granted Sen release on bail in 2011.

The state of Chhattisgarh has taken draconian measures to silence journalists and intimidate social workers and social scientists. In the district of Bastar, journalists are repeatedly subject to arrest, torture, and intimidation, and many have been forced to flee the area. In November 2016, the situation took a bizarre turn when Archana Prasad, a professor at Jawaharlal Nehru University, and Nandini Sundar, the chair of the Department of Sociology at Delhi University and an expert on India's Maoist conflict, were among ten people charged with murder in the case of a villager in Bastar who allegedly had been killed by a Maoist. They were also charged with rioting and conspiracy.

Sundar was not in Bastar at the time of the murder, but police accused her and the others of fomenting an atmosphere that emboldened the Maoists. A local police officer revealed the real motive behind the bizarre charges: "Bastar knows to handle its own problems. We don't like any kind of interference." More chillingly, Chhattisgarh State Reserve Policeman Kalluri said, "Activists are enemies because they incite the people of India." Silencing the press and hounding social activists and social scientists studying the conflict will only ensure that local people will be more vulnerable than ever to human rights abuses committed by authorities and Maoists alike.

What are the politics around caste in India today?

The British codified caste to facilitate their administration of India, and the Republic of India largely adopted their codification after independence. It has since been expanded upon and modified, especially with a view to redressing historical caste discrimination through affirmative action programs for members of lower-caste groups. In recent decades, caste-based political parties have emerged in India, propelling lower-caste politicians to positions of state power and changing the nation's political dynamics.

In India there are *"jati*-clusters," federations of similar-status *jatis*, or castes, that are recognized by the state and that act on behalf of their members for political and social purposes. India's convoluted caste administration seeks to provide relief from discrimination against lower-caste Indians through quotas for government jobs and university admission. As we saw in an earlier question on the Mandal Committee, this has sparked violent demonstrations by members of castes not historically subject to discrimination who demand that they too be categorized among what are known as the Other Backward Castes, Scheduled Castes, and Scheduled Tribes in order to secure government jobs and university admission.

Thanks to affirmative action and government scholarships for economically disadvantaged students, there are more Dalit students in Indian universities than ever before, but these students continue to face terrible discrimination. In January 2016, Rohith Vemula, a Dalit PhD student at Hyderabad University, committed suicide after the university's administration barred a group of Dalit student activists from the campus's residence halls and dining facilities. The university had suspended payment of his student living stipend, and Vemula's family was poor. Members of the Hindu nationalist militant student group Akhil Bharatiya Vidyarthi Dal had complained that the Dalit students were troublemakers. Smriti Irani, then minister of human resources in the Modi government, reportedly demanded the Dalit students be punished after her office was alerted to the Hindu nationalist students' complaint.

"My birth is my fatal accident," Vemula wrote in his suicide letter. His suicide made national and international news. Prime Minister Narendra Modi expressed his regret that "a mother has lost a son," but he made no reference to the caste politics that played a part in Vemula's death.

What is AFSPA?

Caste is not the only arena where gross social injustice against particular groups is institutionalized in India. AFSPA is an acronym for India's Armed Forces (Special Powers) Act. The Indian government drafted the act in 1958 in response to a Naga insurgency in the country's northeast. AFSPA grants wide powers and confers immunity from prosecution to India's military and security forces deployed in "disturbed areas." It remains in force in seven states in the northeast and, since 1990, in the Kashmir Valley.

AFSPA is blamed for encouraging Indian troops and security forces to terrorize civilians. The government and military denies abuses occur, though they admit troops may commit "mistakes" in situations where it is not always easy to tell insurgents from civilians. As of 2017, India's Defense Department had not sanctioned a single prosecution under AFSPA since 1991, despite thirty-eight specific requests to do so.

In 2015, twenty-five years after AFSPA was applied in the state of Jammu and Kashmir, Amnesty International published a detailed report on human rights abuses committed in the state, and on the impunity of Indian security forces. According to the report, 96 percent of complaints brought against the Indian army "have been dismissed as false and baseless," and many abuses go unreported or are not recorded by police. Alleged abuses include kidnapping, torture, murder, and rape. After an official visit to India in 2012, Christof Heyns, the United Nations special rapporteur on extrajudicial, summary, or arbitrary executions, declared he was "of the opinion that retaining a law such as AFSPA runs counter to the principles of democracy and human rights."

AFSPA has been in force in the state of Manipur, where ethnic groups have long waged secessionist insurgencies, since 1980. In 2004, a woman named Manorama Devi was raped, tortured, and killed after being picked up by security forces from her home in Manipur. Her body was later found with gunshot wounds to her genitals and thighs. Her death provoked a dramatic demonstration by Manipuri women who stripped naked and invited the soldiers of the Assam Rifles, an elite Indian army unit, to rape them. Nicknamed the "Sentinels of the Northeast," the Assam Rifles traces its founding to 1835, when a group of fighting men was raised by the British to combat unruly tribes in the hills of Assam.

In 2004, the Manipuri activist Irom Sharmila Tharu began a protest fast she vowed would not end until AFSPA was repealed. She was soon arrested by the authorities and charged with attempting to commit suicide. She was subsequently released and arrested several times, and kept alive by a feeding tube at the All India Institute of Medical Sciences in New Delhi and the Jawaharlal Nehru Institute of Medical Sciences in Imphal. In 2013, Amnesty International called Sharmila a prisoner of conscience. In 2016, after a court in Imphal acquitted her of the charge of attempting suicide, Ms. Sharmila ended her fast and announced her intention to enter politics.

In July 2016, India's Supreme Court ruled that AFSPA could not be used to give blanket immunity to India's armed forces, and that soldiers could not shoot civilians on "the mere allegation or suspicion that they are 'enemy.'" The court warned that abuses committed under AFSPA put "not only the rule of law but our democracy" in grave danger. While it remains to be seen whether investigations into abuses committed under AFSPA will now yield criminal charges against perpetrators, the court's landmark decision is a welcome development for justice and human rights in India.

Will the violence in Kashmir ever end?

In Part I, we looked at the early roots of the still tense situation in Kashmir. More than half a century later, a political solution that could finally bring peace to the region appears as unlikely as ever. In March 2016, after much wrangling, the Bharatiya Janata Party entered into a coalition government with the People's Democratic Party (PDP) in the Indian states of Jammu and Kashmir. PDP politician Mehbooba Mufti was tapped as chief minister. This coalition between the Hindu nationalist party and a Kashmiri party asserted that peace could only come to Kashmir from a trilateral dialogue that included India, Pakistan, and the Kashmiri people, giving hope that a political solution might finally be reached in Kashmir.

Then, on July 8, 2016, Indian security forces killed Burhan Wani, a charismatic twenty-two-year-old self-defined militant advocating for an independent Kashmir who had built up a popular following among Kashmiri youth by means of social media. Thousands of Kashmiris attended Wani's funeral, and the Kashmir Valley erupted in violent confrontations between stone-throwing youths and armed Indian security forces. Within weeks, thousands had been injured, mostly civilians. Police and security forces relied on pellet guns to control the angry crowds, and hundreds, including many children and teens, were blinded by pellets lodged in their eyes.

By mid-September 2016, eighty-three people had died. In an attempt to quell the uprising, Indian authorities imposed curfews, cut communications—including cell phones and Internet services—and raided local newspaper offices.

The political conflagration unleashed by Wani's death was long in the making. The insurgency that raged in Kashmir in the 1990s had given way to a period of relative calm in the first decade or so of the twenty-first century, though it never completely disappeared. The number of militants crossing over from Pakistan, where they found sanctuary and support, had declined to a trickle. But Kashmiris chafed under their brutal treatment by Indian security forces, which had operated in the Indian state with complete impunity for decades due to AFSPA. By the time the insurgency of the 1990s ended, more than 70,000 people had been killed, with both Indian soldiers and militants committing atrocities. Most Kashmiri families had been affected by the violence in some way. Indian security forces had grown to an occupying force of some 700,000.

Meanwhile, young Kashmiris were swept up by the rising global tide of Islamist militancy, embracing the glories of jihad and martyrdom as valiant alternatives to lives emptied of hope under Indian occupation. It was this inheritance of loss and rage, as Kashmiri author Basharat Peer wrote in the *New York Times*, that pushed boys as young as twelve to revolt in 2016. That fall, arsonists destroyed more than thirty schools in Kashmir, and the prospect for Kashmiri youth of finding another path to adulthood than through the crucible of insurgency dimmed further.

Only a political solution can bring peace to Kashmir. In addition to Pakistan ceasing to use militant incursions to wage a proxy war against India, the Indian government should finally accord Kashmiris the autonomy granted to them by Article 370 of India's Constitution, calling for Jammu and Kashmir to be a "special autonomous state." India should withdraw army personnel and security forces not directly charged with border protection, and hold perpetrators of human rights abuses committed against the Kashmiri people accountable. But with Hindu nationalism's rise, and a fresh attack by militants who crossed over the border from Pakistan in September 2016, killing eighteen Indian soldiers, the prospect of peace in Kashmir appears more distant than ever.

What is Hindutva?

Hindutva is a term that was coined by writer and activist Vinayak Damodar Savarkar in 1923 when he published his book *Hindutva: Who Is a Hindu*? For Savarkar, Hindutva, or "Hindu-ness," arises from the geographical unity of the Indian subcontinent, a common Hindu culture, and a common race. Hindutva seeks to define Indian culture in terms of Hindu values, recognizes the entire subcontinent as the natural home of Hindus, and seeks to redress what it views as harm done to Hindus by Muslim and other foreign invaders historically. Hindu nationalists blame the National Congress Party for relegating Hindus, who make up 80 percent of India's population, to the role of a "bystander" in their natural homeland, and for cravenly catering to India's Muslims.

Hindutva forms the basis of policies pursued by the BJP government of Prime Minister Modi. The BJP is part of the Sangh Parivar (Family Organization), which groups several Hindu-nationalist entities under the umbrella of the Rashtriya Swayamsevak Sangh (RSS), or National Volunteer Organization. Other major groups associated with the Sangh Parivar are the Vishva Hindu Parishad (VHP), whose "objective is to organise—consolidate Hindu society and serve—protect Hindu dharma," according to its official website; the Bajrang Dal, which is the youth wing of the Vishva Hindu Parishad; and the Akhil Bharatiya Vidyarthi Parishad, a student organization that polices anti-Hindu or anti-Hindutva activities on India's university campuses.

The RSS is a militant Hindu nationalist group whose mission, as stated on its website, is "to carry the nation to the pinnacle of glory through organizing the entire society and ensuring the protection of Hindu Dharma." The RSS was founded in 1925 by Keshav Baliram Hedgewar in response to Hindu-Muslim riots that rocked India during the 1920s. Inspired by European fascism and the Nazis' German ethnic nationalism, the RSS envisions India as a land with a shared race, culture, religion and geographical unity that must be purified of contaminating foreign influence. To that end, its primary object is to defend Hindu India against what it sees as foreign elements, namely, Muslims and Christians, and to restore Hindu India to past greatness.

The RSS has been banned several times during India's history for its political extremism. Prime Minister Jawaharlal Nehru banned it in 1949 following the assassination of Mahatma Gandhi by Nathuram Godse. Godse had a long association with far-right Hindu nationalist groups—though the RSS disputes that he was a member when he killed Gandhi. The RSS was banned again during the national state of emergency under Prime Minister Indira Gandhi in 1975–77, and it was banned for six months following the destruction of the Babri Masjid, a mosque built on the ruins of a Hindu temple dedicated to the Hindu god Ram, in Ayodhya on December 6, 1992.

The RSS is organized into *shakhas*, or local branches, which in turn are organized into hierarchical groupings. RSS cadres are called *paracharaks*. At the top of the membership hierarchy is the supreme leader, the *sarsanghchalak*. Its members wear a uniform, known as a *ganvesh*, of baggy khaki shorts cinched with a wide canvas belt, white shirts, black shoes, and black caps. In 2016, the RSS replaced the shorts with long khaki pants.

During marches and drills, members wield long wooden *dandas*, long bamboo sticks, and bring their right hand parallel to their chests in salute. *Shakhas*, composed of males only, meet daily, weekly, or monthly, and perform a series of symbolic actions, such as raising the group's trademark saffron flag and reciting a prayer in Sanskrit that ends with the cry

"Bharatmata ki jai!"—"Long live Mother India!" There are also regular camps where *shakhas* gather to practice martial exercises. Most senior figures in India's current government are longtime members. The RSS is gaining ground in India. There were more than 50,000 *shakhas* in 2015.

Who is Narendra Modi?

Narendra Modi was named prime minister of India when the Bharatiya Janata Party won the 2014 general elections. Modi was born in the state of Gujarat on September 17, 1950. Much has been made of his humble origins as the son of a grocer who helped out at his father's tea stall. Modi discovered the RSS at the age of eight and formally joined the organization at age nineteen, steadily moving up its ranks. In 1988, he was elected organizing secretary of the BJP in Gujarat. In 1990, Modi helped Lal Kishan Advani organize and carry out what became the 1992 Rath Yatra procession to Ayodhya to destroy the Babri Masjid.

Modi was elected chief minister of Gujarat in 2001. In February and March 2002, horrific communal violence broke out in cities across Gujarat in the wake of an attack on a train carrying Hindu Ayodhya militants when it made a scheduled stop in the town of Godhra, a town of no particular significance before the attack but whose name became a rallying cry for revenge attacks on Muslims in its wake. What exactly triggered the attack on the train and who was responsible remains unclear. But after the attack, more than 1,000 people were killed, most Muslims, in the state of Gujarat. The complicity of state and local officials and police in targeted killings of Muslims in their homes and businesses has been well documented by human rights organizations, including India's own National Human Rights Commission. In 2005, the United States government denied Modi a visa to visit the United States for failing to stop the carnage in Gujarat in 2002. Under US law, "severe violations of religious freedom" are grounds for visa denial. As head of state, however, now Prime Minister Modi is welcome to travel to the United States.

While chief minister of Gujarat, Modi pursued an aggressive business-friendly politics, attracting large amounts of foreign direct investment. Gujarat was held up as a model of what India could achieve if it could unfetter itself from the stifling bureaucracy of the socialist-inspired economic policies of the Congress Party. Though Gujarat's human development rankings remained low under Modi's government, business flourished and the state posted strong economic growth.

That success, as well as Modi's image as a man of the people, helped define him as a candidate who would bring integrity to India's government after a series of spectacular corruption scandals we outlined earlier at the highest levels of the incumbent Congress Party–led United Progressive Alliance government. Modi campaigned on a promise to unleash India's economic potential, bring new opportunity to its poor and aspiring middle class, and transform the country into a twenty-first-century global power. In 2014, the BJP won enough seats in parliament to govern without coalition partners, the first elected national government in India to achieve one-party rule in a quarter of a century.

What has changed since Narendra Modi was elected in 2014?

Modi has traveled the world since becoming prime minister, cementing alliances and drumming up foreign investment in India. He has launched a series of ambitious programs to stimulate India's economy, including, as we have seen, Make in India to boost manufacturing and Digital India to leverage digital technologies to fuel economic growth. In 2015, he dissolved India's Planning Commission, which had charted India's development with a series of five-year plans for sixty-five years, replacing it with a new National Institution for Transforming India. Modi's government has moved aggressively to expand the use of Aadhaar (discussed earlier), India's unique biometric identification number, for the delivery of government services. And Modi has moved to expand India's tax base, institute nationwide taxes on goods and services, and eliminate "black money" from India's economy through a 2016 demonetization order (examined earlier).

At the same time, Modi has moved just as quickly to fulfill the promise of Hindutva. He has staffed his cabinet with longtime members and supporters of the RSS. Minister of Culture and Tourism Mahesh Sharma, moved early to put India's leading cultural and educational institutions under the direction of Hindu nationalist ideologues. Sharma, a doctor by training, says on his personal website that he became in involved with the RSS "at the tender age of fourteen." He later joined the Akhil Bharatiya Vidyarthi Parishad (ABVP) before becoming an "active member" of the Bharatiya Janata Party." Since Sharma was named minister of culture, the boards or governing bodies of the Nehru Memorial Museum and Library, the Indira Gandhi National Centre for the Arts, and the Lalit Kala Akademi (National Academy of Art) have been disbanded, with directors either replaced or their posts left vacant. The director of India's National Museum, Venu Vasudevan, was removed halfway through a three-year term. Prominent Indians involved in culture, including the historian Romila Thapar and the playwright Girish Karnad, petitioned the ministry of culture to have Vasudevan reinstated. Eminent art historian B. N. Goswamy wrote to Modi, also asking for Vasudevan to be allowed to finish his term. These efforts fell on deaf ears.

In June 2015, students and alumni of the Film and Television Institute of India in Mumbai went on strike in protest over the Modi government's appointment of Gajendra Chauhan to lead the country's premier film school. Chauhan's main qualification for heading the film institute was not his role as Ydhisthira in the *Mahabharata* film series of the 1980s but his fealty to the BJP and the RSS. Students at the film school were still on strike a year later when, in June 2016, Chauhan made a trip to RSS headquarters in Nagpur to meet with the head of the organization, Mohan Bhagwat. Chauhan claimed his visit had nothing to do with the film school upheaval, explaining that he had only wanted to invite Bhagwatji, "a father figure to me," to his son's wedding.

Modi's government has also moved to shut down or curtail the activities of foreign foundations and Indian nonprofits that accept foreign donations. In April 2015, the government placed the Ford Foundation on a national security watch list, barring the organization from disbursing funds to any Indian group without prior government permission. The Ford Foundation, present in India since 1952, had made $500 million in grants to organizations in India for projects aimed at reducing poverty, improving education, advancing democracy, and fighting injustice. The move appeared to be payback for the foundation's grants to Sabrang Trust, whose founder, Teesta Setalvad, has worked on behalf of victims of the rioting that took place in Gujarat in 2002 when Modi was the state's chief minister.

The same month, India's Home Ministry temporarily suspended Greenpeace India's registration under the Foreign Contribution Regulation Act (FCRA), effectively preventing the organization from receiving foreign funds. In January 2015, Modi's government barred Greenpeace activist Priya Pillai from boarding a flight to London, where she was to brief British legislators on the environmental and human rights impact of coal mining in India. In both instances India's courts stepped in. Ruling that Pillai's travel ban was illegal, Justice Ravi Shakdher of the High Court warned, "You cannot muzzle dissent in a democracy."

In November 2016, India's Home Ministry refused to renew the registration licenses under FCRA of twenty-five Indian nongovernmental organizations. Human Rights Watch and Amnesty International condemned the move, arguing that the list of affected groups included several human rights organizations. In June 2016, United Nations special rapporteurs on human rights called on the Indian government to repeal

FCRA, warning the act was "being used more and more to silence organizations involved in advocating civil, political, economic, social, environmental or cultural priorities, which may differ from those backed by the government."

In 2015, more than forty Indian novelists, essayists, poets, and playwrights returned their Sahitya Akademi literary awards to protest a growing climate of intolerance. The writers were distraught over the lynching of a Muslim man accused by a Hindu mob of eating beef in October 2015 as well as the assassination of the seventy-six-year-old award-winning scholar Malleshappa Kalburgi, whose campaign against superstition and what he called "false beliefs" had angered right-wing Hindu groups. Writer Nayantara Sahgal, imprisoned during the 1975–77 Emergency, wrote in a letter that she was returning her award "in memory of the Indians who have been murdered, in support of all Indians who uphold the right to dissent, and of all dissenters who now live in fear and uncertainty." Novelist Salman Rushdie explained that the reason for the writers' action was the degree of "thuggish violence" that had now "crept into Indian life."

What are gau rakshas?

A cursory glance at Indian and international news about India since Narendra Modi became prime minister reveals a host of expressions the uninitiated non-Indian reader or television viewer would be hard-pressed to understand. These include the Hindi expressions *gau rakshas*, meaning "cow protectors," and *gar wapsi*, meaning "return home"—that is, to the Hindu faith—and the expressions "love jihad" and "pink revolution." Hindu *gau raksha* vigilantes now roam India, attacking Muslims and Dalits accused of killing cows or eating beef. In September 2015, in a village near New Delhi, an angry Hindu mob dragged a Muslim man from his home and killed him on the suspicion his family had beef in their refrigerator. In July 2016, two Muslim women were attacked by an angry Hindu mob that accused them of transporting beef. In September 2016, a cattle trader's mutilated body—his genitals had been chopped off—was found in a field near the village of Dholahat in the state of West Bengal.

Cow vigilantes have become so bold that in August 2016, as the BJP prepared for key state elections, Modi was compelled to condemn the violent actions of *gau rakshas* after a videotape of five Dalits being beaten for supposedly killing a cow in the state of Gujarat went viral in the press and on social media. The Dalit men had been simply doing their caste-imposed job of disposing of an animal that, the cow's owner insisted, had died of natural causes.

Modi has himself contributed to the zeal of *gau rakshas*. During his 2014 election campaign, he accused the Congress Party of waging a "pink revolution" of beef exports in order to profit from the killing of cows. The expression alludes to the Green Revolution, involving cereal grains, and the White Revolution, associated with India's huge dairy industry. India's beef exports—to sixty-five different countries— accounted for 20 percent of global beef exports in 2014. Exporting cow meat is now illegal in India, though buffalo meat may be legally exported as beef. Modi's "pink revolution" campaigning was a call-out to Hindus to vote against both the Congress Party and India's Muslims.

Gar wapsi, or "homecoming," refers to the conversion— Hindu nationalists say "reconversion"—of Indian Muslims and Christians to Hinduism. "Love jihad" refers to the supposed determination of Muslim men to convert Hindu women by making them fall in love with them. Individuals and gangs associated with right-wing Hindu groups, including the RSS, the Bajrang Dal, and the BJP, hunt down mixed couples and kidnap Hindu women, returning them to their parents. Hindu anti–"love jihad" militants have stopped interfaith weddings and have even forced Hindu women to leave their Muslim husbands and marry Hindu men.

Hindu nationalists regularly refer to secularism as "pseudo-secularism" or, sneeringly, "sikularism" (presumably because secularism is "sick"). Hindu nationalist media commentators and trolls on Twitter label as a "pseudo-sikularist" any person who is perceived as challenging the notion that India should be a Hindu state, anyone who champions free speech, or anyone who appears to defend Muslims. Journalists who don't toe the Hindu nationalist line are labeled "presstitutes."

What role do social media play in Indian politics?

Barbs aimed at journalists on Twitter are only one symptom of the politicization of social media in India. Social media has become a powerful force in Indian politics, as well as a tool for government surveillance. During the 2014 general election campaign, the Electoral Commission of India asked social media providers to monitor their sites for fraud after politicians were accused of artificially boosting the number of their followers on Twitter and Facebook. Social media was credited with helping the Aam Aadmi Party, founded on an anticorruption platform in 2012 by social activist Arvind Kejriwal, previously known for his work on behalf of India's poor, to sweep Delhi elections in March 2015, less than a year after Narendra Modi and the BJP's landslide victory. In 2016, as we have seen, the death of Burhan Wani, a Kashmiri militant who was extremely active on social media, led to a popular uprising that brought thousands of protestors into the streets. A violent crackdown by Indian security forces left thousands injured, many blinded by pellet guns, and killed at least ninety people in 2016. The pellet gun injuries and blindings in turn sparked a social media campaign, originating in Pakistan, that showed the faces of famous people pocked with pellet wounds, shocking images that quickly went viral.

Images disseminated on social media are also blamed for sparking communal violence in India. In 2013, Hindu militants circulated a video that they claimed showed two Hindu men being killed by Muslims. The video was, in fact, filmed in 2010 and showed two Muslim men being killed in Pakistan.

It nonetheless sparked attacks in Muzaffarnagar, a city in the state of Uttar Pradesh near India's capital, New Delhi, that left more than sixty Muslims dead and displaced 50,000 people.

Indian government officials have used the 2008 Information Technology Amendment Act to monitor and censor individual social media accounts, with police swooping in to arrest people shortly after they post comments on Facebook deemed to offend local or national politicians. Cartoonists and journalists have had their social media accounts closed. In 2015, India's Supreme Court struck down a law making the posting of "offensive" comments on social media illegal. In 2016, the government announced it would track journalists' articles online as well as websites they visited in order to identify journalists whose stories were critical of the government and to counter them with positive stories.

Do Indians have freedom of speech?

The right to freedom of speech and expression in India is not absolute. Article 19 of India's constitution guarantees the right "to freedom of speech and expression." However, the constitution also allows the government to limit freedom of expression "in the interests of the sovereignty and integrity of India, the security of the State, friendly relations with foreign States, public order, decency or morality, or in relation to contempt of court, defamation or incitement to an offence."

There are also several sections of the penal code that criminalize certain speech. Section 153A, for example, criminalizes "promoting enmity between different groups on grounds of religion, race, place of birth, residence, language, etc., and doing acts prejudicial to maintenance of harmony by words, either spoken or written, or by signs or by visible representations or otherwise." Section 292 criminalizes obscenity. Section 295A criminalizes "deliberate and malicious acts intended to outrage religious feelings of any class" of citizens. Section 298 criminalizes "uttering any word or making any sound" with "the deliberate intention of wounding the religious feelings of any person."

The Indian government has used these laws to ban books, such as Salman Rushdie's novel *The Satanic Verses*, and movies, such as *India's Daughter*, a 2015 documentary film made by Leslee Udwin for the BBC on the 2012 gang rape of a Delhi college student. In 2014, RSS member and self-appointed cultural vigilante Dina Nath Batra forced Penguin India to withdraw University of Chicago scholar Wendy Doniger's book *The Hindus: An Alternative History*, and to agree to pulp all copies in its possession, by bringing a series of civil and criminal actions against the book on the basis that it violated Section 295a.

Then there is sedition. In an effort to quash rebellion, the British made sedition a crime in India in 1860. And so it remains. Section 124 of the Indian Penal Code states: "Whoever, by words, either spoken or written, or by signs, or by visible representation, or otherwise, brings or attempts to bring into hatred or contempt, or excites or attempts to excite disaffection towards the Government established by law in India shall be punished with imprisonment for life." India's Supreme Court has limited sedition to speech that is "incitement to imminent lawless action." Few have been convicted of sedition, but it suffices to bring the charge against someone to unleash a legal process that can take years before the individual is, as is usually the case, acquitted.

Charges of sedition have recently multiplied in India as a way to curb free speech and to intimidate government critics. India's Crime Records Bureau recorded forty-seven cases of alleged sedition in nine Indian states in 2014. A folk singer, students cheering at a cricket game, and the author Arundhati Roy are just some who have been charged with sedition. In February 2016, Kanhaiya Kumar, the leader of the student union of Jawaharlal Nehru University, was charged with sedition under politicized circumstances we will discuss in the next section. The case kicked up a media storm and attracted worldwide attention. India's Supreme Court ordered Kumar released on bail.

Censorship also comes in the form of physical intimidation. In January 2015, celebrated Tamil author Perumal Murugan posted on his Facebook page: "Perumal Murugan, the writer, is dead." Murugan declared literary suicide after being hounded by local chapters of right-wing Hindu groups affiliated with the BJP and the RSS that found passages in his novel *One Part Woman* offensive. After copies of his book were burnt by an angry mob and he'd received threatening phone calls, Murugan met with local authorities and agreed to apologize and withdraw copies of his book from sale.

In July 2016, the Madras High Court delivered a decision in defense of the author and of free speech in general. Chief Justice Sanjay Kaul wrote in the court's decision: "One of the most cherished rights under our Constitution is to speak one's mind and write what one thinks." He told the book's detractors: "If you do not like the book, throw it away." It was a stinging rebuke to self-appointed censors of the Hindu right.

The charge of defamation is also used to silence free speech. Sections 499 and 500 of the Indian Penal Code criminalize defamation in terms so broad anyone can claim to be aggrieved by something said or written about them. This includes powerful Indian corporations, which do not hesitate to sue authors, journalists, or activists for defamation, backed up with claims for damages no author, publishing house, newspaper, or non-profit group can afford to pay. In addition to the threat of colossal punitive damages, filing a defamation suit against someone is a sure way to tie the person up with legal fees and court proceedings, potentially for years.

According to the Index on Censorship, in 2014, seven legal notices of defamation were served in India: five to media companies, including publishing houses; one to a marketing federation; and one to journalists Subir Ghosh, Paranjoy Guha Thakurta, and Jyotirmoy Chaudhuri for a book on Reliance Industries Ltd., India's biggest corporation, run by Mukesh

Ambani. Reliance sought 1 billion Indian rupees, or about $16,400,000, in damages. Environmental journalist Keya Acharya was slapped with a defamation suit by industrialist Sai Rama Krishna Karaturi, of Karaturi Global Ltd., also demanding a billion rupees in damages. The same year the Sahara Media Group dropped a defamation case asking for 2 billion rupees in damages against journalist Tamal Bandophadhyay for his book *Sahara: The Untold Story* after the author agreed to include a disclaimer by the company in his book.

In May 2016, India's Supreme Court upheld Sections 499 and 500 of the Penal Code in a challenge filed by twenty-four leading politicians and other individuals, saying in its decision that, as India's legislature had "not thought it appropriate to abolish criminality of defamation in the obtaining social climate," apparently referring to the current social climate of great tensions over freedom of expression, the court would take no action either. The two-judge bench's decision in this case was widely criticized, the more so, perhaps, as the court has made important decisions upholding Indians' basic constitutional rights. The complainants had argued that colonial-era defamation laws were criminalizing dissent in a democratic nation. In 2017 the Supreme Court dismissed Greenpeace activist Priya Pillai's petition to the court arguing that Sections 499 and 500 were so overly broad and vaguely worded that they violated her constitutionally protected right to free speech in a defamation suit filed against her by Mahan Coal Ltd. for exposing the social and environmental impact of the company's coal-mining ventures. The court's decision is a boon to Indian corporate goliaths seeking to muzzle investigative reporters and environmental activists, and has critical implications for free speech in India going forward.

What about freedom of the press in India?

India's media has become increasingly concentrated in the hands of powerful, family-owned corporations. High-profile journalists whose views do not toe the new line have been pushed out or quit their jobs. Self-censorship by journalists is a growing problem. Those who do speak out regularly face harassment and threats. Reporters Without Borders ranked India in 133rd place out of 180 countries in its 2016 World Press Freedom Index.

India has become a dangerous place to be a journalist. The Committee to Protect Journalists (CPJ) sounded the alarm in February 2016 after two journalists, one working for the BBC, were forced to flee the Indian state of Chhattisgarh after threats to their lives, and lawyers for imprisoned journalists were evicted from their offices. Chhattisgarh is in the grip of a violent confrontation between security forces, mafia gangs, and Maoist insurgents, and journalists trying to report on what is going on find themselves targeted on all fronts. CPJ said it had documented a pattern of police in Chhattisgarh harassing, abusing, and threatening journalists to silence their reporting, while Maoists had attacked journalists they accused of being police informants.

And then there are the journalists who are killed for doing their job. Reporters Without Borders documented nine journalists killed in India in 2015, five while doing their job. "Their deaths confirm India's position as Asia's deadliest country for media personnel, ahead of both Pakistan and Afghanistan." In May 2017, two journalists were shot dead in eastern India in a single twenty-four-hour period. Shock waves rippled through India's press in August 2017 when senior journalist Gauri Lankesh was shot dead in front of her home in Bengaluru by a gunman who sped away on a motorcycle. Defiant in her critical reporting on the Hindu right, her death eerily recalled the murder in 2014, previously mentioned, of rationalist Malleshappa Kalburgi. Both killings had all the hallmarks of a hit job, and investigators later determined that, in fact, Lankesh and Kalburgi had been killed by the same gun. The month after Lankesh was gunned down, Shantanu Bhowmick, a television journalist reporting on a political altercation involving Adivasis in the state of Tripura, was beaten to death.

In November 2016, India's Ministry of Information and Broadcasting ordered television station NDTV off the air for a day as punishment for reporting on a terrorist attack in Pathankot in January of that year, on the grounds the reporting threatened national security. The Editors Guild of India responded with a sharply worded rebuke, saying the action recalled the dark days of press censorship under the 1975 Emergency and demanding the ban be immediately rescinded.

Who are India's "anti-nationals"?

On February 20, 2016, star television news anchor Rajdeep Sardesai published a statement in the *Hindustan Times* announcing that he was proud to be labeled an "anti-national" because, he said, he believed "in an expanded definition of free speech as spelt out in Article 19 of the Constitution." Sardesai was moved to write his statement in response to the arrest of Jawaharlal Nehru University student union president Kanhaiya Kumar on charges of sedition. Kumar, as noted earlier, was arrested after students chanted slogans in support of Afzal Guru, a Kashmiri who was convicted of being a participant in the 2001 terrorist attack on India's Parliament and hanged under suspicious circumstances in 2013. The campus chapter of the Akhil Bharatiya Vidyarthi Parishad, a right-wing Hindu student group, alerted the university's new chancellor, who had been appointed by the Modi government, and the chancellor called in the police. When Kumar was later produced in court, he was subjected to supporters chanting "Glory to Mother India!" and "Traitors leave India!" BJP politician Om Prakash Sharma, a member of India's legislative assembly, said: "There is nothing wrong in beating up or even killing someone shouting slogans in favor of Pakistan." Rajnath Singh, then home minister in Modi's cabinet, announced on the day that Kumar was arrested that should anyone raise anti-India slogans or question the nation's unity and integrity, "they will not be spared."

Hundreds of Indian journalists marched in protest in New Delhi in response to the police action and Kumar's arrest, and thousands of students and faculty at universities across India turned out to protest the government's actions. Some 500 scholars and university professors from around the world signed a protest statement condemning the police action at Jawaharlal Nehru University and the threat it seemed to pose to academic freedom. Pratap Bhanu Mehta, now vice chancellor of Ashoka University, warned that members of Modi's government "have threatened democracy." Sardesai spoke for many when he pointed out that the "right to dissent is as fundamental as the right to free speech."

Public fury over an attack in September 2016 by militants who had crossed over the border from Pakistan that killed eighteen Indian soldiers in Kashmir led to threats of violence against a new Bollywood film simply because it co-starred a popular Pakistani actor. As previously discussed, the film's director, Karan Johar, felt compelled to issue a videotaped statement defending his patriotism and begging for thugs not to attack movie theatres where his new film was to be screened. "For me, my country comes first," he pleaded. "Nothing else matters but my country."

The public has become so inflamed over the issue of patriotic nationalism that a wheelchair-bound man was beaten up in a movie theater in October 2016 because he did not stand when India's national anthem was played. On October 22, 2016, the *Economist* published an editorial entitled "All Hail," which denounced the role India's media has played in whipping up hypernationalist feeling, noting: "The Indian media have vied to beat the war drums loudest."

What does the political future of India look like?

Narendra Modi is not Recep Tayyip Erdogan, nor is he Vladimir Putin. But there is no doubt that under his leadership India is becoming an increasingly illiberal democracy. Whether or not Modi, the BJP, and its affiliated organizations in the Sangh Pariwar will be able to achieve their dream of turning India into a Hindu state in the twenty-first century is an open question.

India's Congress Party was severely weakened after its defeat in 2014. Rahul Gandhi, Indira Gandhi's grandson and Jawaharlal Nehru's great-grandson, has not yet been able to inspire voters, and the Congress Party appears incapable of breaking with dynastic politics. Surprisingly, however, the Congress Party did far better than expected in Gujarat state—Modi's stronghold—elections in December 2017. And there are other still strong regional and caste-based parties that do not subscribe to the ideology of Hindutva: the relatively new Aam Aadmi party beat the BJP in Delhi elections in February 2015, and the Janata Dal party was victorious over the BJP in Bihar state elections in November 2015. If the BJP fails to deliver on its election promises to bring the fruits of economic growth to India's poor, to create enough jobs, and to improve living conditions both in cities and in the countryside, it may yet find itself voted out.

7

GEOPOLITICS

Who are India's neighbors?

India is by far the largest economy in South Asia, dominating neighboring Pakistan, Sri Lanka, Bangladesh, Myanmar, and Nepal, not to mention tiny Bhutan and Sikkim. It also shares a disputed border with China, a nuclear power whose military and economic might dwarf India's. India's relations with its neighbors are constantly evolving—trade between India and its neighbors has increased, and even boomed with China, in recent years—but tensions remain. These tensions hamper greater economic integration and cooperation on interests vital to all, such as combatting terrorism and equitably managing dwindling water resources. They also pose a serious, ongoing risk to regional security.

India's former external affairs minister Jaswant Singh famously justified India's 1998 nuclear tests by saying the country was situated in a "dangerous neighborhood." As if to underline the point, Pakistan immediately followed India's tests with nuclear tests of its own. China was already an acknowledged nuclear power. The region where these three nuclear powers meet has been called the most dangerous place on earth. One must hope that the consequences of any conflict escalating to the point of an exchange of nuclear weapons would be so horrifying that no country would be foolhardy enough to risk them. That hasn't prevented all three countries from pursuing the expansion of their military forces, including their nuclear weapons' capabilities. The risk of a nuclear conflict between India and Pakistan or between India and China remains one of the twenty-first century's worst nightmares.

What about India and China?

Though, as noted, China's economy and military might dwarfs India's, the two Asian giants are locked in a constant, if uneven, competition for global resources and regional influence. Bilateral trade between India and China was worth over $70 billion in 2016, but most of that value came from Chinese exports to India, resulting in a trade deficit for India of nearly $53 billion. The military and economic partnership between India and the United States that has bloomed in the last few years has been fueled as much by economic potential as by a shared desire to counterbalance China.

India's relations with China remain haunted by a brief war in 1962 in which China succeeded in wresting from India territory along the two countries' still-disputed border, known as the Line of Actual Control. When Prime Minister Modi visited China in May 2015, following fresh incidents along the border, he reported that he and Chinese president Xi Jinping had agreed to find a "fair, reasonable and mutually acceptable resolution" to the border dispute. That resolution remains elusive. In early 2016, China banned all maps that did not represent its claimed borders. The Indian government followed suit in May 2016 by introducing legislation to ban maps of the region that did not depict India's border claims. In 2017, India and China faced off again over a stretch of the disputed border that runs between Bhutan and China on the Doklam Plateau. India sees the area, near the Siliguri Corridor, a narrow strip that connects India's main body to the part of its northeastern territory known as the "chicken's neck," as strategically vital. Both India and China eventually agreed to withdraw their troops from near the border, but the issue of where that line runs remains unresolved.

Will there ever be peace between India and Pakistan?

India and Pakistan have fought four wars—two of them over Kashmir—since the two countries gained their independence in 1947. Relations between the two countries have varied between tepid and frigid over the years. On December 25, 2015, Modi "dropped in" to visit Pakistan's president, Nawaz Sharif, on his birthday. But peace talks set to begin after that visit in mid-January 2016 were derailed by a terrorist attack in early January on an Indian air force base in Pathankot, in the Indian state of Punjab. India blamed the attacks on Jaish-e-Mohammed, a terrorist group, based in Pakistan.

In September 2016, India blamed militants from Pakistan for the deaths of eighteen Indian soldiers at a camp on India's side of the Line of Control that separates the two countries in Kashmir. The militants, India's military said, had crossed over from Pakistan. India retaliated with what it called "surgical strikes" across the Line of Control, inflicting, it claimed, "significant casualties" on militants in Pakistan. Pakistan denied the strikes occurred. India subsequently boycotted a meeting of the South Asian Association for Regional Cooperation held in Islamabad in October 2016, diplomatically isolating Pakistan but also casting new doubt on that group's ability to unite divided South Asian nations in any kind of cooperative venture. Relations between the two countries entered a new, highly fraught period.

India has long complained that Pakistan supports terrorist groups that target India, including an attack on parliament in 2001 and terrorist attacks in the city of Mumbai in 2008 that killed 247 people. The motive behind these attacks is to call attention to Pakistan's claim that the whole of Kashmir, with its majority Muslim population, rightfully belongs to Pakistan. They also perennially distract Pakistanis from their government's failure to deliver promised improvement in many citizens' lives. That a majority of Indian Kashmiris may prefer independence or a semi-autonomous status within India is generally ignored by both India and Pakistan.

Meanwhile, Pakistan, fearful of India's growing economic and military clout, has been building up its nuclear arsenal at a furious clip, with the capacity to produce twenty nuclear warheads annually against India's estimated five—a number India could increase if it wished to do so. And Pakistan has been developing tactical (short-range) nuclear weapons that appear aimed at India. It is in India's, Pakistan's, and the world's interests to find ways of stabilizing the nuclear arms race in South Asia. But without a durable political solution to the crisis in Indian Kashmir and a willingness by Pakistan's military to clamp down on terrorist groups that operate with impunity on its territory, that goal remains elusive.

What about India's relationship with Sri Lanka?

India's relationship with Sri Lanka has been improving since 2009, when a bloody civil war in Sri Lanka that pitted ethnic Tamils in the country's north against a Sinhalese-dominated government ended. The election of Maithripala Sirisena as president in January 2015 resulted in a warmer Sri Lankan posture toward India—his predecessor, Mahinda Rajapaksa, had shown a pronounced tilt toward China. Modi visited Sri Lanka in March 2015. A free trade agreement has been in effect between the two countries since 2001. Sri Lanka imported more from India than from any other country in 2015.

Why is India building a fence along its border with Bangladesh?

India plans to complete a fence along its 4,000-mile-long border with Bangladesh by 2017. Construction of the fence began in 1995. The territory that is now Bangladesh was carved from the former Indian region of Bengal in 1947 as a Muslim-majority homeland that was originally part of Pakistan. Called East Pakistan, the region won independence from Pakistan in 1974 with, as we have seen, India's help in a bloody war and became the nation of Bangladesh. Bangladesh's first parliament passed a Land Boundary Agreement in November of that year that was meant to be followed up by a similar agreement in India, establishing a mutually acceptable border between the two countries, but India's parliament never passed the legislation.

The Land Boundary Agreement was finally ratified by both India and Bangladesh in 2015. Prime Minister Modi hailed the agreement as a "meeting of hearts." Where these hearts meet, a fence—meant to prevent large-scale migration of Bangladeshi Muslims to India—is, to India's mind, insurance the two countries remain good neighbors. The fence is a legacy of an influx of Bangladeshi Muslims seeking land and employment in India that began in the 1980s, provoking a backlash in India. Official estimates put the number of Bangladeshis living illegally in India at 2 million.

The fence slices through economically interdependent, culturally homogenous zones and has inflicted hardship for many who live along the border. Every year, India's Border Security Forces kill or wound Bangladeshis attempting to breach the fence.

Meanwhile, the government of Bangladesh's Prime Minister Sheikh Hasina has embraced India as an important partner in the fight against Islamist terrorism, which both governments view as a threat. In the wake of Modi's visit to Bangladesh in 2015, India announced the signing of a $2 billion line of credit to Bangladesh and memoranda of understanding covering new cooperation on transportation, human trafficking, cattle smuggling, and coastal shipping.

What about India and Nepal?

In the fall of 2015, violent protests erupted in Nepal in the Terai region, which borders India. At issue was a new constitution that an ethnic group of Indian-origin people called the Mahdesis, along with some other ethnic groups, believed disenfranchised them. In the wake of the protests trade between India and landlocked Nepal ground to a halt, with Nepal accusing India of an economic blockade. Subsequent fuel shortages caused great hardship in Nepal. The government in power at the time subsequently fell, amid accusations of India meddling in Nepali affairs.

The month after he was elected Nepal's prime minister in August 2016, Pushpa Kamal Dahal traveled to India on a visit aimed at mending ties. Sandwiched between India and China, Nepal is viewed by India as a strategically important country. China has been wooing Nepal, where a nearly decade-long Maoist insurgency that ended in 2006 left some 16,000 people dead. Nepal has also yet to recover from a devastating earthquake that struck the country in April 2015.

What is India's "Act East" policy?

During the 1990s, under former Indian prime minister Narasimha Rao, India took a fresh look at its strategic and economic interests in Southeast Asia. A new "Look East" policy was born out of a world changed by the collapse of the former Soviet Union—India's major ally during the Cold War—and by India becoming a nuclear power in 1998. Countering China's growing influence in the region was also a factor. In 1992, India began a dialogue-level partnership with ASEAN, the Association of Southeast Asian Nations, and became a summit-level partner of ASEAN in 2002. After his election in 2014, Prime Minister Modi pledged to change India's "Look East" policy into an "Act East" policy, with a focus of expanding trade and security ties with Bangladesh, with Myanmar, and beyond across Southeast Asia. During a 2015 visit to India, US secretary of defense Ashton Carter cited the important convergence of India's Act East policy with the United States' efforts to "rebalance" the Asia-Pacific region away from China, especially in the area of maritime security. But the election of President Donald Trump, his abandonment of the Trans-Pacific

Partnership, questions about his commitment to a geopolitical partnership with India in Asia, and uncertainty over how the United States will manage growing Chinese influence in Southeast Asia are forcing India to rethink how it should now pursue its Act East policy.

As part of that policy, Prime Minister Narendra Modi paid a visit to Myanmar in September 2017 to enhance economic and security cooperation with the country. In a speech in Myanmar's capital, Naypyidaw, Modi expressed India's support for Myanmar authorities' treatment of the Rohingya Muslim minority in Rakhine state even as a brutal ethnic cleansing operation by Myanmar's military was sending hundreds of thousands of Rohingya fleeing for their lives to neighboring Bangladesh. His government later softened its stance slightly, recognizing that there were "Rohingya refugees" heading to Bangladesh, but it continued to cast the problem as a security issue involving Islamist terrorism. Citing them as a security risk, India threatened to deport 40,000 Rohingya who had earlier taken refuge in India.

In July 2017, New Delhi rolled out a red-carpet welcome for Myanmar's top military commander, General Min Aung Hlaing, the man most responsible for the ethnic cleansing of the Rohingya and other alleged human rights violations in Myanmar. But with China being Myanmar's top investor and arms purveyor, and with the anti-Muslim hatred of radical Buddhists in Myanmar aligning with far-right Hindu nationalists' attitude toward Muslims in India, India is unlikely to retreat from supporting Myanmar's military-dominated government anytime soon. India sees defense deals, like the many it has signed with Myanmar, as a way to strengthen ties with Southeast Asian countries and counter China's outsized influence in the region.

What about India and Russia?

As noted, the Soviet Union was India's major superpower partner during the Cold War, supplying much of its military hardware. After the fall of the Soviet Union, India began shifting toward the United States but remained close to Russia, on which it continued to depend for servicing of its existing military hardware. By 2016, the United States had become India's biggest military supplier. Still, in October 2016, India signed billions of dollars' worth of military and energy deals with Russia, ceding a controlling stake to Russian oil giant Rosneft in India's Essar Oil. Commenting on the deals, Modi said India's relations with Russia remained important, and that the two countries shared views on Afghanistan and the Middle East.

What was the 2008 US-India Civil Nuclear Agreement?

On October 1, 2008, the United States Congress approved a civil nuclear agreement between the United States and India. The agreement ended a thirty-year moratorium on nuclear trade with India, allowing India to purchase nuclear fuel and supplies from members of the Nuclear Suppliers Group. In return, India pledged to allow inspections of its civil nuclear reactors and to place four of its twenty-two reactors under permanent safeguard of the International Atomic Energy Agency. The administration of President George W. Bush saw the agreement as an important step in bringing India's relationship with the United States in from the Cold War era, when the two countries were more estranged than engaged. It also saw an opportunity for American companies to build nuclear energy plants in India. Critics of the agreement fretted that these realpolitik arguments did grievous harm to a rules-based nonproliferation regime, but the Bush administration argued that by allowing inspections, the agreement would bring India into some compliance and oversight of its nuclear program. The civil nuclear agreement capped off a strategic partnership initiated between India and the United States in 2005. A shared perception that closer India-US cooperation was needed to counterbalance a rising China was one of the main drivers of the nuclear agreement.

What is the future of India's relationship with the United States?

Building on progress in India-US relations following the historic nuclear deal of 2008, the United States and India issued a sweeping joint statement during Prime Minister Modi's June 2016 visit to the United States. The statement proclaimed India and the United States to be "enduring global partners in the twenty-first century" and cited a deepening strategic partnership, as well as the two democracies' shared values, in pledging the two countries would work together to encourage economic growth, strengthen democratic institutions, and provide global leadership on shared interests. There was no mention of China in the statement, but it nonetheless loomed large.

In recognition that climate change will, perhaps more than any other factor, define the twenty-first century, the statement gave first priority to climate change and clean energy. Nuclear nonproliferation followed. The statement applauded the two countries' joint cooperation on the 2015 US-India Joint Strategic Vision for the Asia-Pacific and Indian Ocean Region. The United States recognized India as a major defense partner, pledging to share technology with India and to support the country's Make in India campaign to develop local industries. The 2016 statement recalled a 2015 joint statement to make the US-India partnership a defining "counterterrorism relationship for the twenty-first century" and talked about cooperation in space, science, and technology. Finally, the two countries' leaders reaffirmed their commitment to a reformed UN Security Council with India as a permanent member. In 1998, then Indian prime minister Atal Behari Vajpayee declared India and the United States "natural allies." The 2016 joint statement, and the many joint initiatives pursued by the two countries since 2008, made Vajpayee's pronouncement more concrete than ever.

The election of Donald Trump in the United States in 2016 has cast uncertainty on the future of India-US relations. Trump is involved in several real estate ventures in India, as he is in many countries around the world, but his "America first" policies, including his opposition to outsourcing and his proposed immigration reforms that eliminate family reunification—something Indian immigrants to the United States have greatly benefited from—in favor of highly skilled, English-speaking immigrants are not helpful to India. Trump's withdrawal of the United States from the Paris climate change accord and his denial of global warming are also unhelpful to a country that is already feeling the effects of a warming world and that is taking strong steps to reduce its future carbon emissions.

What about India's diaspora?

Some 30 million people of Indian origin are scattered across the world, from Australia to Fiji, from Guyana to Britain, from Canada to South Africa. The history of the emigration of people out of India is a long and varied one. Some left in the nineteenth century as indentured laborers, known as "coolies," for work on plantations in Fiji or Guyana. Others left to pursue business opportunities in Africa or Southeast Asia in the early twentieth century. Many went to the United States, Canada, Britain, or Australia to pursue higher education and then stayed. Still more travel to the Gulf States to work in construction.

According to the World Bank, India was the world's top destination for foreign remittances in 2015, receiving $69 billion from Indians overseas. Prime Minister Modi is trying to boost foreign direct investment (FDI) from the Indian diaspora. In 2015, his government approved amendments to the country's FDI policy to make it easier for members of the Indian diaspora to invest. Modi told members of the Indian diaspora in Singapore in 2015 that *FDI* stood for "first develop India."

India does not allow dual citizenship. However, the government has extended special rights to diaspora Indians according to their status as Nonresident Indians (NRIs), Persons of Indian Origin (PIOs), or Overseas Citizens of India (OCIs). NRIs are

Indian citizens who live abroad. The PIO and OCI categories were merged in 2015. PIO and OCI status relieves people of Indian origin who are not Indian citizens from registering as foreigners with local police stations when they visit India. They may also travel to India on a lifetime visa, and they enjoy all the rights Indian citizens do with regard to employment and property ownership, with the exception of holding some government posts and the purchase of agricultural land.

Nowhere is the Indian diaspora growing faster or becoming more influential than in the United States. According to a 2014 report by the Pew Research Center, there were more than 3 million Indian Americans in the United States. At this rate, by 2065, Indians will overtake Hispanics to be the United States' largest immigrant group. Indian Americans are, on average, highly educated (with 70 percent of those over the age of twenty-five holding a college degree) and prosperous (with a median household income of $88,000, compared to $49,800 for US households overall).

Prominent American residents with origins in India include the actor Kal Penn; musician Norah Jones; Satya Nadella, CEO of Microsoft; Indra Nooyi, CEO of Pepsi; comedian Aziz Ansari; filmmaker Mira Nair; the economist Amartya Sen; scholar Gayatri Spivak; television journalist Fareed Zakaria; and a slew of novelists and writers, including—to name only a few—Amitav Ghosh, Salman Rushdie, Jhumpa Lahiri, and Chitra Banerjee Divakaruni. In November 2016, Kamala Harris, a Democrat whose mother immigrated to the United States from India, was elected US senator from California.

Indian entrepreneurs have played an outsized role in Silicon Valley, accounting for a third of immigrant-founded companies there between 2006 and 2012. While Indian immigrants make up less than 1 percent of the US population, they account for 14 percent of Silicon Valley start-ups. Successful Indian high-tech entrepreneurs in Silicon Valley have founded venture capital firms focused on investing in Indian technology. Many have returned to India to start companies in Bengaluru or Hyderabad, the country's two main technology hubs.

In 2014, Modi put in what was more a rock-star appearance than one by a head of state in a ceremony at Madison Square Garden in New York to a sold-out house of 19,000. That November, 75,000 British Modi fans turned out to see him at Wembley Stadium in London. No doubt Modi can count on enthusiastic support from many diaspora Indians, but not all share the BJP's vision of transforming India from a secular republic into a Hindu state, and most are focused on making new lives for themselves in the countries in which they have settled.

What is India's role in the BRICS?

The "BRICs" acronym was coined in 2001 by Goldman Sachs' chairman Jim O'Neill for a set of fast-emerging economies that included Brazil, Russia, India, and China. These countries then formed a formal BRIC group. South Africa joined the group in 2010, and the acronym became BRICS. Since then, China's economy has surged ahead and India has also posted high economic growth, with the two expected to outstrip the economy of the United States well before the end of the twenty-first century. Brazil, Russia, and South Africa have not fared as well.

The BRICS countries began meeting as a bloc in 2009. In 2014, the group founded a New Development Bank as an alternative to the Bretton Woods institutions of the World Bank and the International Monetary Fund. In October 2016, India hosted the BRICS conference, which saw members call for increased cooperation across a wide range of areas, from digital technology to film festivals. The goal of the BRICS is nothing less than to shape a new global agenda, one that better represents the interests of the large emerging economies that will shape the twenty-first century than do the Western-dominated institutions created in the immediate wake of World War II.

What role does India play in the G20?

The G20 group of finance ministers and central bankers was founded in 1999 in the wake of the Asian financial crisis. India has been a member since the inception of the group. The G20 held its first Leaders Summit in 2008 to respond to the global financial crisis that year. The G20 works on issues related to the global economy, international financial institutions, financial regulation, and economic reform. On the sidelines of the G20 meeting in China in 2016, which saw tensions between China and the United States, Prime Minister Modi met with President Xi Jinping. Xi underlined the need for each country to be sensitive to the other's concerns as they work together in the G20. As India's economic and military powers grow, it will likely find itself playing an increasingly delicate balancing act between China and the United States.

What about India and the World Trade Organization?

In 2008, talks in the Doha round of World Trade Organization negotiations collapsed when India, China, and the United States fell out over efforts to protect poor farmers from international price fluctuations in basic food commodities and Indian minister of commerce Kamal Nath famously declared. "I reject everything." Disagreement over protections for farmers in developing countries continued to haunt WTO trade negotiations for several years, finally resulting in a breakthrough in 2014 when the WTO agreed that developing countries' food stockpiles would not be challenged until a permanent solution could be found on which all parties could agree. The next bone of contention between the United States and India at the WTO was over Indian domestic requirements on solar power that the United States found inconsistent with WTO rules and damaging to US solar exports. In 2016, a WTO panel weighed in on the side of the United States.

Trade policy in India, as for most countries, is driven by domestic politics. Farmers' lobbies are powerful, and food security is a core issue for India, which has never forgotten its dependency on food aid in the post-independence decades, nor the terrible famine in Bengal under British rule in 1943. Yet India's economy is expanding rapidly, and the country is courting international investment. To that end, India ratified the WTO's Trade Facilitation Agreement in 2016, but only after the requirement to implement the agreement was linked to each country's ability to do so. Food security nonetheless remains a critical matter to India, home to one-quarter of the world's malnourished people, and it is likely to continue to defend domestic support programs against WTO efforts to liberalize global food trade and agriculture.

Will India get a permanent seat on the UN Security Council?

Global realities have changed since the United Nations Security Council was founded at the end of World War II in 1945. The Security Council consists of five permanent members— the United States, Russia, China, France, and Britain—and ten nonpermanent members elected for two-year terms by the United Nations General Assembly. Only the permanent members have veto power over resolutions presented to the Security Council.

Momentum is growing to reform the Security Council to better reflect current and projected global realities in the twenty-first century, including the rise of India. In 2004, the leaders of Germany, Japan, India, and Brazil declared they supported each other's candidacies for permanent membership. In 2010, US president Barack Obama said the United States supported India becoming a permanent member of the Security Council, a pathbreaking declaration since no changes can be made to the Security Council without US support.

India's candidacy is strong. Its population will soon be the world's largest, and its economy is slated to become the second largest after China's. India is a major contributor of troops to UN peacekeeping forces, and its military might is growing. China, however, has little interest in India becoming a permanent member, especially given its relationship with the United States. Still, at some point soon, the disconnect between the countries it made sense to include as permanent members in 1945 and a world that has changed radically since that time risks rendering the Security Council irrelevant.

How much is India investing in its military?

India was the world's fourth-largest spender on defense in 2016–17. Its military budget is expected to grow faster than those of other major defense spenders over the next several years, reaching a total of $63 billion in 2020. The prospect of lucrative defense contracts has major defense vendors, including the United States, France, and Israel, lining up to sell their fighter jets, submarines, aircraft carriers, surveillance systems, and other related military hardware to India.

India's determination to defend itself in a troubled region and its ambition to become a major regional and global power are fueling growth in military spending, much of it dedicated to modernizing defense capabilities. In June 2015, the United States and India signed a ten-year defense cooperation agreement, focused on the two countries working together to develop new military capabilities that both can use and which would produce spin-off innovation for civilian use and help boost industrialization in India.

India also has defense partnerships or cooperative agreements with Israel, Russia, Japan, and the European Union. In October 2016, following India's signing an $8.8 billion deal to purchase Rafale fighter jets from France, the Rafale's manufacturer, Dassault Aviation, joined with Indian Anil Ambani's

Reliance Group to form Dassault Reliance Aerospace. The new entity will work on defense research and development.

Will India be a superpower in the twenty-first century?

There is no doubt that India's stature on the world stage is growing, and that it has much potential to expand its already considerable role as South Asia's largest power and as an important player in global institutions. But the definition of a "superpower" is a state that can project its military and economic might around the world. India is not there yet. Whether or not India becomes a superpower in the twenty-first century will largely be determined by how well it deals with the enormous challenges it faces, including tackling poverty, improving the status of women, blunting the impact of climate change, calming communal and caste-based violence, resolving tensions on its borders, and preserving the considerable "soft power" it derives from being an open, plural, and tolerant democracy.

For many Indians, India's ascent to superpower status seems inexorable. But, given India's—and the world's—problems, perhaps the better question is not whether India will become a superpower in the twenty-first century but how India may use its growing power to address serious problems at home, as well as global challenges the world can solve only with India's help.

8

ENVIRONMENT

How will climate change affect India?

With its large population, long coastlines, and location near the equator, India is particularly vulnerable to the negative effects of global warming. Rising sea levels will threaten the country's many coastal cities, including the financial capital, Mumbai, and the metropolises of Kolkata and Chennai. India's annual monsoon rains are becoming more erratic, resulting in both severe drought and devastating flooding. Drought following two years of weak monsoons caused grave suffering for more than 330 million Indians in 2016, especially in rural areas where crops had withered and water for livestock dried up. In November 2015, Chennai experienced the heaviest rainfall in a century, causing massive flooding and killing some 300 people. In August 2016, the Ganges broke all previous flood records, displacing thousands of people and killing 150. In August 2017, Mumbai was paralyzed after as much rain fell in twelve hours as usually falls during a twelve-day period during a typical monsoon. Across South Asia, flooding and landslides from heavy monsoon rains that summer affected at least 41 million people.

India has is already recording record-setting high temperatures. In May 2016, the highest ever temperature recorded in India—51 degrees Celsius or 123.8 degrees Fahrenheit—was hit in the state of Rajasthan, where the town of Phalodi recorded several days of temperatures above 50 degrees Celsius. In New Delhi, the temperature rose to 47 degrees Celsius. In 2015, some 2,500 Indians died during a heat wave.

In response, the government launched regional warning and assistance plans in 2016 to help its population cope with severe heat waves. The plans call for opening cooling centers, training medical personnel, and reaching out to the most vulnerable, including the poor and the elderly.

In the coming years, rising temperatures and erratic rainfall will stress India's capacity to produce enough food for its growing population, and threaten the livelihood of the 70 percent of Indians who depend on agriculture for survival. Global warming will also have an impact on India's forests and fisheries. Rising temperatures could also favor a rise in insect populations, including agricultural pests and disease-carrying mosquitos.

Meanwhile, shrinking glaciers in the Himalayas threaten future water security for hundreds of millions of Indians. Lower river levels and higher river water temperatures threaten power production by thermal plants that depend on water for cooling. Millions of climate refugees, both within India's borders and potentially crossing over from Bangladesh, could pose a threat to political stability.

In terms of adaptation to climate change, India's 2008 National Action Plan on Climate Change calls for efforts on sustainable agriculture and housing, water, preserving the Himalayan ecosystem, and reforestation. Urgent action is also needed to prepare urban and rural populations for severe flooding and temperatures approaching the limits of what people, animals, and plants can survive.

How much does India contribute to global warming?

India is the world's third-largest emitter of greenhouse gases, emitting 2.4 billion metric tons of carbon dioxide in 2013.

With the fastest-growing world economy, India is determined to seek out adequate energy to fuel its economic growth and industrial development, including the increased use of fossil fuels, and so India's greenhouse gas emissions will increase over the next several decades. India has declined to commit to a year when it anticipates its emissions will peak. In 2015, the Brookings Institution set a plausible peak at 2043.

However, on a per capita basis, India's rate of greenhouse gas emission is low. India has contributed only 4 percent of total historic emissions of greenhouse gases, and it currently produces 2 metric tons of carbon dioxide per person, compared to a per capita output of 20 metric tons in the United States and 8 metric tons in China. India's position has long been that while it will make a concerted effort to reduce the rate of the rise of its greenhouse gas emissions over a "business-as-usual" scenario, it will not sacrifice its economic development by forgoing an increased consumption of fossil fuels.

What is India doing to tackle climate change?

In October 2015, India submitted its Intended Nationally Determined Contribution (INDC) on carbon emissions to the United Nations in advance of the December 2015 meeting of the COP21 climate change negotiations in Paris. India pledged that by 2030 it would reduce its carbon emissions by 30 to 35 percent over 2005 levels. It also pledged to increase the portion of non-fossil-fuel energy power sources to 40 percent by 2030. In addition, India promised to increase tree cover to create a "green sink" to absorb 2.5 to 3 billion metric tons of carbon dioxide. Given the stakes for India—and the world—one hopes that India will do even better than it pledged in 2015 to reduce the rate of increase of its carbon dioxide emissions. One must also hope that the United States will recommit to the 2015 Paris climate deal and reduce its emissions of greenhouse gases.

How bad is air pollution in India?

According to a 2016 report from the World Health Organization, six of the world's ten most polluted cities are in India. New Delhi is one of the most polluted cities in the world. Indoor air pollution, primarily from wood- or cow-dung-burning cooking stoves that are used by more than 800,000 million Indians, also leads to premature deaths. Together, outdoor and indoor air pollution are killing 1.5 million Indians every year.

Tens of millions of Indian children are growing up in environments with highly polluted air, compromising the health of India's future working-age population. A 2015 study indicated that a shocking 35 percent of Indian school-age children suffered from poor lung health, a proportion that rose to 40 percent in India's capital, New Delhi. Asthma rates among Indian children have skyrocketed.

A 2016 World Bank study estimated that air pollution cost India's economy 8.5 percent of GDP. At that rate, air pollution is more than offsetting India's economic growth of around 7.5 percent. Air pollution is also having an impact on agriculture. Black carbon and ozone pollution are blamed for cutting India's wheat yields in 2010 by 36 percent, and rice yields by 15 percent. The OECD projects that annual deaths in India from outdoor air pollution could reach 2.5 million by 2060.

So far, India has made piecemeal efforts to tackle the problem. The city of Delhi imposed a temporary odd-even license plate system to restrict automobile use to alternate days in January 2016, and again in April 2016, in an attempt to reduce vehicle emissions. The government's 2016–17 fiscal year budget included a new tax of up to 4 percent on new car sales to dampen demand. And in 2016, India's Supreme Court temporarily banned the sale of some diesel cars and imposed a 1 percent "green" tax on diesel car sales.

India could do more, such as better monitoring of air pollution and penalties for polluters. With large numbers of rural citizens heading to the country's cities, public urban transportation networks in India's need to be expanded rapidly: the Delhi Metro urban rail transport system saw ridership jump to an average of 2.75 million passengers per day during the odd-even license plate restriction period in January 2016. Developing dedicated freight rail lines to shift the transport of goods from diesel trucks would help. So would tougher vehicle emissions standards and a shift to hybrid and electric cars. India's automobile industry is booming: in 2015, new automobile sales jumped nearly 10 percent over the prior year, with more than 2 million new cars hitting India's already strained roads.

Industry also contributes to India's urban air pollution. Factory emissions must be better monitored, and penalties levied against polluters. Cleaner coal-burning power stations need to be built, and better coal-washing facilities are needed to rid India's plentiful but low-quality coal of its high ash content. Shifting as much energy production as possible, as rapidly as possible, to renewable energy sources such as wind and solar will also help. More than anything, the government must put forward a national action plan to deal with urban air pollution, backed by sufficient resources for reducing emissions and enforcing air quality standards.

What about coal in India?

Despite record levels of air pollution in its cities, and the imperative to reduce the rate of increase of the release of carbon dioxide into the atmosphere, India moved ahead to open more coal mines and to build more coal-burning power plants after the 2014 election of Narendra Modi as prime minister. The reason was simple: coal is plentiful in India—the country has the third-largest coal reserves in the world—and India's growing population, its rapid economic growth, and the shift of its people to cities where the demand for electricity is higher led the government to argue that India could simply not afford to forgo coal as a source of power if it is to rapidly industrialize and urbanize its economy.

Coal accounts for more than 70 percent of power generation in India. But falling prices for solar and wind power are making coal less attractive, and India is planning to increase substantially the proportion of renewable energy sources in its total energy mix. This will reduce the reliance on coal as an energy source for India, even as its total consumption of coal will increase for some time to meet growing demand for power.

Is India investing in renewable energies?

India is making an ambitious bid to increase its energy production from renewable energy sources, including solar, wind, and hydropower. In 2010, India launched the Jawaharlal Nehru National Solar Mission, which set a goal in 2014 to hit 100 gigawatts of solar installations by 2022. In 2016, Prime Minister Modi announced a plan to pump $3.1 billion into India's solar panel manufacturing industry. The goal is not only to increase power production in India from solar but also to turn India into a global solar manufacturing leader and to reduce the current dependency on imported solar panels from China. During the first six months of 2016 alone, India imported 18 percent of China's solar production, making it one of China's biggest solar customers. The government's goal is to raise India's 2016 renewable energy capacity of 45 gigawatts to 175 gigawatts by 2022.

In 2014, India had the fifth-largest installed wind capacity in the world—23 gigawatts—and planned to increase that capacity to 60 gigawatts by 2022. In 2016, India's Ministry of New and Renewable Energy announced a scheme to facilitate interstate transmission of wind power, allowing India's eight windier states to send power to less windy ones, and encouraging more of India's state governments to sign up to purchase wind power.

There is also potential for India to further develop hydropower. At 45 gigawatts of installed capacity in 2016, hydropower accounts for only 15 percent of India's total power capacity of 300 gigawatts. Jawaharlal Nehru famously called large hydropower dams the "temples of modern India." But as the problems associated with big dam projects—high cost, ecological damage to waterways, drowning of vast amounts of land—have become better known, small hydro projects of less than 25 megawatts have attracted new interest in India. Small-scale hydro has great potential to provide clean, renewable power to remote areas currently not on India's power grid.

What about nuclear power?

One of the main arguments behind the 2008 US-India Civil Nuclear Agreement, which, as we have seen, allowed India to purchase nuclear technology, reactor parts, and uranium from members of the Nuclear Suppliers Group, was to spur the development of nuclear power as a non-carbon option to meet India's growing energy needs. As of 2016, India had twenty-one operating nuclear reactors at seven sites. An additional six reactors were under construction. Nuclear provides a small fraction—just 3 percent—of India's total energy capacity.

India's nuclear power expansion has met stiff resistance from concerned citizens where new plants are planned. The damage to nuclear reactors in Fukushima, Japan, by a tsunami in 2011 spooked many around the world, including in India, about the safety of nuclear power. A new Kudankulam nuclear plant that opened in 2016 in the state of Tamil Nadu sparked violent protests from local fishermen and other citizens who cited the threat from tsunamis as well as fears about potentially defective parts fabricated in Russia. Construction of the Kudankulam reactor went six years and $1 billion over budget. More than a million people live within twenty miles of the reactor.

Another drag on the development of nuclear power in India has been American manufacturers' concerns over liability should an accident occur. But in 2015 India and the United States reached an agreement over liability that greenlighted the construction of six new nuclear reactors in India by Westinghouse. The issue of liability is particularly sensitive for India in the wake of the deadly chemical leak in Bhopal, India, in 1984 at the site of a Union Carbide fertilizer plant. As we have seen, the leak killed as many as 15,000 people, and it remains the worst industrial accident in history.

Does India have enough water?

India is facing a multifaceted water crisis in the twenty-first century. With 18 percent of the world's population but only 4 percent of the planet's fresh water, India's growing economy and population are straining the country's capacity to deliver sufficient water for increasing agricultural and urban demand. The amount of available water per capita has declined over the past fifty years in India by nearly two-thirds, from 3,000 to 1,123 cubic meters. India's underground aquifers—which provide over 50 percent of India's total water supply—are disappearing at a startling rate, with farmers forced to dig wells deeper and deeper to reach water for irrigation. Ninety percent of groundwater consumed in India is for irrigation, of which 60 percent comes from ground sources.

There is also the question of the quality of India's water. Much of India's surface water is highly polluted from untreated sewage and industrial effluents. Pesticide residues are also present in much of the country's water.

The issue of sharing water from the Cauvery River sparked a dispute between the Indian states of Tamil Nadu and Karnataka in 2016 and triggered violent riots in India's high-tech hub Bengaluru. Prime Minister Modi threatened to take a hard look at the 1960 Indus Rivers Treaty that governs use of water from the Indus River and its tributaries—important sources of water for both India and Pakistan—after an attack on Indian soldiers in Kashmir near the Pakistani border in September 2016. India is building a dam on a tributary of the Indus, the Jhelum. Water from the Indus irrigates 75 percent of Pakistan's cropland, including its vital cotton-growing region.

Using water as a weapon sets a dangerous precedent: India is dependent on water that flows from rivers originating in China, including the Indus and the Brahmaputra, and China is constructing dams on rivers in Tibet that provide water to India. Altogether, India, China, Bhutan, and Pakistan are on track to construct some 400 hydroelectric dams in the Himalayas, risking severe environmental damage to the region and complicating the issue of water sharing. Whether there will be sufficient water to power these dams is an open question: warming global temperatures are causing glaciers in the Himalayas to shrink, reducing water flow from glacial melt by an anticipated 10 to 20 percent by 2050.

The prospect of violent conflict, even war, over water has never loomed larger as a threat to India and its region. According to a 2016 study by scientists at the Massachusetts Institute of Technology, India and China will face severe water stress by 2050 unless steps are taken immediately to address the growing gap between the region's water supply and its burgeoning demand.

What is the "sand mafia" and how is it affecting the water supply?

India's urban construction boom has boosted demand for sand, an essential ingredient in concrete. Because obtaining legal permits to mine sand is a cumbersome process, and because demand for sand outstrips the legal supply, a powerful "sand mafia" has taken over illegal sand mining in India, which generates some $17 million in profits every month.

India's Supreme Court and National Green Tribunal have handed down strong judgments to regulate sand mining in India and to stop illegal activity, but these judgments have had little effect at the local level, where corrupt officials often look the other way in exchange for bribes. Indian citizens who protest illegal mining face brutal intimidation from sand mafia goons.

The damage to India's already stressed waterways by illegal sand mining is severe—and potentially irreversible. In addition to disrupting the ecology of riverbeds, stripping sand prevents water from percolating down into already dwindling underground aquifers used for drinking and irrigation. It also makes rivers more prone to flooding when monsoon rains arrive.

What about pesticides in India?

India is the world's fourth-largest pesticide manufacturer and the sixth-largest exporter of pesticides. Pesticides—along with chemical fertilizers, hybrid seeds, and irrigation—helped India increase crop production dramatically after the arrival of the Green Revolution in the 1960s. India became self-sufficient in food after a period of being dependent on food imports during the first decades following independence in 1947.

But pesticide use in India is largely at the discretion of farmers. Illiterate farmers may not understand the risk of exposure, may not protect themselves from pesticides as they handle them, and may apply pesticides too liberally or misapply them. Concern is growing about high levels of pesticide residues in Indian fruits, vegetables, eggs, milk, and meat. The European Union and Saudi Arabia have banned the import of some fruits and vegetables from India because of high pesticide residues. Contamination of groundwater by pesticides is blamed for high cancer rates in Punjab, where intensive agriculture and irrigation are common. Pesticides that are banned elsewhere are either legal or easily available in India, including DDT, monocrotophos, and endosulfan. The Food and Agriculture Organization of the United Nations recommended that developing countries phase out monocrotophos after the pesticide was blamed for the tragic death of twenty-three children in India in 2013 that were fed a school meal from food stored in containers that had contained the product. Residues of a variety of pesticides, including endosulfan, DDT, endrin, aldrin, dieldrin, methyl parathion, and heptachlor, are found in public water supplies in the territory around New Delhi, in the Yamuna and Ganga Rivers, in Allahabad, and elsewhere in India.

India is taking action to address pesticide pollution. The government has agreed to phase out endosulfan—banned by the Stockholm Convention on Persistent Organic Pollutants in 2011—by 2017, and to eliminate all existing stocks of the pesticide past their expiration date. In 2015, the Indian government offered victims of endosulfan poisoning in Kerala 50,000 Indian rupees of credit against outstanding agricultural loans. In 2016, the government moved to ban eighteen pesticides linked to cancer, birth defects, and other adverse health effects. State governments are also moving to crack down on the sale of banned pesticides by seizing stocks and alerting farmers about which pesticides they should avoid using.

What about organic farming in India?

A combination of concern with the overuse of pesticides and chemical fertilizers in India and an eagerness to capture some of the growing global market for organic food products is pushing growth in organic farming in India. India's organic food exports—including tea, rice, honey, and spices—nearly doubled from 11.6 billion rupees (about $203 million) in 2012–13 to 21 billion rupees (about $350 million) in 2014–15. Still, as of 2016, India had only 0.4 percent of its total cropland under organic cultivation.

India's domestic organic market remains tiny. But several Indian states are going organic. In January 2016, the state of

Sikkim declared itself to be a 100 percent organic state. The states of Meghalaya, Nagaland, Mizoram, Arunachal Pradesh, and Kerala are in the process of following Sikkim.

What genetically modified crops are grown in India?

Introduced in India by Monsanto in 2001, so-called Bt cotton—cotton plants genetically modified to resist the cotton bollworm—quickly gained popularity among India's cotton farmers. By 2010, 6 million Indian farmers had planted Bt cotton on 90 percent of India's cotton-growing land. Genetically modified cotton is now grown on 95 percent of India's cotton-growing land.

But a whitefly infestation of Bt cotton crops in 2015 dampened enthusiasm for the genetically modified seeds, which cost far more than conventional seeds. Monsanto's sales of cotton seed fell in 2015, and in 2016, the company found itself embroiled in an intellectual property dispute with India's National Seed Association after the government limited the price that could be charged for Monsanto's patented cotton seeds and regulated the royalties paid to producers of genetically modified seeds. In August 2016, Monsanto notified India's Genetic Engineering Approvals Committee that it was withdrawing its application to sell a new variety of Bt cotton seed in India.

In 2010, the government barred the cultivation of genetically engineered eggplants after widespread public protest against the crop. As of 2016, no genetically modified food crops were authorized for cultivation in India, but a genetically modified mustard seed produced by Bayer (which purchased Monsanto in 2016) was nearing approval for cultivation by the government. India imports 60 percent of its edible oils, and mustard oil is a popular cooking oil in India. Prime Minister Modi's government authorized field trials of twenty-one genetically modified food crops in 2015. But Modi faces stiff resistance on genetically modified crops from Hindu nationalist groups he counts among his staunchest supporters, who view these crops as foreign interlopers and favor indigenous plant varieties. The states of Rajasthan and Madhya Pradesh, governed by the BJP, said in 2016 that they would not allow the cultivation of the new genetically modified mustard in their states.

What role genetically modified crops will play in India's agricultural future—and who will hold the patent rights to those seeds—remains to be seen.

Will India be able to feed its growing population?

After a period during which, as we have seen, Green Revolution techniques boosted India's agricultural production and helped the country achieve food self-sufficiency, India is again importing many basic food items. Food grain production declined by 3 percent in 2014 and 2015, a decline largely blamed on poor monsoons. There is no doubt that Indian agriculture faces tougher times ahead, as climate change takes a toll on yields even as the country's growing population increases demand.

India's National Mission for Sustainable Agriculture is tasked, as part of the country's National Action Plan on Climate Change, with making Indian agriculture sustainable. To address this challenge, the body is focusing on water use efficiency, integrated farming, soil health, and the conservation of resources. One of the biggest challenges facing India is that 60 percent of its agricultural land, producing 40 percent of the nation's food, depends on rainfall, and rainfall is becoming less predictable. Another challenge is posed by rising temperatures, which, as noted, will stress food crops and reduce yields. A 2007 report on the impact of climate change on global agriculture indicated that by 2080, India's agricultural production will decline by 38 percent over 2007 levels as a direct result of climate change. During this period, its population will increase by one-third.

In 2011, the United Nations put forward a proposal that agroecology—the application of principles of ecology to food production—could increase global food production tenfold, and was the only truly sustainable approach to feeding the world. Conventional agriculture, dependent on fossil-fuel-derived fertilizers, contributes 17 percent of greenhouse gas emissions, depletes soils, and contaminates groundwater. In the long term, conventional large-scale agriculture is simply not sustainable, critics say.

In India, several organizations, including the Centre for Sustainable Agriculture and Navdanya, are pushing for ecologically sound, integrated approaches to food production that protect the health of farmers and consumers as well as the environment while boosting yields. But in India, as elsewhere in the world, powerful commercial interests in the agribusiness sector—companies that produce chemical fertilizers, pesticides, and patented seeds—have little interest in seeing food production weaned from the inputs they sell.

Still, there are intriguing experiments across India with alternative agriculture, using traditional fertilizing and pest control techniques, intercropping, soil conservation, micro-irrigation, and indigenous food plants that have evolved under less than optimal growing conditions. If India can find a way to produce enough food to feed its anticipated population of 1.7 billion in an era of rising temperatures and erratic rainfall, it has the potential not only to ensure its own food security but to offer solutions to a world that will increasingly struggle to produce enough food on a changing and ever more hostile planet.

Will India's Bengal tiger become extinct?

Due to poaching, habitat destruction, decline of prey populations, and encroachment from human settlement, the wild Bengal tiger population dropped by 96 percent over the last century. In 2006, India's wild tiger population had dwindled to just 1,411. But vigorous conservation efforts, including a crackdown on poaching, appear to be paying off. The government of India's environment ministry announced in 2015 that India's wild tiger population had risen to 2,226 individuals, according to a 2014 survey conducted under the auspices of India's Project Tiger.

The tiger is a proud and beloved symbol of India independence. The recent success of conservation efforts in saving the tiger gives hope for the future of this magnificent animal, and for India's ability to tackle the many problems it faces in the twenty-first century.

FURTHER READING

The following suggestions are hardly exhaustive. Many books not mentioned here will spring to the minds of Indians and India experts. Still, the following will open new horizons to readers unfamiliar with India who wish to learn more.

An excellent general book on India is Stanley Wolpert's beautifully written and succinct *India* (University of California Press, 2009), a classic that has gone through several editions. For concise histories of India, Stanley Wolpert, again, does a superb job in *A New History of India* (Oxford University Press, 2008). Sunil Khilnani's *Incarnations: A History of India in Fifty Lives* (Farrar, Straus and Giroux, 2017) provides a novel and fascinating approach to India's history. For the history of early India, acclaimed Indian historian Romila Thapar's many books, including her recently updated *The Penguin History of Early India, From the Origins to 1300* (Penguin, 2015), set the gold standard.

To delve deeply into Hinduism, the seven-volume translation of *The Ramayana of Valmiki: An Epic of Ancient India* (Princeton University Press) by Robert P. Goldman and Sally Sutherland Goldman and the fifteen-volume translation of the *Mahabharata*, edited by Sheldon Pollock for the Clay Sanskrit Library are the best available. Another excellent and more wide-ranging source is *Brill's Encyclopedia of Hinduism* (Brill, 2009–2014), edited by Knut A. Jacobsen and more. Less ponderously, William Dalrymple's *Nine Lives: In Search of the Sacred in Modern India* (Vintage, 2011) offers a sense of the richness of India's multiple religious traditions and how they may be lived today.

On the Indian mutiny of 1857 and its aftermath, Dalrymple's *The Last Mughal* (Vintage, 2008) is superb. *Righteous Republic: The Political Foundations of Modern India* by Ananya Vajpeyi (Harvard University Press, 2012) examines Indian influences on the founders of independent India, while Ramachandra Guha's *India After Gandhi: A History of the World's Largest Democracy* (Harper Perennial, 2008) looks to India's diversity to explain how democracy took hold in a country where many expected it couldn't. Of course, India's founders wrote important books of their own. Nehru's *The Discovery of India* (Penguin, 2004), Gandhi's *An Autobiography or the Story of My Experiments with Truth: A Critical Edition*, translated by Mahadev Desai, introduction by Tridip Suhrud (Penguin, 2018), and Ambedkar's *The Annihilation of Caste* (Verso, Annotated, Critical edition, 2016) are good introductions to their work.

Sunil Khilnani's *The Idea of India* (Farrar, Straus and Giroux, 1999) is a profound meditation on Indian democracy, while Shashi Tharoor's *India: From Midnight to the Millennium and Beyond* (Penguin Books, 2012) ably charts the greatest challenges to India during the first decades of independence. In *Indira: India's Most Powerful Prime Minister*, Sagarika Ghose (Juggernaut Books, 2017) offers an intimate portrait of Indira Gandhi as well as a sweeping view of the history of India during her lifetime.

Sujata Gidla's *Ants Among Elephants* (Farrar, Straus and Giroux, 2017) powerfully tells the story of a century of modern Indian history from the point of view of a Dalit family and the crushing discrimination they face. For a searing look at the scourge of rape in India, there is no better book than Sonia Faleiro's *13 Men* (Deca Stories, 2015). Snigdha Poonam's *Dreamers: How Young Indians are Changing the World* (Hurst 2018) recounts searing stories of the aspirations, too often frustrated, of India's youth.

On the rise of Hindu nationalism, I recommend Thomas Blom Hansen's *The Saffron Wave: Democracy and Hindu*

Nationalism in Modern India (Princeton University Press, 1999), Christophe Jaffrelot's *Hindu Nationalism: A Reader* (Princeton University Press, 2007), and Arvind Rajagopalan's *Politics After Television: Hindu Nationalism and the Reshaping of the Public in India* (Cambridge University Press, 2001). Amartya Sen's *The Argumentative Indian* (Picador, 2006) marshals India's considerable traditions of dialogue and dissent against these forces, while Shashi Tharoor's *Why I Am a Hindu* (Aleph Book Company, 2018) argues for a Hinduism of tolerance and questioning, rather than of hate and bigotry.

Wide-angle books on India's rise include my own *Planet India: The Turbulent Rise of the Largest Democracy and the Future of Our World* (Scribner, 2008), Edward Luce's *In Spite of the Gods: The Rise of Modern India* (Anchor, 2008), Pavan Varma's *Being Indian: Inside the Real India* (Arrow Books, 2011), Patrick French's *India: A Portrait* (Vintage, 2012), and Adam Roberts' *Superfast Primetime Ultimate Nation: The Relentless Invention of Modern India* (Public Affairs, 2017). A more critical take is found in Pankaj Mishra's *Temptations of the West: How to Be Modern in India, Pakistan, Tibet and Beyond* (Picador, 2007) and *From the Ruins of Empire: The Revolt Against the West and the Remaking of Asia* (Picador, 2013).

On the cruel fate of India's poor, I recommend Katharine Boo's *Behind the Beautiful Forevers: Life, Death and Hope in a Mumbai Slum* (Random House, 2014), P. Sainath's *Everybody Loves a Good Drought: Stories from India's Poorest Districts* (Penguin, 2017), and Siddharth Dube's *In the Land of the Poor: Memories of an Indian Family, 1947–97* (Zed Books, 1998). Suketu Mehta's *Maximum City: Bombay Lost and Found* (Vintage, 2005) remains the definitive book about Mumbai. Meera Subramanian's *A River Runs Again: India's Natural World in Crisis, from the Barren Cliffs of Rajasthan to the Farmlands of Karnataka* (Public Affairs, 2015) offers a passionate look at India's environmental crisis.

On the Indian diaspora, my *Motiba's Tattoos: A Granddaughter's Journey from America into Her Indian Family's Past* (Plume, 2001) traces one path Indian emigration took over the last century and Gaiutra Bahadur's *Coolie Woman: The Odyssey of Indenture* (University of Chicago, 2013) traces another.

Sumit Ganguly's *Engaging the World: Indian Foreign Policy Since 1957* (Oxford University Press, 2015), together with *The Oxford Handbook of Indian Foreign Policy* (Oxford University Press, 2015), edited by David Malone, C. Raja Mohan, and Srinath Raghavan provide a substantial peek into the evolution of India's foreign policy.

Of course, one of the best ways to learn about a country is to read its fiction. Many Indian novelists are mentioned in this book but there are many others—as well as poets, playwrights, and short-story writers, not to mention folk tales, ancient epics, and poetry—that I wish I had the space to list.

INDEX